John D. MacDonald

John D. MacDonald

David Geherin

Frederick Ungar Publishing Co. / New York

To Diane
and to
Christopher, Peter, and Daniel

Copyright ©1982 by Frederick Ungar Publishing Co., Inc.
Printed in the United States of America

Library of Congress Cataloging in Publication Data

Geherin, David, 1943–
John D. MacDonald.

(Recognitions)
Bibliography: p.
Includes index.
1. MacDonald, John D. (John Dann), 1916–   —Criticism and
interpretation.
I. Title. II. Series.
PS3563.A28Z66   813'.54   81-70123
ISBN 0-8044-2232-X   AACR2
ISBN 0-8044-6173-2 (pbk.)

Contents

Before the Fact

The two most obvious statements that can be made about John D. MacDonald as a writer are, one, that he is prolific (sixty-three novels and hundreds of short stories to date) and, two, that he is immensely popular (at least twenty-six of his titles have sold more than a million copies each). While popularity is certainly no assurance of quality, neither is it necessarily evidence of inferior work. What is readily apparent to any reader of MacDonald's novels is that he is a writer of great versatility and talent whose high standards have combined with high productivity to produce a significant body of outstanding fiction.

Slip F-18, Bahia Mar, Ft. Lauderdale, Florida, has become as famous an address as Sherlock Holmes's 221b Baker Street flat or Nero Wolfe's West 35th Street brownstone. Object of his own fan club, inspiration for a shirt once marketed under his name, friend and fantasy hero to millions of readers, Travis McGee has joined the small but select company of fictional characters who manage to transcend the boundaries of the books in which they appear. However, thanks to MacDonald's care in creating a character with substance as well as stature, McGee has also become an effective spokesman for public and private themes. An endlessly fascinating man, his growth, development, and faithful adherence to principles of moral behavior in an increasingly amoral world are sources of continuing interest. Equally important, he serves as a prism through which MacDonald is able to reflect his own views and opinions on dozens of issues of contemporary relevance. Whether assailing the venality and corruption he sees around him, bemoaning the regrettable decline in the quality of much of our contemporary culture, or deploring the shameless assaults on the environment, McGee has become an impassioned commentator on the way we live today—a feature that elevates his exciting adventures to a level of seriousness beyond mere escapist entertainment.

In an impressive body of fiction, which comprises considerably more than the Travis McGee novels, MacDonald has shown that writing for a mass-market audience (most of his books have first appeared as paperback originals) and adhering to the general patterns of genre fiction—activities that some would dismiss as second-rate— are in his case no impediments to the creation of first-rate work. His widespread popularity attests to the fact that he knows how to entertain his readers, but even a cursory examination of the novels themselves shows that he also has important things to say about contemporary America, and that he says them uncommonly well. Combining readability with serious intentions, MacDonald enjoys the enviable status of a writer who appeals both to those readers who claim they never read mysteries and to the legions of devoted fans who do.

The following study begins with a brief biography of MacDonald, the man and the writer. Chapter 2 examines the forty-some books published prior to the introduction of McGee, with special emphasis on those works that best exemplify MacDonald's novelistic skills, including several which feature protagnoists that can be seen as early versions of the hero who will eventually become McGee. Chapters 3 through 6 provide detailed examinations of each of the nineteen McGee novels in chronological order, with special emphasis on MacDonald's growing mastery of his successful formula, the growth and development of McGee's character, and the important themes and issues that emerge in the series. Readers are cautioned that in order to discuss each novel thoroughly, it has been necessary to disclose endings of the books. Chapter 7 focuses on the character of McGee himself: on his background, personality, philosophy, and place in the American private-eye tradition. Chapter 8 is a consideration of the elements of MacDonald's artistry, especially his talent for storytelling, his skill in characterization, and his colorfully effective prose. The book concludes with a bibliography of MacDonald's works and a selected listing of important works about him.

For their assistance in the preparation of this book, I would like to thank John D. MacDonald, who kindly answered my queries, Carmen Williams, who guided me through the John D. MacDonald collection at the University of Florida library in Gainesville, and Dick Riley, for his encouragement in this project.

1

Getting Started

John Dann MacDonald was born on July 24, 1916, in Sharon, Pennsylvania, the only son of Eugene Andrew and Marguerite Dann MacDonald. When he was twelve years old, his father, an executive with the Standard Tank Car Company, accepted a position with the Savage Arms Company, and the family (which also included a younger sister, Doris) moved to Utica, New York. At about the same age, MacDonald was stricken with mastoiditis and scarlet fever and was confined to bed for a year, during which time he read voraciously: "I think that long episode of reading and being read to made a considerable difference in my mental climate. I entertained myself by exercises of imagination, and still do." He graduated from Utica Free Academy at the age of fifteen and in 1934, at his father's insistence, enrolled in the Wharton School of Finance at the University of Pennsylvania. He withdrew during his sophomore year, moved to New York City, worked at a variety of odd jobs (dishwasher, busboy, waiter, fruit stand operator, bookstore duster), and eventually returned to upstate New York, where he enrolled at Syracuse University, obtaining a degree in business administration in 1938.

While at Syracuse he met Dorothy Prentiss, an art major, whom he married in 1937. Following graduation, he and Dorothy moved to Cambridge, Massachusetts, where he began studies at the Harvard University Graduate School of Business Administration. He received

1

his M.B.A. in 1939, the same year his only child, Maynard John, was born. Following a series of "brief and mutually unsatisfactory encounters with several employers" (he was a trainee with the Burroughs Adding Machine Company, an insurance salesman, and an installment credit collection agent, among others), his termination in each case usually attributable, he now confesses, to a "virulent case of Boca Grande (Big Mouth)," in 1940 he accepted a commission in the U.S. Army as a lieutenant in the Ordnance Department. In 1943 he was sent to the American Staff Headquarters in New Delhi, India. Later recruited by the Office of Strategic Services (forerunner of the Central Intelligence Agency), he served in the China-Burma-India Theater during the war, eventually rising to the rank of lieutenant colonel.

Because of the secret and sensitive nature of his work with the OSS, his outgoing mail was subjected to strict censorship, so as a diversion he wrote a 2,100-word short story about life in New Delhi, which he sent to his wife instead of a letter. Unbeknownst to him, she typed the story and submitted it to *Esquire* magazine, which, although rejecting it, wrote an encouraging reply. She then sent it to Whit Burnett at *Story* magazine, who purchased it for $25. (It appeared in the July–August 1946 issue as "Interlude in India.") When MacDonald arrived back at Fort Dix, New Jersey, in September 1945, Dorothy surprised him with the check from *Story*; for the first time, he entertained seriously the possibility that he might become a professional writer:

> I had no idea of actually being a writer until I was twenty-nine. I read everything I could reach from the day I learned to read. I thought that to be an author would be the best thing anyone could ever do—to put down the words for others to read. But I did not think it could ever be me. Not ever.

MacDonald returned to Utica and, encouraged by his single sale and supported by four months' terminal leave money, decided to see if he could make it as a professional writer. What struck his friends and relatives as a severe postwar readjustment problem was actually the beginning of a period of intense literary apprenticeship:

> During those first four months of effort, I wrote about 800,000 words of unsalable manuscript, all in short-story form. That is the

classic example of learning by doing. Had I done a novel a year, it would have taken me ten years to acquire the precision and facility I acquired in four months. I could guess that I spent eighty hours a week at the typewriter. I kept twenty-five to thirty stories in the mail at all times, sending each of them out to an average of ten potential markets before retiring them.

The secret of MacDonald's eventual success is simple: his works were—and are—the result not of poetic inspiration but of hard work, products of a no-nonsense attitude toward writing derived from his early training for a business career. Having known no other writers, he had no clear idea how a writer ought to go about his work.

> I thought you got up in the morning and went to work and worked till lunch and then went back to work until the day was over—with good business habits, as in any other job.
> It wasn't until my habit patterns were firmly embedded that I discovered that writers tended to work a couple of hours and then to brood about it the rest of the day. . . . The thing to do is to do it. Get the fissures in the piles and the varicosities and the pressures on the disks and keep the ass on the chair and *do it*!

Five months of feverish activity later, MacDonald managed to sell his second story to *Detective Tales* for $40, bringing his lifetime earnings from his new career to a grand total of $65: "I had a wife, a son, two cats—and almost one thousand form letters of rejection." Undaunted, he continued writing and optimistically mailing out stories until by the end of 1946 he managed to get twenty-three of them published in a variety of popular pulp magazines (*Detective Tales, Dime Detective, Dime Mystery, Doc Savage, Mammoth Mystery, The Shadow Magazine*). He also earned enough money—about $6,000—to prove that he could support his family as a professional writer.

MacDonald's short story output in the next four years is nothing short of breathtaking. According to the listing compiled by Jean and Walter Shine in the 1980 John D. MacDonald bibliography (which, because of the ephemeral nature of pulp magazines, may not be complete), he published at least thirty-five stories in 1947, fifty in 1948, seventy-three in 1949, and fifty-two in 1950, when he also began writing novels. He wrote all kinds of stories—sports stories, adventures, westerns, science fiction, mystery—which appeared in virtually every pulp on the market (including the venerable *Black Mask*), as well as in such "slick" magazines as *Collier's, Esquire, Liberty,* and *Cosmopolitan.* MacDonald published so many stories during this period that often more than one of his works would appear in the same issue of a magazine, under his name as well as such house names as "John Wade Farrell," "Robert Henry," "John Lane," "Scott O'Hara," "Peter Reed," and "Henry Rieser." (In the July 1949 issue of *Fifteen Sports Stories,* for example, four of his stories appeared.) To date, he has published perhaps as many as six hundred stories, well over four hundred of which are listed in the Shine bibliography.

In a brief but helpful survey of MacDonald's pulp fiction ("The Making of a Tale-Spinner," see bibliography), Francis M. Nevins, Jr. provides an informative look at the range and variety of his mystery and suspense stories. From among the more than two hundred stories MacDonald published between 1946 and 1950 (many of them admittedly little more than apprentice pieces), Nevins singles out four as being among the finest examples of his efforts in the short story format: "You've Got to Be Cold" (*Shadow Mystery Magazine,* April-May 1947); "The Tin Suitcase" (*Doc Savage Magazine,* May-June 1948, written under the name "Peter Reed"); "A Corpse in His Dreams" (*Mystery Book Magazine,* February 1949); and "Heritage of Hate" (*Black Mask,* July 1949). The bulk of MacDonald's pulp output is difficult to obtain today, although MacDonald is reportedly preparing a collection of his early pulp stories for publication.

Three volumes of MacDonald's short stories are, however, readily available: *End of the Tiger and Other Stories* (1966), *S*E*V*E*N* (1971) and *Other Times, Other Worlds* (1978), a collection of his science fiction tales. Most of the stories in the first two volumes were published in popular "slick" magazines rather than the pulps (*Cosmopolitan, Collier's, This Week, Playboy*) and are frequently marred by heavy doses of sentimentality. Far better examples of MacDonald's skill in the mystery-suspense genre are such often anthologized stories as "Man in a Trap" (reprinted in *Alfred Hitchcock Presents: Stories That Go Bump in the Night,* Random House, 1977), "Hit and Run" (reprinted in *A Treasury of Modern Mysteries,* Doubleday, 1973), "Homicidal Hiccup" (reprinted in *Alfred Hitchcock Presents: The Master's Choice,* Random House, 1979), and an outstanding recent effort, "Finding Anne Farley" (reprinted in *Best Detective Stories of the Year: 1978,* E.P. Dutton, 1978), which features a Travis McGee-type insurance investigator.

The pulp market not only provided MacDonald with a vital source of income (at the rate of a penny or two a word), it also served as a valuable training ground in which to learn his craft. The pulp editors forced improvement on him "by acting as filtering agents for the great flood of words. The ones which were improved were sold." One piece of advice he found he couldn't follow, however, was to write for a specific magazine or market. Then, as now, he concentrated on telling it well first before trying to sell it; once he completed a story to his satisfaction, he would submit it to the appropriate market—thus preserving his freedom to write what he wished while developing an arsenal of narrative skills.

Despite his success at selling his work, certainly not everything he wrote was publishable. In a newspaper column written in 1948, he commented on his budding writing career:

> The thing which gives us pause is the fact that not yet have we ever written a story of which we are completely proud. We are serving an apprenticeship to the Angry Gods of the Typewriter, but we can't bury our lesser efforts. We have to sell them for grocery money. It's a good thing they don't let doctors practice this way.

He also confessed that he once spent an entire afternoon supervising his eleven-year-old son in the burning of over two million words of unsalable work. Nevertheless, through an industrious trial-and-error method, MacDonald quickly developed as a writer and in the process learned invaluable lessons about how to tell a good story, how to create believable characters, how to maintain suspense, and, above all, how to entertain the reader.

During these apprentice years, MacDonald and his family lived in upstate New York, first in Utica (where for three months in 1946 he served as executive director of the Taxpayers' Research Bureau), later in nearby Clinton (where in 1947–48 he wrote thirty-two weekly columns for the local *Clinton Courier*). But he was soon making enough money from his writing to move his family south each year— to places like Ingram, Texas, Cuernavaca, Mexico, and Clearwater Beach, Florida—in order to escape the severe New York winters. In the fall of 1951, the MacDonalds rented a small cottage on Casey Key near Sarasota, Florida, and the following spring, thanks to his increasing success, they were able to purchase their first home on nearby Siesta Key. They have resided on Siesta Key ever since, except for a time each year when they return to a summer home on Piseco Lake in the Adirondacks and for periods of extensive traveling, recently to such far-off places as Russia, South America, the People's Republic of China, and New Zealand, where their son and his family live.

By 1950, with the pulp market dwindling rapidly, MacDonald discovered a new market for his work as a writer of paperback novels. He continued writing short stories but, between the publication of *The Brass Cupcake* in 1950 and his most recent Travis McGee adventure, he has published sixty-three novels, most of them paperback originals. In addition, he edited an anthology of mystery stories by women writers, *The Lethal Sex* (1959), and has written two nonfiction books: *The House Guests* (1965), an amusing account about life with Geoffrey and Roger, MacDonald's two cats, and *No Deadly Drug* (1968), an ambitious 600-page account of the notorious murder trial of Dr. Carl Coppolino which, MacDonald claimed, took him seventeen months to write and cost him at least three McGees. Today all but two of MacDonald's novels are still in print: *Weep for Me* (1951), a pale imitation of James M. Cain, and *I Could Go On Singing* (1963), a novelization of a Judy Garland movie, both of which have been withdrawn at his request.

As widespread as his popularity became after a decade and a half of writing paperback novels, it was the creation of Travis McGee in 1964 that brought MacDonald his greatest fame and fortune. Like his early novels, the McGee books first appeared as paperback originals, but since 1973, when Lippincott published *The Turquoise Lament* hardbound, all new McGee books have been published first in hardcover and most of the earlier paperback editions have been reprinted in hardcover form. Many of his books have also been made into films: *Man Trap* (1961), based on *Soft Touch*; *Cape Fear* (1962), with Gregory Peck and Robert Mitchum, based on *The Executioners*; *Darker Than Amber* (1970), with Rod Taylor as Travis McGee and Theodore Bikel as Meyer; *The Girl, the Gold Watch, and Everything* and *Condominium*, films made for television, both telecast in 1980.

MacDonald's popularity has also been accompanied by widespread critical acclaim. One of his early stories, "The Bear Trap," won the Benjamin Franklin Award from the University of Illinois as the best magazine short story published in 1955; the French edition of his novel *A Key to the Suite* was awarded the Grand Prix de Littérature Policière in 1964; *The Last One Left* was nominated for an Edgar

Award as the best mystery novel of 1967; *The Green Ripper* received the American Book Award as the best hardcover mystery published in 1979. MacDonald himself has been honored by being elected president of the Mystery Writers of America in 1962 and also by being awarded its prestigious Grand Master Award in 1972. Since 1965 he has been the subject of a journal devoted entirely to an appreciation of his work, the *JDM Bibliophile*, begun by a California couple, Len and June Moffatt, and now published by the University of South Florida. In 1971 MacDonald received the George Arents Pioneer Medal, awarded by Syracuse University to its most prominent alumni. In 1978 he was presented an Award for Distinguished Achievement in the Popular Arts by the Popular Culture Association and was also the subject and honored guest at "The John D. MacDonald Conference on Mystery and Detective Fiction," sponsored by the University of South Florida. He has, in addition, been awarded honorary degrees by Hobart and William Smith Colleges (1978) and the University of South Florida (1980).

Equally important, he has earned the accolades of his fiction-writing colleagues. Fellow mystery writers like Raymond Chandler, Rex Stout, Mickey Spillane, and Ian Fleming have all praised his work; Chandler, for example, admitted that MacDonald was one of the few writers he reread every year and Fleming remarked that he automatically bought every McGee novel as it came out. Novelist Richard Condon called him "the Great American storyteller" and journalist and mystery writer Pete Hamill proclaimed him to be "the best novelist in America." Kurt Vonnegut, Jr., another writer of paperback originals who eventually gained international recognition, singled out MacDonald's accurate portrayal of contemporary life in his books, predicting that to archaeologists a thousand years from now, "the works of John D. MacDonald would be a treasure on the order of the tomb of Tutankhamen." British novelist Kingsley Amis went so far as to assert that MacDonald is "by any standards a better writer than Saul Bellow," but that because he writes thrillers and Bellow is a "human-heart chap" he is denied the higher honors.

Only a writer with MacDonald's disciplined methods could have produced the amount of work he has. An outgrowth of his admitted ignorance about how writers are "supposed" to work, his strict regimen is the obvious key to his enormous productivity. After a period of

morning exercise (sit-ups and push-ups), he begins writing about 9:00
A.M. and, except for a lunch break, continues until late in the day,
with Friday and Sunday afternoons off. (MacDonald once computed
by counting the empty spools of typewriter ribbon he used that during
one twenty-six-month period, he wrote two million, ten thousand
words, or 6,700 manuscript pages.) Such a strict regimen, MacDonald
found, produced quality as well as quantity:

> I just think that most professionals in writing, painting, composing,
> sculpting, acting, etc. etc. *are* professionals because at some point
> they realized that a certain orderliness which one imposes on the
> hours of the days is necessary if one is to free the maximum attention
> for the demands of the projects at hand. Later along, you learn that
> much of the work you do is as good or better when you have done
> it feeling pooped, discouraged, juiceless, as work which turned you
> on at the time you were doing it. Once you know this, then the
> temptation to break off because you don't happen to feel up to par
> is greatly reduced.

He composes on an IBM Selectric (dubbed "The Awesome Beige
Typewriter" by writer Rust Hills); in fact, his typing is so skillful, so
automatic, that he admits he often forgets he is even typing: "It's like
magic," he confesses, "I think and the words appear." He does all his
own editing and, as a measure of the pride he takes in his work, uses
only the highest-quality typing paper he can find:

> I leave my editor with as little to do as possible. My Selectric makes
> nice copy and I use the best available rag content bond paper. It's
> like painting or sculpture. An artist uses the best materials he can
> afford. What my copy looks like has a lot to do with its quality, and
> I have more respect for what I do when I submit the best that I
> can do, the best in every way.

Unlike many writers—and perhaps surprisingly, given his usually
tightly structured plots—MacDonald does not outline a novel in
advance. Instead he decides on an approximate ending, works to
develop a good beginning, and then begins to write, thereby preserving
a sense of the unexpected in his work:

> I do not plan the middle portions of a book. Once I have found a

solid beginning-place, and know where it will end, I then have multiple choices of how to find my way through the thickets and jungles of the middle portion. When such portions get too far off the track because a side trail becomes too enticing, I can take out that portion and set it aside as something to read over the next time I am in the process of selecting a story to write. For me, too much preplanning destroys freshness and spoils my own fun. I do not know what each day of work will bring. I know the compass direction, but not the specific destination of each day.

Only a writer whose disciplined habits ensured ample productivity would feel comfortable revising the way MacDonald does, namely by throwing out whole chunks of work. Sometimes a section will be saved, perhaps as inspiration for another book, but hunks of unsatisfactory manuscript usually end up in the wastebasket:

> I revise by throwing away. I might, for example, throw away thirty thousand words of a novel in first draft because it begins to feel progressively worse and beyond repair. Or I might discard the final twenty thousand of the first fifty thousand words by rereading it enough times to be able to detect the approximate arena where it began to feel wrong.

Such a method no doubt contributes to the fluid movement of most MacDonald novels, for rather than patching and pasting over troubled sections, his habit of discarding entire unsatisfactory sections gives a greater organic unity to the work as a whole, thus preserving its freshness. MacDonald also normally works on more than one book at a time, so that when he encounters problems in one, he can put it aside and turn to another project. At times, MacDonald admits, he has had as many as three or four "cripples" on the shelf to one of which he would eventually return, usually with a successful solution to the problem that first caused him to put it aside.

And finally, only a writer with a deep and abiding love for his work would continue to adhere to such a rigorous schedule for as long as he has. MacDonald freely admits that his primary motivation in writing is neither money, nor fame, nor a drive for success: "I just enjoy the hell out of writing," he confesses; and what gives him special joy are those moments when he writes a page that is exactly right, that expresses precisely what he wishes it to say. It is this drive to satisfy himself, and the pleasure he gets when he does it, that has kept him at his desk for thirty-five years and will continue to keep him there as long as he is still able to do the work.

> I will do as many more stories as time, energy, and self-knowledge will permit. It has meant sixty hours a week at this machine for more years than I care to confess. But there is not a day that I cannot get a quick, electric feeling of joyous anticipation when I roll the white empty page into the machine. A day, a week, a month, or a half year of work may leave me without a page I can keep. But sooner or later there will be a day when the satisfaction at the end of the day matches the anticipation at the beginning.
> And that's what keeps my machine going.

Although he no longer turns out books at the prodigious rate he once did, he continues to publish works which provide convincing evidence that popular success and critical acclaim can happily coexist and which demonstrate that "serious" fiction and "popular" fiction are not mutually exclusive. In his long and illustrious career, he has produced a body of work that includes some of the best mystery and suspense fiction of the past three decades and has created a protagonist who has become one of America's most famous fictional heroes.

2

From Pulps to Best Sellers

Between 1950 and 1964, when Travis McGee made his first appearance, MacDonald published forty-two novels, frequently at the rate of four a year. What is so impressive about this is not so much the sheer quantity of the output but its range, variety, and quality. Although half the novels can be classified as crime or mystery works, the rest fall into a number of other categories: science fiction (*Wine of the Dreamers, Ballroom of the Skies*), fantasy (*The Girl, the Gold Watch, and Everything*), romantic comedy (*Please Write for Details*), sociology (*The End of the Night*), novels about marriage (*Clemmie, Cancel All Our Vows, The Deceivers*), about business in America (*A Man of Affairs, Area of Suspicion, The Crossroads, A Key to the Suite*), and *Grand Hotel/Airport*–type novels about people thrown together by circumstances or crises (*The Damned, Murder in the Wind, Cry Hard, Cry Fast, Condominium*). While one should be careful about making extravagant claims for the excellence of the work in toto, one should be equally wary about dismissing it too cavalierly as the hurried output of a writer obviously too busy to take much care with his work.

Searching for quality in this massive outpouring of words is a far more productive enterprise than panning for gold in a muddy stream. A surprisingly large number of the novels are fully realized, accomplished, and entertaining works of fiction. Unfortunately, despite the fact that they comprise over two-thirds of MacDonald's total novelistic

11

output, the pre–Travis McGee novels have been overshadowed by the enormous success of the later books. From the perspective of his current popularity, MacDonald is widely perceived as the creator of the McGee books who happened to write some earlier, lesser-known works; from the perspective of his entire career, MacDonald can more accurately be judged as a versatile and skilled writer whose creation of McGee should be seen as only the culmination of a long and successful career as a mystery and suspense writer. Adding to the relative obscurity of the early works is the fact that because most were published as paperback originals, they received scant critical attention. (A fact which has never overly concerned MacDonald, who once admitted, "It doesn't matter to me if a story is bound in Kleenex or crocodile hide. Why, for the prestige and the implication that hardcover means 'good writing,' should I bother? I'd rather deal more directly with the troops and get the profits." Quite the businessman, MacDonald reportedly resisted efforts to have his books, including the early McGee novels, published in hardcover because then he would have had to share his substantial paperback royalties with his hardcover publisher. With publication in paperback, solely he received all the royalties.) Only Anthony Boucher of *The New York Times* regularly reviewed these early novels; praising MacDonald as "one of the first-rate craftsmen of crime," he compared him favorably with Georges Simenon as an example of a writer who combined high quality and prolific output.

MacDonald rarely writes criticism, but in a review of James M. Cain's *The Institute*, his comments provide a revealing insight into his own formula for success as a writer:

> There is a special debt we owe them, a debt to Chandler, Hammett and Cain. They excised pointless ornamentation, moved their stories forward with a spare, ruthless vigor and so superimposed the realities we already knew with characterizations we could believe, that they achieved a dreadful, and artistic, inevitability.
>
> They were the big guys, changing the definitions of suspense and readability, forcing all of us smaller fry to cut more cleanly and deeply, to delete the windiness of tortuous explanation, to get on with it—showing instead of telling.

MacDonald learned from the masters well, for his stories are always interesting, his plots well constructed, his narratives well paced; his characters are thoroughly believable; his prose is lively and readable, precise and polished, not precious or plodding. Above all, he adheres to the dictum that showing is vastly preferable to telling in the creation of good mystery and suspense fiction. Although it is difficult to generalize about the overall accomplishment of a body of work as large and varied as MacDonald's, one can isolate the basic qualities that have contributed so much to his enormous success.

First of all, MacDonald seldom fails to tell interesting stories and tell them well, one of his greatest strengths in this regard being the knack of getting a story moving quickly, grabbing the reader's attention immediately. *The Empty Trap* (1957), for example, begins with a dramatic scene in which Lloyd Westcott is pushed off a mountain in his car by three men hired to kill him. Miraculously, he is thrown from the car and survives. The incident raises a multitude of questions which only reading the rest of the novel can answer. In *You Live Once* (1956), Clint Sewell is awakened by the police, who want to question him about the disappearance of Mary Olan, a friend of his. After they leave, he showers and, opening his closet to get some clothes, is shocked to find her body there. MacDonald had honed his narrative skills by writing for the pulps, and one of the things he had learned best was how to control the pace of a story, how to narrate with economy while at the same time generating tension, suspense, and mystery.

But if openings are his strength, endings are sometimes his downfall. Either because he lost interest in his story, or rushed to finish, or his material simply proved intractable, the resolution of many promising plots is disappointing—a weakness of which Mac-Donald himself is not unaware: "I tend to neaten things up too carefully at the end," he has confessed. "Many of my solutions are too glib." In *The Soft Touch* (1958), the murderer is dramatically exposed when he gets amnesia after suffering a blow to the head and unwittingly digs up the body of his wife (whom he had murdered), thinking he was recovering loot he had buried. The impending takeover of the Harrison Corporation by entrepreneur Mike Dean in *A Man of Affairs* (1957) is averted at the last moment when he suddenly drops dead of a heart attack.

Furthermore, MacDonald also strains to provide what Thomas Doulis, in an interesting study of the formulaic elements of these early novels, calls "terminal reassurance." The villain is invariable punished, the good guy always amply rewarded, usually in the company of the beautiful woman he meets during the course of the novel. Even when the villains appear to have triumphed, as in *April Evil* (1956), retribution awaits them: one is killed when her car rams into a speeding train; the other, who has escaped in a boat with hundreds of thousands of dollars, perishes at sea, a victim of exposure and lack of water. When the plot of a novel requires victims, it is seldom the innocent who are sacrificed. In both *Cry Hard, Cry Fast* (1955), about a multiple traffic accident, and *Murder in the Wind* (1956), about a hurricane, it is an escaping convict and his girlfriend who are killed off. Darby Garon is punished for his infidelity by being killed by a stray bullet in *The Damned* (1952); he is where he shouldn't be, having temporarily abandoned his wife and children for a quick fling in Mexico with a woman he had just met. Most of the female characters who die in these novels are either hookers, like Toni Rasselle in *A Bullet for Cinderella* (1955), or in some way morally damaged, like Lucille Branson, who, in *The Price of Murder* (1957), has been unfaithful to her devoted husband. One of the most blatant examples of MacDonald's compulsion for "terminal reassurance" occurs in *The Beach Girls* (1959), which concludes with a letter written several years after the events of the story, bringing the reader up-to-date concerning the various rewards and punishments doled out to each of the characters.

Just as implausible as the retribution meted out to the evildoers are the happy endings awaiting most of the good characters. In *Judge Me Not* (1951), Barbara Heddon, a prostitute whose face has been disfigured in a knife attack, is nursed back to health, cured of her prostitution, and introduced to real happiness for the first time in her life thanks to the unselfish devotion of Teed Morrow, who has fallen in love with her despite her unsavory past. Tal Howard solves his difficult adjustment problems following his release from a P.O.W. camp during the Korean war simply by falling in love with Ruth Stamm in *A Bullet for Cinderella*. Betty Larkin is cured of her frigidity in *Deadly Welcome* (1959) and Jill Townsend overcomes her painful shyness in *Murder for The Bride* thanks to the loving ministrations of understanding men who provide happily-ever-after lives for them. Often the rewards are professional as well as emotional. Clint Sewell not only marries his secretary in *You Live Once*, he is also promised a major promotion in his company. There is, of course, nothing wrong with happy endings in themselves; the flaw is primarily an aesthetic

one in that the happy endings are frequently arbitrarily tacked on at
the end. Not demanded by the plot, they simply tie things neatly
together and offer the kind of reassurance that was, to be fair to
MacDonald, common in stories and movies of the fifties. In retrospect,
however, MacDonald's endings are sometimes as unconvincing to
contemporary tastes as the Doris Day films so popular at that time.

Despite such lapses, MacDonald's storytelling ability is outstanding. Even when the endings sometimes prove disappointing, the
reader cannot fail but become caught up in the story, which, thanks
to MacDonald's skillful handling of plot, generates its own compelling
rhythm, and what contributes so much to the success of his stories is
his ability to create characters. Whether focusing on the interrelation-
ships of people living at a seaside marina (*The Beach Girls*), operating
a family-owned business (*The Crossroads*), jockeying for power at a
business convention (*A Key to the Suite*), vacationing together (*All
These Condemned*), or simply thrown together by crisis (*Murder in
the Wind* and *The Damned*), he depicts the rich variety of the human
animal's interplay with his fellow creatures so skillfully that Anthony
Boucher was prompted to dub him "the John O'Hara of the crime-
suspense field." His insights into the mysteries of male–female relationships, particularly their more erotic and sensual forms, suggest a
comparison more with D. H. Lawrence than with O'Hara. His probings
of modern marriage in such novels as *Clemmie, The Deceivers,* and
Cancel All Our Vows compare favorably with John Updike's acute
explorations of the marital condition. The point is that MacDonald's
primary interest is people and their interactions, and his skill in
creating credible individuals and endlessly fascinating relationships
provides the flesh-and-blood substance to his usually deft plots.

Not surprisingly, given so large a fictional output, characterizations
occasionally become stereotyped. Many of his women, for example,
approach human perfection in their virtues, both physical and sexual,
and the breathless rhapsodizing between male and female characters
sometimes gets out of control. In a few instances, villains are melo-
dramatically overdrawn: in *The Price of Murder* (1957), Johnny Keefler,
a sadistic parole officer obsessed with avenging his uncle's murder by
a gang of youths, continually beats his artificial hand against his thigh
"so as to feel more clearly the aching and the pain." Dwight McAran,
in *One Monday We Killed Them All* (1961), kicks dogs, rapes young
girls, shoots his own sister, and even cuts the heads off the cardboard

cutout dolls she made when they were children—like William Faulkner's Popeye. Admittedly, MacDonald's villains are usually motivated
by the more understandable vices of greed, lust, power, and the like
rather than by such offbeat psychotic quirks.

Finally, each of the early novels is distinguished by MacDonald's
clear, clean prose. Recognizing the primacy of story and character, he
conscientiously avoids a prose that is too ornate or too self-conscious.
But eschewing an overly mannered style does not as a consequence
result in a bland, lifeless prose. Far from being merely serviceable,
MacDonald's prose is colorful, his language expressive, his rhythms
graceful. One would not expect a writer who turned out three or four
books a year to be as exacting as, say, Flaubert. Nevertheless,
MacDonald is a consummate craftsman and his descriptions, observations, and dialogue are the result of care, attention to telling detail,
affection for the language, and control over its power to generate
emotional responses in the reader.

Although categorization is often arbitrary and misleading,
MacDonald's pre–Travis McGee novels can easily be divided into two
groups: those that are primarily crime, mystery, or suspense thrillers,
and those that are not. Into the latter category falls some of his best
work. *Cancel All Our Vows* (1953) and *The Deceivers* (1958), for
example, are perceptive explorations of marriage and infidelity. *A Key
to the Suite* (1962), which MacDonald consistently lists among his
favorites, is an uncompromising look at the new corporate ethics. The
action of the novel takes place during a business conference at a Florida
resort hotel, during which MacDonald exposes the rituals of conventions and the machinations of corporate intrigue and position-jockeying
with acute perception. The success of the novel is due to MacDonald's
uncompromising honesty in his depiction of Floyd Hubbard, an
ambitious up-and-coming executive who is given the task of informing
the company sales manager that he is finished. He carries out his
superior's commands, thus demonstrating he has what it takes to move
up into the higher echelons of the company. However, his actions also
expose the costly damage to his humanity that such ruthlessness
demands.

Some of MacDonald's best fiction is, surprisingly, comic. *Please
Write for Details* (1959), a romantic comedy set at a Mexican hotel
that has been turned into an artists' colony, is populated by a delightfully
loony bunch of characters. *The Girl, the Gold Watch, and Everything*

(1962), an entertaining blend of the serious and the fanciful, starts out as a novel of corporate intrigue but is soon transformed into an antic comedy when Kirby Winters discovers that the gold watch his millionaire uncle bequeathed him can magically stop time. With the assistance of lusty, free-spirited Bonnie Lee Beaumont, Kirby investigates his newfound toy in a variety of amusing ways. The novel raises serious questions—such as how should one handle power, in this case the ultimate power to alter the outcome of future events—in a light, whimsical manner which is an unexpected though pleasing departure for the usually serious MacDonald. His ability to create entertaining comic characters is also demonstrated in *The Beach Girls* (1959), a sort of Atlantic Coast *Cannery Row*.

One of MacDonald's most impressive and ambitious novels, *A Flash of Green* (1962), depicts the fierce battle between environmentalists, who are trying to save a small bay on the west coast of Florida, and local developers, who seek to fill it in in order to erect a housing development there. Despite their success in stopping an earlier attempt, the conservation group is doomed to defeat at the hands of the powerful moneymen, who use any means, including blackmail, bribery, and intimidation, to get their way. Although MacDonald is clearly on the side of the environmentalists (the book is dedicated to three friends and "all others opposed to the uglification of America"), *A Flash of Green* manages to avoid becoming a shrill polemic. There is anger in much of the writing—a character, for example, looking at the coast of Florida from the air, comments: "The land was some great fallen animal. And all the night lights marked the long angry sore in its hide, a noisome, festering wound, maggoty and moving, draining blood and serum into the silent Gulf"—but a feeling of resignation hangs over the account of the defeat of the environmentalists' efforts. The novel focuses on the human battle between men and women of good will and principle on one side, and men of power and money, men used to getting their own way, on the other. In the end, the losers include not only the environmentalists but also those, like newspaperman Jimmy Wing, who are compromised and corrupted by the battle. This eloquent protest against the ongoing rape of the environment and the exploitation of natural resources and beauty was an early warning shot in what has become a full-scale fusillade in our present day.

Perhaps the most popular of MacDonald's non-mystery novels is

Condominium (1977), which appeared on *The New York Times* best-seller list for six months. The novel, which follows the *Grand Hotel–Airport* pattern of many of his books, is ambitious (more than a third longer than any of his other novels), sprawling, serious in intention, and chock-full of information. One critic remarked that in *Condominium* MacDonald reminded him of the man who, when asked for the time, explained instead how to make a watch. While it is true that MacDonald has forsaken the pace, economy, and taut structure of his best work, his sprawling narrative style allows him to tell the stories of dozens of characters and to include an encyclopedic array of information about condominiums, their construction, management, financing, etc., as well as technical data about the geological history of Florida, the development of hurricanes, and the devastating power of nature.

The novel details what happens to some poorly constructed condominiums perched on a key off the west coast of Florida when a massive hurricane strikes. This simple plot is buttressed by a multitude of subplots involving the private dramas of his many characters, each of whom is given his or her own history, quirks, interests, foibles, and dreams in the shorthand individualization MacDonald does so well. Everything leads up to the hurricane itself, a masterpiece of realistic writing. MacDonald, as is his wont, combines an impressive amount of factual information about hurricanes in general, their history and effects, with a gripping, almost documentary-like account of the death and destruction left in the wake of the one which strikes in *Condominium*.

One of the weaknesses of the novel, at least in comparison with his finest work, is the lack of a clear emotional center in the novel. Instead, MacDonald focuses his attention on an entire group, namely the elderly and retired who have come to Florida in pursuit of the golden years—which, for many, consist of little more than waiting around to die. He writes with compassion and sympathy about the many issues surrounding the treatment of the elderly, who have become almost a race apart in America. Although *Condominium* is not MacDonald's best work, lacking the emotional depth of his better fiction, it is distinguished by brutal authenticity in its description of the awesome destruction of the hurricane, by MacDonald's compassionate portrayal of the plight of the elderly in America, and by his denouncement of man's folly in thinking he can control the forces of nature, especially when such efforts are vitiated by his greed and stupidity.

Our primary focus, however, is on the crime/mystery genre, and it is here where MacDonald's reputation and greatest fictional accomplishments lie. His first published novel, *The Brass Cupcake* (1950), is a mystery patterned after the hard-boiled stories of Dashiell Hammett and Raymond Chandler. Its hero is a private investigator, which strongly suggests that MacDonald gave more than passing consideration to entering the private-eye sweepstakes with his own fictional hero. (*The Brass Cupcake* was published only a year after Chandler's *The Little Sister* and Ross Macdonald's *The Moving Target*, the first Lew Archer novel.) However, well aware of the limitations imposed by a series character and anxious to retain maximum freedom in his writing, MacDonald chose not to develop his hero beyond a single book. Nevertheless, *The Brass Cupcake* is important as an early indication of an interest that would lead, some fourteen years later, to the creation of Travis McGee.

Cliff Bartells is an insurance investigator for the Security Theft and Accident Company in Florence City, Florida. A former lieutenant with the Florence City police department, he was forced to quit when he refused to cooperate in a department-engineered framing of an innocent man. An honest cop, his gold badge reduced in his eyes to what he now cynically calls a "brass cupcake," Bartells has managed to begin a new career as an insurance investigator. Like his hard-boiled fictional predecessors, Bartells is tough, incorruptible, indestructible; like them, his attitude is irreverent and his wisecracks, quips, and witty comments give his narrative a colorful flavor.

Bartells is hired to investigate the theft of several jewels—insured by his company for $750,000—from wealthy Elizabeth Stegman, who was murdered during the robbery. However, his desire to get revenge against the corrupt officials of Florence City causes him to become something more than a simple insurance adjustor. During the course of the novel, he retrieves the jewels, solves the murder of Elizabeth Stegman, brings her killer to justice, and exposes the corruption of his former police colleagues (who, as he suspected they would, steal the $300,000 he delivers to the thieves for return of the jewels). In the process, he is beaten up and shot at, but in the end he prevails and returns to the force as Deputy Chief.

Having him rejoin the police force is one way MacDonald resists the temptation of continuing Bartells's career as a private investigator. Nevertheless, his choice of a hero like Bartells, who is mindful of the morality of his actions and who doggedly pursues his course of action to its conclusion despite the risks, is significant. For although Mac-Donald chooses not to develop his character beyond *The Brass Cupcake*, he does not entirely forsake the private-eye hero, as several of his subsequent novels will demonstrate.

Dead Low Tide (1953) rises above the level of much of MacDonald's early fiction by virtue of its excellent plot, interesting characters, polished style, and protagonist—who is yet another prototype of Travis McGee. Andrew McClintock, like his creator a graduate in business administration from Syracuse University, has come to the Gulf Coast of Florida to join John Long's construction company. Working in his office late one evening, he is visited by Long's worried wife, Mary Eleanor, who wants his help in finding out what is bothering her husband. But before he can learn anything, Long is found dead, an apparent suicide. Thanks, however, to some incriminating evidence (Long's death was caused by McClintock's harpoon gun) and the perjured testimony of Mary Eleanor (who falsely claims to have been having an affair with him), McClintock is shortly arrested for murder. The subsequent discovery of the body of his neighbor, friend, and former lover, Christy Honeywell, murdered while he was in jail, temporarily frees him from suspicion, but provides him with more than enough impetus to solve the mystery of the two deaths.

Circumstances thus transform McClintock from a businessman into a private detective; and a very effective one he proves to be. His snooping uncovers several interesting facts: he finds an envelope in the apartment of Joy Kenney, a secretary recently hired by John Long, which contains explicit photographs of Mary Eleanor Long making love with a man whose face has been scissored out of the pictures; he discovers that Mary Eleanor recently borrowed $40,000 and concludes that someone, perhaps the man in the pictures, is blackmailing her; from a waitress who used to work with Joy Kenney, he learns about a suspicious boyfriend of Joy's who used to work at the same diner. As the pieces begin to fall into place, he determines to question Mary Eleanor further, only to discover that she too has been murdered.

The key to the solution of the mystery comes as a real surprise when the police produce an unexpected witness—the supposedly dead Christy Honeywell. After befriending Joy Kenney, Christy learned from her that her brother (whom everyone mistakenly assumed was her boyfriend) was blackmailing Mary Eleanor Long over the pictures; when John Long discovered the photographs, Kenney killed him and later murdered Mary Eleanor when he feared she would expose him as her husband's murderer. When he learned that his sister was confiding in Christy, he killed her too. Or thought he did. But she survived and has been cooperating with the police in setting a trap for Kenney. However, in the confusion caused by the happy reunion between Christy and McClintock, Kenney slips away. When he later returns to finish the job on her, McClintock, using a casting rod, kills him by embedding a fishing spoon in his neck, the third such grisly death by a neck wound in the novel.

In their *Catalogue of Crime*, Jacques Barzun and Wendell Hertig Taylor cite *Dead Low Tide* as one of MacDonald's "best stories of sex and violence." It is unquestionably one of his better novels, yet while there is no denying its violent elements (although its sex is largely implied), it is misleading to categorize the novel so baldly. For despite the more exciting aspects, its success is equally due to other qualities. For example, the plot is masterfully constructed; from a quiet beginning, the novel picks up momentum with the sudden and unexpected death of John Long. From this point on, the plot moves swiftly and in unexpected directions, and MacDonald's handling of both mystery and suspense is outstanding. Also, the characterizations are excellent, especially Roy Kenney, whose brief but memorable appearance in the novel reveals him as a character whose bright, articulate manner effectively obscures the fact that he is a calculatingly vicious psychopath.

Above all, there is the character of McClintock. Instead of the tough-talking, wisecracking style appropriate for a character like Cliff Bartells in *The Brass Cupcake*, MacDonald employs a wittier, more thoughtful, more colorfully descriptive style for McClintock's narration that effectively expresses a variety of emotional reactions—from confusion over being wrongly charged with murder, to grief at receiving the news about Christy's death, to joy at learning that she is alive after all. MacDonald also uses McClintock's narration to impart his own opinions on such issues as riparian rights, suicide, the unfairness of life, the changing face of the Florida scene—observations similar to those that will become such an integral part of Travis McGee's character. Typically, these comments are delivered in a succinct and colorful manner. For example, musing about the sexually explicit photographs of Mary Eleanor Long he discovers, McClintock remarks: "They were sick scenes, like the imaginings that sometimes float up out of the stagnant pools in the dark valleys of your mind. They were that ultimate evil which denies and almost refutes the existence of the human soul. They bore that same relation to love that heroin bears to red wine."

What also emerges as an important aspect of his character is his moral sensitivity. McClintock suppresses his sexual longing for Christy Honeywell and his emotional involvement (which he doesn't realize he has until he thinks she is dead) because he knows that "there was more profit to both of us in friendship than in love with a small l." He rejects the explicit advances of Mary Eleanor Long because he knows that if he succumbed, "it would be the kind of memory I couldn't scrub off my soul with a wire brush." Finally, when he is forced into a situation where he must kill a man, he takes no pleasure in the act; in fact, it causes him "an abrupt distortion and dislocation of the soul." McClintock is a believable hero whose personality, situation, and emotional experiences earn the reader's sympathy. Through him MacDonald succeeds in moving the mystery story a step beyond the thriller into the realm of the character study.

Less successful but important nonetheless because its protagonist is yet another ancestor of Travis McGee is *Death Trap* (1957). Construction engineer Hugh MacReedy, home after spending two and a half years working in Spain, happens to read a newspaper account about the upcoming execution of Alister Landy for rape and murder. Landy is the brother of Vicky Landy, a woman MacReedy seduced and then abandoned three years earlier while working in the mid-western town of Warrentown. Despite his adherence to a *Playboy*-inspired pleasure principle ("My basic and instinctive reaction to the female was to attempt to rack up a score, add a pelt to the trophy shelf"), his conscience has been bothering him ever since the episode with Vicky. In fact, only belatedly has he admitted to himself how much she means to him emotionally. Guilty, ashamed, and hopeful of resuming his relationship with her, he heads for Warrentown, locates Vicky, admits his mistake, and declares his true feelings for her. However, she announces that any hope of a resumed relationship depends upon the fate of her brother, for she is so attached to him, and so convinced of his innocence, that if he should die, she will be unfit for marriage with any man. Thus armed with a compelling personal motive for involvement, MacReedy abandons his vacation plans in order to devote all his efforts to proving Alister's innocence.

Less wisecracking and hard-boiled than Cliff Bartells, less the thoughtful commentator than McClintock, MacReedy is characterized more by his physical strength. In fact, MacDonald stresses his physical prowess to the detriment of the novel. MacReedy is involved in four fistfights, two of them with a sadistic local policeman, one with the town tough guy (who takes out his humiliation at losing to MacReedy by stomping his girlfriend to death), none of which have any real bearing on the plot. MacReedy's solution of the mystery as to who murdered the girl Alister Landy is accused of killing is due not to strength but rather to dogged questioning and intuition; as an outsider, he is the only one able to come up with the answer the local citizens have been unable (or unwilling) to look for.

In many ways *Death Trap* resembles the type of mystery novel associated with Ross Macdonald. For one thing, MacReedy discovers that the solution to the crime lies seven years in the past, when eleven-year-old Nancy Paulson was sexually molested by a family friend, Billy Mackin. Five years later, still obsessed with Nancy, Mackin killed her boyfriend by drowning him. However, Nancy's younger sister, Jane Ann, happened to witness the murder and began blackmailing him. So he killed her and framed Landy, Nancy's current boyfriend. There is a good deal of amateur psychoanalyzing in the novel, particularly of Nancy Paulson, who not only bears the emotional scars of her childhood trauma, which she has almost totally suppressed, but whose sexual development has been warped by a puritanical father. Only under hypnosis does the truth come out, finally freeing her from the shackles of the past and exonerating Alister Landy.

The plot of *Death Trap* lacks the pace and narrative drive of his best fiction because undue attention is paid to the side issue of the reckless, self-destructive behavior of America's young, many of whom are portrayed in the novel as being interested only in sex, booze, drugs, and hell-raising. This is a theme that frequently pops up in MacDonald's fiction (cf. *The Neon Jungle*), and one of his better books, *The End of the Night*, is devoted to a careful analysis of the possible causes of this disturbing phenomenon. However in *Death Trap*, the subplot involving sexually precocious Ginny Garson and her fatal involvement with Hardesty Smith, a local hood whose father is president of the bank, only serves to distract from the primary concern of the novel—MacReedy's successful search for the truth, which saves an innocent man from execution and secures the lasting love of the woman he once treated so badly, thereby atoning for his past behavior.

Among the most exciting and suspenseful of MacDonald's early thrillers is *The Executioners* (1958), a chilling study in terror which was the basis for the popular 1962 film *Cape Fear*, starring Gregory Peck and Robert Mitchum. Attorney Sam Bowden, a decent and honorable man, finds his idyllic suburban life disrupted and his family's lives threatened by the unexpected appearance of Max Cady, who has come seeking revenge against Bowden, whom he blames for the thirteen-year prison term he has just completed. Bowden and Cady were stationed in the U.S. Army together in Melbourne, Australia; one night Bowden saw Cady raping a local girl and his testimony at the subsequent court martial resulted in Cady's conviction. During his lengthy imprisonment, Cady's wife remarried and his twelve-year-old son was killed in an accident. Embittered, the crazed Cady has tracked Bowden down in order to get even with him.

The ensuing suspense as the sadistic Cady poses a greater and greater threat to the members of Bowden's family is unremitting. At first satisfied with merely poisoning the Bowdens' dog, he later causes their car to crash by loosening the lug nuts holding the wheel on, and finally shoots and wounds Bowden's son. What makes Bowden's plight so terrifying is that his frantic efforts to obtain protection from the authorities prove fruitless. As an attorney he is confident that the law will protect him from Cady, but he is horrified to discover that since Cady's threats are veiled rather than overt, the police are powerless to prevent his assaults. At first reluctant to go outside the law, in desperation Bowden is reduced to trying unsuccessfully to hire a gunman from a local mobster. Eventually he is forced to take matters into his own hands in order to defend himself against Cady's murderous onslaught, and in the exciting conclusion to the novel he kills Cady when Cady invades his home.

In *The Executioners* MacDonald uses the format of the taut suspense thriller to raise a number of important questions about the inability of civilized society, despite its many laws and elaborate structures of authority, to deal with the savage threats represented by a madman like Cady. The frightening (albeit sometimes melodramatic) elements of the story also serve to embody a kind of existential parable in which the orderly life of an average man is exposed to the sudden intrusion of the irrational and unexpected. Only Bowden's pride at demonstrating his strength and courage under duress mitigates against the disillusionment he suffers thanks to his discovery of the vulnerability of civilized society. MacDonald deftly combines philosophy, psychology, sociology, and old-fashioned mortal terror to produce in *The Executioners* a gripping tale that challenges the mind as it excites the emotions.

While no clear-cut development in MacDonald's artistry can be traced chronologically from one novel to the next (or even from one year to the next), 1960 can be singled out as a turning point in his career, a watershed year that separates the generally skillful work of the fifties from the richer, more mature works that followed. Between 1960 and 1964, MacDonald published many of his best non-mystery novels, works like *A Key to the Suite, A Flash of Green,* and *The Girl, the Gold Watch, and Everything,* as well as several mystery novels of considerable distinction. Beginning with *Slam the Big Door* and *The Only Girl in the Game* in 1960, MacDonald's efforts became more ambitious, his canvas more detailed, his colors more varied and subtler in tone. Moreover, by aiming at more complex characterizations, larger themes, and a more serious purpose than simply telling a good story, MacDonald produced a number of works that successfully blur the distinction between the "thriller" and the "serious" novel.

Slam the Big Door is a sympathetic yet unsparing portrait of a man bent on self-destruction. Troy Jamison wrecked his successful New York advertising career and happy marriage by drinking heavily and by becoming involved with an unsavory woman by the name of Jerranna Rowley. Thanks to the efforts of his Marine Corps buddy, Mike Rodenska, he managed to pick up the pieces of his life, move to Florida, and begin anew with a small construction company. Now, several years later, he has remarried and is in the midst of building an impressive housing development, Horseshoe Pass Estates. However, familiar danger signs are once more beginning to appear: he is drinking heavily again; there are rumors of financial problems involving his new development; and the woman from his past, Jerranna Rowley, has turned up in Florida. It is at this juncture that Mike Rodenska arrives to spend some time with Jamison in order to recuperate from his own tragedy—the recent death of his wife. He isn't there long before he begins to notice the telltale cracks in Jamison's new life.

Rodenska, like so many of MacDonald's characters, including Travis McGee, cannot help but become involved in his friend's problems. A self-described "mister fixit," he suffers from what he calls "the Curse of Rodenska," a natural proclivity for offering a helping hand. When he hears the rumors about the shaky financial status of Jamison's construction project, he noses around like the good newspaperman he used to be, discovers that the project is not as precarious as rumors suggest, and even uncovers evidence that one of Jamison's own partners might be trying to sabotage the project in order to take it over himself. Rodenska bails Jamison out by lending him his $300,000 inheritance, thus solving his immediate cash flow problem. When he learns that Jerranna Rowley is in the area, he finds her and offers her and her boyfriend $1,000 to leave. He also tries to counsel Jamison in an attempt to save his business and his marriage.

But he fails, largely because Jamison is too obsessed with his own dark demons to be saved. In an earlier novel, *Clemmie*, MacDonald created in the character of Craig Fitz a man who loses his job and almost his life after falling victim to the charms of a sexually alluring woman. He comes to his senses in time, however, to salvage his marriage and his life. No such happy ending awaits Jamison, whose plight is more serious, nor does MacDonald flinch from the implications of the situation (as he might have done in an earlier work). Jerranna is not so much the cause as the symbol of Jamison's self-destructive urges, an instrument of his self-hatred; whether driven by guilt over a war experience in which the ten men under his command were killed, or simply by fear of failure (which ironically becomes a compulsion to fail), Jamison cannot save himself and moves as inexorably as a figure from Greek tragedy toward his impending doom. He begins seeing Jerranna again; gets arrested for drunken driving; seduces (or is seduced by) Debbie Ann Hunter, his sexually provocative stepdaughter; later, consumed by self-disgust, he attacks and nearly kills her. The big door is finally slammed on him (MacDonald uses the phrase "slam the big door" the way Chandler used "the big sleep," as a euphemism for death, in this case sudden violent death) when he is killed, along with Jerranna and her boyfriend and the four occupants of another car, in a grinding head-on collision on a lonely Florida highway one evening. (The accident is described in such harrowing detail that Kurt Vonnegut called it "a sort of Beethoven's Fifth for coroners and safety engineers.") Jamison is at last freed from his demons.

Despite the moving portrait of Jamsion, MacDonald's primary interest is Rodenska, whose actions, though they fail to save his friend, clearly embody the obligations of friendship (and in a departure from the pattern of most of MacDonald's books, the friend in question is not a female with whom the protagonist is romantically involved). He is a do-gooder, although his desire to do good operates, as it does in the case of Travis McGee, only on a personal level. He feels no compulsion or desire to redeem the world, only a personal obligation to try to salvage his friend's life. When all of Jamison's New York friends desert him in the midst of his drinking crisis, only Rodenska comes to his aid. His actions, like those of many of MacDonald's protagonists, are motivated by a sense of personal honor, the direct result of a private code of behavior.

Rodenska's personal code not only prompts his decision to help Jamison, it also influences his behavior with women. For example, finding himself drawn to the seductive Jerranna Rowley during their first meeting, he fights to suppress his erotic impulses because he knows that following through would "have irreparably changed his own inner image of himself, made it forever hard for him to have looked deep into his own mirrored eyes." He spurns the advances of the sexually bold Debbie Ann Hunter; such involvement would violate his code. He tells himself:

> It's the subjective harm, Michael. To be desperately old-fashioned, the loss of honor. It would be just a switch on the salesman and the farmer's daughter. You were asked down to relax and mend. The services of the daughter of the household were not included in the facilities available. And, because you have years to live, and nobody cares deeply how you live them, and sons to raise, let's beware of the sophistry that nobody gives a damn what you do. Because you do give a damn. When there's nothing left but your own image of yourself, it somehow becomes a more grievous sin to smear it.

Rodenska's behavior is based on what he calls "old-timey" morality, on a recognition that he is "still on this good and evil kick" and mustn't violate the image he has of himself as a moral man. Although there is more than a hint of self-righteousness in his character, and a touch of what Debbie Ann calls "the reek of church talk" in his philosophizing, MacDonald clearly intends us to admire Rodenska's moral sensitivity and his faithful adherence to a self-designed code of behavior that determines his relationships with others. Integrity. Personal honor. Authenticity. These are the qualities of the ethically responsible individual that are standard components of the MacDonald protagonist, attributes that will become crucial elements in the character of Travis McGee.

Troy Jamison's stormy personal tragedy unfolds beneath the bright Florida sunshine on Ravenna Key and Riley Key, fictional settings off the state's west coast. Most of MacDonald's early novels are set in small towns in the Midwest or in upstate New York; only a few are set in Florida (*The Brass Cupcake, Dead Low Tide, April Evil, The Beach Girls*) and in these the locale is not particularly significant. But with *Slam the Big Door*, MacDonald for the first time uses the setting for something more than local color. In one sense the sparkling Florida sunshine can be seen simply as an ironic counterpoint to the bleak story detailed in the novel, but MacDonald is interested in something more substantial than this. Just as the West was viewed as the land of opportunity beckoning Americans in the nineteenth and early twentieth centuries, the Sun Belt states have in recent years become the new frontier, the place for new beginnings and get-rich dreams. Troy Jamison illustrates the point. After his defeat in New York, he was able to start anew and achieve success as a land developer in Florida. Once he makes a mistake, however, he becomes a sitting duck for the likes of such local wizards as Purdy Elmarr, whose good-ole-boy appearance belies his shrewdness, his knowledge of everything worth knowing, and his ability to profit from the slightest mistake anyone makes, especially newcomers from the North.

But it isn't just as a symbol of new opportunity that MacDonald is interested in exploring the Florida setting. Florida also attracts other types, including those looking for what Rodenska sardonically calls "the last outposts of gracious living." These are the people, many of them Jamison's neighbors, with money but no values, no roots, no substance. These are the fun-lovers whose entertainments have a labored, almost strident quality to them. These are the people who have enough money and leisure time to move to Florida seeking the "Kodachrome Life," but who become so caught up in the pursuit of self-gratification that they fail to establish any significant meaning in their lives. These two types—the money-makers and the moneyed but aimless pleasure-seekers—are among the more interesting local flora and fauna of the New Florida that MacDonald will henceforth examine more closely in his fiction.

MacDonald offers in *The Only Girl in the Game* a behind-the-

scenes glimpse into one of the most exotic of all American businesses—
Las Vegas. The reader learns about the ticklish relationship between
the hotel and casino operations of a Vegas showplace, how cash is
skimmed off the top, how big rollers are subtly manipulated to continue
playing, despite their losses, how drunks, suicides, and employees
who cannot refrain from gambling are dealt with. But as usual
MacDonald is careful to locate his characters so naturally in their
milieu that the background, however exotic, never overwhelms them.

Hugh Darren is a promising young executive hired to salvage the
foundering Cameroon Hotel in Las Vegas. Within a few months he
straightens out the mess he inherited, puts the hotel on a sound
paying basis, and earns the admiration of both his superiors and
underlings. However, he has no long-term ambitions in Vegas; he is
the proud owner of Peppercorn Cay, a tiny sixty-acre tropical island
in the Bahamas, and has mapped out an ambitious plan, with the help
of friendly investors, to build a resort hotel there. He intends to stay
in Vegas for just three years, long enough to save the money he figures
he will need to realize his dream. He works hard, taking time out for
only one diversion—Betty Dawson, a beautiful entertainer in the
Cameroon with whom he has become romantically involved. Lady
Luck soon stops smiling, however, and deals him a hand that only
confirms his suspicion that the odds never favor the players.

The key figure in the unfortunate turn of events is Homer
Gallowell, a seventy-year-old Texas multimillionaire who lost $200,000
at the gaming tables on his previous visit to Vegas. Although the loss
of money is no more than a mere annoyance to Gallowell, the insult
to his pride is unbearable, so with the assistance of the best mathematical minds in his employ, he devises a betting system that he feels
confident will enable him to win back his money. Gallowell is one of
MacDonald's most interesting characters, a good-ole-boy type whose
calculating shrewdness makes him a formidable opponent in any
scheme. He returns to Vegas with but a single purpose, coolly follows
his system, and wins $225,000, thus upsetting the owners of the
Cameroon, who are disinclined to allow anyone to leave town with so
much of their money.

Unbeknownst to Darren, his girlfriend, Betty Dawson, has a
shady past she is unable to escape. As a struggling performer she
auditioned for a job at the Cameroon and found it required that she
first entertain a big winner. Unfortunately for her, her activities were

filmed by the casino owners, who threatened to send the films to her father, a prominent San Francisco physician, unless she did their bidding. Casino manager Max Hanes uses her sparingly, only when he needs her special charms to keep a really big winner in town, thus improving the house's odds of winning its money back. Only the timely news that her father (from whom she has sought to hide her indiscretions) has suddenly died spares her from being forced to deceive Gallowell, whom she had befriended on his previous visit to Vegas. She immediately confesses the situation to Gallowell, who graciously thanks her for her honesty and returns to Texas with his winnings.

Things take a tragic turn at this point. Hanes orders a couple of thugs to rough Betty up, to knock some sense into her. Unfortunately, while scuffling with them, she hits her head on a table and is critically injured. Taken to the desert, she is killed and unceremoniously buried. Her sudden disappearance deeply disturbs Darren, even though she has left behind a note telling him she was leaving (freed from her situation by her father's death, she had decided to leave Darren in order to spare him the agony of learning about her past). When a private investigator comes to Vegas looking for her after she failed to appear for her father's funeral, Darren's sorrow turns to concern. He snoops around, turns the hotel into an elaborate espionage network, and finally learns what happened. He then seeks the assistance of Homer Gallowell, who gives him $130,000 to set a trap for those responsible for Betty's death. Darren plants the money so that the hotel owner, Al Marta, will suspect that his associates have been skimming cash from him. Marta orders them all executed, then suffers the same fate when his superiors decide he can no longer be trusted.

MacDonald's early novels would never have ended like this, with the hero denied the woman he loves. But as he did in *Slam the Big Door*, MacDonald sacrifices happy endings for the good of his material. Not only is Betty murdered but Temple Shannard, Darren's old friend and one of the investors he is counting on to help him fund the Peppercorn Cay project, also ends up dead. Shannard came to Vegas in hopes of raising some quick cash to help him finance a current project. The Vegas moneymen like the deal, but instead of agreeing to become his partners, as he hoped, they offer only to buy him out. So he decides to try to raise the money at the gaming tables. Before his wife and Darren are able to stop him, he loses $63,000. When he

sobers up the next morning and realizes the full magnitude of his
losses, he leaps from his balcony to the pavement eight floors below.
The big green money machine has claimed another victim; "it never
faltered," MacDonald writes, "chomping and grinding that innocent
flesh, spewing out disillusion—and keeping the money."

The deaths of Shannard and Betty underscore the destruction
that money leaves in its wake when it becomes the all-consuming goal.
They also emphasize the proximity of the threat to Darren himself.
Although wary of the "stench" permeating Vegas, the moral corruption
surrounding him, he believes he can maintain his immunity. Nevertheless, he finds himself compromising more and more, accepting cash
bonuses for little favors he does for Max Hanes, with the result that
his confidence in his immunity begins to sound more and more like a
rationalization:

> I am adjusting, Hugh told himself. That's all. When your stance is
> too rigid, they knock you down. So you stand loose, ready to bob,
> weave and sidestep. Flexibility is the clue to local survival. So I
> shall stand under the money tree and hold my pockets wide open,
> and if some falls in, it isn't my doing. It's just gravity. This doesn't
> have to touch me in any basic way. I'll make what I have to make,
> and then I shall pack up and leave, and run my own show in my
> own way.

But when he sees what the money machine does to his friends, he
resolves to strike back at it. Motivated by a combination of grief and
guilt, he seeks revenge not only in the name of love and friendship
but also as a purgative, as a way of cleansing his own conscience for
having himself participated in such an odious system. After gaining
revenge against Max Hanes and the others, he accepts a physically
demanding job on one of Gallowell's oil rigs in the Gulf of Mexico as
his personal penance.

With his fascination for intricate moneymaking schemes, it is only
natural that sooner or later MacDonald would get around to examining
Las Vegas, the granddaddy of them all. The American Dream for
many of MacDonald's characters can be defined simply—striking it
rich—and the casinos of Las Vegas are the temples where the dreamers
worship. A character like Gallowell is able to move unscathed through
the green-felt world because moneymaking to him is nothing more

than a coldly rational mathematical process. He is not without feeling or emotion (although he doles it out in small quantities for a selected few, like Betty, whom he genuinely likes), but when it comes to business, his eyes are "cold as geometry, merciless as a drill bit." On the other hand, big dreamers like Shannard are tragically vulnerable to money's siren song. And people like Betty Dawson often become innocent victims of the malignancy lurking behind the glittering neon façade.

In addition to *Slam the Big Door* and *The Only Girl in the Game*, 1960 also saw the publication of *The End of the Night*, a chilling novel about four young misfits, known collectively as "The Wolf Pack," whose violent wave of terror and crime foreshadows such later sixties phenomena as the Manson murders in Los Angeles. Written, according to MacDonald, as a result of his curiosity about the involvement of increasing numbers of upper-middle-class adolescents in mindless vandalism and crime, the novel offers several penetrating insights into the sociological and psychological aspects of group murder and violence.

The foregoing three novels, published in the space of less than a year, give ample evidence of a new direction in MacDonald's fiction, one which indicates that the demands of the material are to be given precedence over the desire for a tidy conclusion or an arbitrarily imposed happy ending.

MacDonald returns to the fictional town of Florence City, Florida (used in his first novel, *The Brass Cupcake*) and to the private-eye format in *Where Is Janice Gantry?* (1961). (He also foreshadows the continuity a series provides by including the Sarasota pianist, Charlie Davies, who appeared in *Dead Low Tide*, as well as a reference to the automobile crash that killed Troy Jamison in *Slam the Big Door*.) What distinguishes the Travis McGee prototype in this novel from his predecessors in *The Brass Cupcake* and *Dead Low Tide* is his complexity as a character. No longer satisfied with a protagonist who is simply shrewd enough or strong enough to solve a crime, MacDonald creates in Sam Brice a figure of considerable substance and depth, whose investigation of a crime becomes inextricably bound up with the resolution of his internal conflicts.

Brice has returned to his boyhood home of Florence City under a cloud of suspicion. A former local hero and All-State football player, he has come home after a three-year career as an offensive tackle in the NFL. Although the rumor is he was kicked out of professional football for cheating, the truth is he was banned for failing to report to league officials an unsuccessful attempt to bribe him to throw a game. The affair also cost him his wife, who left following the incident. He has started a new career in the insurance business (as Cliff Bartells did in *The Brass Cupcake*) as owner and operator of a one-man agency called Automotive Appraisal Associates. However, his personal setbacks have left him so wary that his fear of emotional involvement has caused the recent breakup of his affair with Janice Gantry, although they have remained good friends and she has continued to work as his secretary.

Among the authors MacDonald admires most are Joseph Conrad and William Faulkner, both of whom created protagonists with a philosophy of noninvolvement similar to Brice's. But like Conrad's Axel Heyst (in *Victory*) and Faulkner's Gail Hightower (in *Light in August*), Brice learns the painful lesson that you cannot enjoy immunity from the human condition, that isolation from emotional relationships is self-destructive. Brice's emotional isolation is challenged early one morning by the appearance of Charlie Haywood, a local boy who has escaped from the state prison where he was serving a sentence for attempting to rob a safe in the home of Florence City resident Maurice Weber. Haywood has sought out Brice because he felt he would understand how it felt to be treated unfairly. Brice is willing to offer food, clothes, and overnight shelter, but nothing else. When he drops Haywood off at a public telephone, he is dismayed to learn that he calls Janice Gantry, who, unlike himself, is eager to help. It was she who nursed Haywood's emotional wounds during the darkest days following his return to town and Brice knows that "anything with a broken wing would get her immediate attention." His dismay turns to concern, however, when she fails to show up for work the following day.

So, despite his philosophy of noninvolvement, Brice finds himself searching for Janice. His first step is to try to talk with Charity Weber, reclusive wife of the man whose safe Haywood was caught robbing. (Haywood had mentioned to Brice that he intended to contact her.) But instead of Charity, he meets Peggy Varden, her stepsister and houseguest, with whom he quickly begins to fall in love. From her he learns about the mysterious Webers, who have a fetish about privacy, and about the two strange men who recently stayed at their house. Later Brice gets an opportunity to examine the damaged railing on Weber's expensive yacht and, after noticing a black smear on it, concludes that this could have been caused by the black sports car Janice was driving when last seen. His suspicions aroused, he tries to question Weber, but when he arrives at his house he is attacked and knocked unconscious; when he awakens, he finds himself and Peggy tightly bound and about to be delivered to the same watery fate that, he learns, befell Janice and Haywood when they too tried to talk with Weber.

Weber had once been a small-time political official who documented the corruption of his superiors and then used the evidence to blackmail them into financing his early retirement, complete with yacht, servants, even a couple of hired thugs to ensure his safety. What Charlie Haywood was caught trying to steal from the Webers' safe was not money; spurred on by Charity Weber (with whom he was having an affair), he agreed to steal the evidence Weber hid there implicating her in the murder of her former husband. It turns out that she isn't even Weber's wife, but has been forced into becoming his full-time companion by fear of exposure of her past. When Haywood finally realized that he was simply being used by her, he escaped from prison and returned to establish his innocence. Weber, to protect himself, had Haywood and Janice killed and their bodies placed in her car, which damaged the railing of his yacht when it was dumped into the ocean. Only Brice's superhuman effort in breaking the wire binding his wrists saves him and Peggy from the same fate as they escape overboard and swim to safety.

Brice solves the mystery of Janice's disappearance and uncovers the secret of the Webers, but he is powerless to save Janice or Haywood. This offers further evidence of MacDonald's departure from the simplified system of rewards and punishments operative in his early novels, where the good guys are always rewarded and the evildoers punished. This more mature (and realistic) view also affects the portrayal of his hero, who, although rewarded by being granted a promising future with Peggy Varden as his bride, must also acknowledge the painful fact that his stubborn refusal to help Haywood cost Janice Gantry her life. The guilt, he admits, is something he is going to have to live with for the rest of his life.

MacDonald portrays Brice's gradual change from isolation to involvement convincingly. At first only his pride is affected by Charlie Haywood's accusation that he has pulled himself into a hole, but later he is more deeply stung by the comments of longtime family friend

Ackley Bush, who, in his conversations with Brice, foreshadows the role later played by McGee's friend Meyer. Bush derides Brice for his reluctance to get involved and chastises him for the immaturity of his attitude: "They wouldn't let you climb the apple tree any more, so you went home to sulk." It is Bush who persuades him to try to speak with Charity Weber as the first step in locating Janice. Eventually, Peggy Varden teaches him the benefits of emotional involvement. Like him, she is vulnerable, having lost her husband, but unlike him she is willing to commit herself emotionally, and he soon finds himself responding to her invitation: "With that special tone of voice and the look in her eyes she had pried open the last crypt, letting the stale cold air out, filling that corner of me with a warmth I had never known before." In something of a departure from the usual pattern of MacDonald's books, it is the woman who unlocks the man's frozen heart and becomes the instrument enabling him to overcome his emotional deficiencies.

MacDonald's final novel before the introduction of Travis McGee, *The Drowner* (1963), features his only protagonist who is by profession a private eye. Paul Stanial, an employee of a Miami detective agency, is hired by Barbara Larrimore to investigate the death of her sister, Lucille Hanson, who drowned while swimming alone in a small deserted lake. Barbara received a letter from her sister shortly before her death which has made her suspicious about the drowning and she wants it investigated. The novel follows the typical pattern of the private-eye novel, with Stanial uncovering clues, questioning people, following leads until he finally discovers the identity of the killer. But what distinguishes *The Drowner* is MacDonald's talent for sharp delineation of character, including another interesting variation of the type of protagonist who will in his next book become Travis McGee.

Like Sam Brice and Andrew McClintock, Stanial is in the midst of a personal crisis. After six years with the police force of a northern city, Stanial quit when the department became weakened due to the interference of local politicians and moved to Miami, where he joined a local detective agency. But after two years of investigative work largely confined to what he sarcastically calls "the bedroom circuit," he needs a change, something to challenge his abilities before he finds he stops "giving a damn what he had to do, so long as he was paid." He is also emotionally restless, torn as he is between the hedonistic pleasures of the Miami area—"One big noisy cauldron of busy butts and ripe red mouths, rare steaks and guitars, skinny-dipping and party games, twisters and gin, kicks and tits, laughter and brass horns, oiled brown backs and tall teased hair"—and a desire for something deeper, more lasting, more emotionally fulfilling. The solution to his problem comes with his assignment to investigate Lucille Hanson's death.

His snooping quickly leads him to Sam Kimber, a local business-man who was having an affair with Lucille. He too has reason to believe she might not have died accidentally, for he tells Stanial that a package containing $106,000 in cash, which he stashed in her apartment in order to hide it from the scrutiny of government tax investigators, is missing. Kimber names two possible suspects with enough motive to murder Lucille: Kelsey Hanson, her estranged husband, and Gus Cable, Kimber's lawyer, who knew about the money. But Hanson is cleared and Cable himself is soon murdered. Stanial's suspicions eventually lead him to the most unlikely suspect of all—Angie Powell, Kimber's beautiful and devoted secretary. Although she is widely liked and appears to have had no possible motive for killing anyone, under Stanial's probing her girl-next-door façade slips enough to reveal lurking beneath it the demented mind of a religious fanatic who envisions herself as the Lord's avenger.

Once before, in *You Live Once*, MacDonald created in the character of Wally Pryor a person driven by religious delusions to kill as a self-styled instrument of God's justice. But Angie Powell is more complex, more credible, and ultimately more frightening than Pryor. Despite her tantalizingly sexy appearance (she is six feet tall with a statuesque body and golden hair), she is a sexual neuter, a prude in every sense of the word. She fends off all sexual advances, is embarrassed by any reference to sex—and even alters her bowling delivery to prevent her body movements from becoming too suggestive. But as MacDonald focuses in more closely on her character, her puritanism is revealed to be a pathological fear of sex induced at an early age by a mother who harped on the message that marriage is "vile bondage . . . where a woman has no rights at all and is turned into a soiled vessel for the brute pleasure of some dirty-minded man, crying herself to sleep night after night after he's shamed her and sickened her." Angie has become so sexually repressed that, to assuage her guilt, she has devised such masochistic mortifications of the flesh as burning her arms under a candle and kneeling on hard wooden beads for an hour at a time.

Angie's loyalty to her boss led her to believe she could remove temptation and save his soul by killing Lucille and taking the money he was hiding from the government. When Kimber fired Gus Cable, she took it upon herself to punish Cable for his disloyalty by killing him (incredibly, by reaching up under his ribs and squeezing his heart). When she reluctantly concludes that Kimber is beyond saving, she kills him too and then lures Stanial to the same isolated lake where she killed Lucille. She hides beneath the dock and when Stanial walks to the end of it, she grabs his leg and pulls him under the water. Stanial struggles desperately but cannot overpower the Amazon-like Angie; only the timely arrival of Barbara Larrimore and the sheriff saves him from a watery grave.

Angie is a religious fanatic whose insane behavior is made credible by MacDonald's decision to present portions of the book from her point of view. Her religious delusions are so well hidden that no one is led to suspect her of the murders. Only the reader is privy to the darker side of her personality. Consequently, despite the horror of her cold-blooded and brutal murders, she is presented with a measure of sympathy by MacDonald, in part because he wishes to show her as a victim herself, tragically warped by the paranoia of her mother. But there is something more at issue here. Doc Hines, who delivered Angie into the world and who understands her background and upbringing, offers this view:

> She's an extreme case, certainly. But spare a little sorrow for the rest of them. More people than you could count have bitched up lives on account of this crazy culture. The puritan heritage says that sex is nasty. Life says sex is constructive fun. So we go around smirking, sneaking, making it a nasty mystery. The most self-conscious, sex-oppressed nation in history. . . . Such a stinking fuss over the simple beautiful mechanics of fertilization. If clothes were against the law, we'd be cured in one generation.

MacDonald's point is that what is so disturbing about Angie's behavior is the suspicion that it perhaps represents only an extreme manifestation of a disease he fears is infecting the culture at large.

MacDonald has published only one non-McGee mystery novel since 1964, *The Last One Left*, which appeared in 1967, shortly after *One Fearful Yellow Eye*, McGee's eighth adventure, was released.

Among his most impressive works, the novel was nominated for an Edgar award as the best mystery of the year and cited by Anthony Boucher as "one of the major suspense novels of the 1960's." Based on a true incident, the 1961 wreck of a boat off the Bahamas and the subsequent revelation that the skipper had killed his passengers in order to collect on an insurance policy, *The Last One Left* at first appears to be about a similar tragedy at sea. The *Muñeca*, sailing from Florida to the Bahamas, has apparently exploded and burned, killing all six passengers aboard; only the captain, Garry Staniker, rescued several days later badly burned and in critical condition, has survived the accident. What gradually and deftly unfolds from this initial situation is a taut suspense novel in which robbery, murder, and doublecross are the main ingredients.

Eight days after the tragedy aboard the *Muñeca*, a small boat containing one of the six passengers, Leila Boylston, presumed dead but barely alive, drifts ashore on a small mangrove island whose sole inhabitant is a mentally damaged recluse by the name of Sgt. Carpo. The mystery deepens when Leila's brother Sam, a tough Texas lawyer investigating the incident, learns that there was over $800,000 cash aboard the *Muñeca*. It turns out that Captain Staniker isn't the fortunate lone survivor of a terrible tragedy at sea, as first thought, but in reality the killer of his passengers and beneficiary of the missing $800,000. As soon as Leila Boylston can talk to the authorities and explain what actually happened aboard the ship, Staniker will be exposed. But the paranoid Sgt. Carpo, fearful of what the authorities will do to him if he should appear with the young girl, decides to nurse her back to health himself, thus making her a virtual prisoner on his little island. While the tension builds as we worry about the fate of the terrified girl at the hands of the primitive Carpo, and wonder whether she will live to tell her story, the plot takes another interesting turn. Staniker is found dead in his bathtub, his wrists slashed, an apparent suicide. Persistent investigation by Boylston eventually leads him to the real villain of the novel, Crissy Harkinson, a thirty-six-year-old ex-call girl who encouraged Staniker to steal the money she learned was to be aboard the *Muñeca*, then talked a young sailing instructor, as enamored of her as Staniker was, into killing the captain.

Instead of settling for a short, fast-paced suspense thriller, MacDonald turns *The Last One Left* into one of his longest (only

Condominium is longer) and most satisfying novels; by carefully developing several of the characters in detail, MacDonald gives his story an emotional dimension that raises it to the stature of a psychological as well as crime thriller. The focus of the emotional interest is Sam Boylston, a tough-minded lawyer admired by an associate because "he didn't have any softness slowing him down" but rejected by his wife (who has recently left him) for the same reason. Feeling guilty for meddling in his sister's affairs by pressuring her to go on the fateful cruise in the first place (in hopes of breaking up her romance with Jonathan Dye, whom he judges not to be a proper match for her), he reluctantly agrees to help Dye search for Leila. Before long, however, his curiosity is piqued and his investigative instincts sniff out enough to enable him to assemble all the pieces of the puzzle.

But while he is solving the mystery of the missing money, he is also solving his own personal problems. His respect for Jonathan Dye's unwavering dedication against all odds to finding Leila, along with his encounters with such other characters as Crissy's Cuban-refugee maid and her journalist boyfriend, cause him to reevaluate his own actions and assess his own motivation in light of their idealistic behavior. Gradually, painfully, he comes to the realization that "it is not so great to be stuck in the world as Sam Boylston." Boylston is a great lawyer, but he comes to appreciate the importance of being a good man first. MacDonald effectively combines the suspenseful investigative elements with Boylston's self-discovery so that the exciting pursuit of the solution to the mystery of the *Muñeca* is never compromised.

While the novel gradually reveals the sympathetic qualities of Boylston, it simultaneously exposes the ruthless inhumanity of Crissy Harkinson. Like many of MacDonald's female characters Crissy has a morally questionable past: she is a former call girl who, for the seven years prior to his recent death, was the well-kept companion of a powerful Florida senator. Aware that she isn't getting any younger and determined to arrange a comfortable future for herself, she uses her knowledge about Texas financier Bixby Kayd's plan to transport a large amount of cash to the Bahamas to bribe some local officials for one last chance to make a big score for herself. Employing all her sexual expertise, Crissy bewitches Staniker and lures him into her deadly scheme by persuading him to kill his passengers (one of whom is his own wife) and take the money. Then, worried about his ability to keep his mouth shut after his rescue from the "accident," she transforms Oliver Akard, her naive young sailing instructor, into her sexual slave and persuades him to kill Staniker. When Akard finds himself unable to carry out her wishes, she calmly slits Staniker's wrists herself and then later just as calmly puts a bullet in Akard's head. Despite her cold-blooded ruthlessness (only the title character of MacDonald's novella "Linda," included in *Border Town Girl*, can match her for heartless villainy), there is something disturbingly human about Crissy. Having lived a hard life, she is determined to grab what she can for herself. Using sex to survive is the only skill she has ever known, and her realization that an aging call girl can expect nothing but a bleak future only adds to the pathos of her desperate situation. Heartless though she may be, her character is as fascinating as a cobra, her alluring beauty lulling one into forgetfulness of her deadly venom.

The subplot involving Leila and her captor, Sgt. Carpo, enhances the dramatic tension of the main plot and also intensifies the human interest of the novel. Carpo's head wounds, suffered during service in World War II, have rendered him unfit for the pressures of everyday life. Suspicious and wary of others, he has at last found peace on his isolated little island. When Leila Boylston invades his world, he must learn to deal with her. He suppresses his sexual attraction for her, watches over her for two weeks, and then, moved by her despair at having become his virtual prisoner, concludes that he must risk discovery and the possible loss of his isolation so that she can return to the mainland safely. Her plight, intensified by her fear and confusion, is equally compelling. When she is finally returned to safety, she repays Carpo's kindness by insisting that he be allowed to remain on his island, living life the only way he is happy.

Reviewing this impressive array of MacDonald's early novels, one sees the handiwork of a true professional, the careful and conscientious efforts of a master craftsman who invariably spins a compelling story and populates it with interesting and credible characters. But more and more, especially after 1960, there is in MacDonald's work evidence of a more serious intention, a desire to extend beyond mere plot and surface realism in order to produce works with substantial emotional and thematic impact. MacDonald once wrote: "The shallowest portions of stories are about the physical things that happen to people, even when they are killed by madmen. The serious parts of stories are about changes in the way the light and shadows fall on the secret and lonely heart." It is his passionate concern with this aspect of his characters that provides such a powerful emotional resonance in the best of his works. No longer interested merely in telling a simple tale of crime and punishment, MacDonald successfully weaves real characters and their very real problems into his stories without diluting their suspense or mystery elements. Moreover, by incorporating his own observations and commentaries about the state of contemporary American culture into his fiction, MacDonald demonstrates that the distinction between the "thriller" and the "serious" novel is illusory. Having fully exercised that artistic freedom he cited as one of the primary reasons he rejected the temptation to begin a series as far back as 1950, and having earned a well-deserved reputation as a writer of immense versatility, he was now ready to apply his fictional talents to virtually the only type of mystery writing he had not yet attempted—the creation of a series character.

3

The Birth of McGee (*Blue, Pink, Purple, Red, Gold*)

Shortly after his first novel was published in 1950, MacDonald's editors at Fawcett Publications began urging him to create a series character, but he declined, knowing only too well the numerous sad accounts of writers who became so locked into a series that they were unable to sell anything else to magazines, which only wanted stories featuring their series hero. Also, a series character, especially if he is the narrator (as he often is), is limiting since everything is restricted to his point of view. So too is the formula that usually emerges in a series. Thus armed with a number of good reasons, MacDonald turned a deaf ear to all such requests and instead devoted his considerable energies to writing some forty-odd novels, several featuring protagonists interesting enough to sustain a series, but none interesting enough to tempt MacDonald to use them more than once.

By 1963 MacDonald's reluctance had weakened. For one thing, he had exercised to the fullest extent the freedom he feared he might lose had he begun a series a decade earlier. By now, having firmly established his reputation as a writer of great versatility, he could not be locked into a series the way he might have been earlier. In addition, his editor at Fawcett, Knox Berger, had just lost one of his most popular writers, Richard Prather (creator of the Shell Scott series), to another publisher and was looking for a replacement. So MacDonald finally agreed to see if he could devise a character he could live with for a series of novels.

In an essay entitled, "How to Live With a Hero," MacDonald describes the birth of Travis McGee. He wrote one novel which he could have sold readily but whose framework, he felt, was too restrictive and whose hero was too somber, "full of dark areas, subject to moody violence." So he scrapped it and tried again, this time swinging too far in the opposite direction with a hero who was a "jolly, smirking jackass," full of quips, puns, and "smartass comments." This too was shelved. A third attempt, entitled *The Deep Blue Good-By* and featuring a hero named McGee, was far more satisfactory. (Originally called Dallas McGee, his name was changed when President Kennedy's assassination gave the name Dallas an unpleasant connotation. A friend, writer MacKinlay Kantor, advised MacDonald: "Hell, name him after an Air Force base. They have good names. Like Travis, in California." Thus, Dallas McGee became Travis McGee.) MacDonald also settled upon the device of using a different color in each title to differentiate the books:

> I did not want to number the books, because that would indicate they should be read in a certain order. I asked friends to help me think of mnemonic devices, and I do not remember if I came up with the idea of using colors, or someone else did. I considered and discarded using months of the year, animals, geographical references, etc. The point is really to enable people to identify the books in the series quickly, and to help them remember whether or not they had bought it previously. A reader who buys the same book twice is a very angry reader.

Although he now had a name for his hero and a gimmick for his titles, he was still cautious, so he wrote another McGee novel.

Primarily, MacDonald wished to ascertain whether his new hero would remain interesting to *him*: "Would subsequent adventures," he wondered, "dull him down to a formula pattern, destroying freshness? Would the quality of his observations and comments become trite through repetition?" Satisfied with his latest effort, called *Nightmare in Pink*, he wrote a third novel, which fell apart, and then a fourth, *A Deadly Shade of Gold*. Now fully committed to his new creation, MacDonald completed a fifth adventure, *A Purple Place for Dying*, then returned to the abandoned third attempt and rewrote it entirely as *The Quick Red Fox*. The series was officially launched in 1964 with the simultaneous publication of *The Deep Blue Good-By* and *Nightmare in Pink* and, later that year, release of *A Purple Place for Dying* (*Red* and *Gold*, though written before *Purple*, still needed work before publication). Thus, prior to Travis McGee's introduction to the reading public, MacDonald had written approximately a million and a quarter words and had completed to his satisfaction five adventures of his new hero. Few characters in fiction have been launched with such care and attention, thanks to MacDonald's desire to be absolutely certain he had a hero he could live with.

The initial book in a series is especially crucial, for it must establish the hero's identity clearly in the reader's mind, set the tone for the rest of the series, and introduce the elements of the formula that will be employed in subsequent books. If readers don't like the hero or his adventures, they simply won't buy future volumes. MacDonald succeeded in hitting the right note in *Blue,* effectively establishing those elements of character and formula that would be refined and modified in each new entry in the series of novels which, despite MacDonald's longstanding aversion, now numbers nineteen volumes and which has become one of the most popular and successful in American publishing history.

The basic facts of Travis McGee's character and life-style are quickly introduced. A large, powerfully built man, six-feet-four, two hundred and five pounds, sporting a deep tan and boyish grin, he lives aboard a fifty-two-foot barge-type houseboat, *The Busted Flush,* moored at Slip F-18, Bahia Mar, Ft. Lauderdale, Florida. (The boat, with its oversized bed and enormous shower stall, was won from "an elderly Palm Beach sybarite" in a poker game and named in honor of the hand that began McGee's streak of luck.) He drives a 1936 blue Rolls-Royce, converted into a pickup truck, which he has christened Miss Agnes after his fourth-grade teacher whose hair was the same shade of blue. A self-styled "reject from a structured society," he admits to being wary of such things as:

> plastic credit cards, payroll deductions, insurance programs, retirement benefits, savings accounts, Green Stamps, time clocks, newspapers, mortgages, sermons, miracle fabrics, deodorants, check lists, time payments, political parties, lending libraries, television, actresses, junior chambers of commerce, pageants, progress, and manifest destiny.

Rather than waiting until sixty or sixty-five to retire, he has decided to take his retirement in chunks, so he works at irregular intervals, usually only when he needs the money. And the work he does is unique—he is a "salvage expert," a retriever of lost items. In other words, if X has something valuable and Y takes it, and X has no way of getting it back, he makes a deal with X to get it and then keeps half of what he retrieves. Stated baldly, the essential facts about McGee suggest nothing so much as a middle-aged playboy who bestirs himself to take lucrative cases only as a way of financing his carefree life-style. What saves him from such stereotyping is MacDonald's care in presenting his character in such a way as to reveal its essentially moral dimensions.

In *The Deep Blue Good-By* (1964), McGee is cleverly finessed by a friend, Chookie McCall, into helping one of her dancers, Cathy Kerr, who needs the services of a man like McGee. At first reluctant (he only takes cases when he begins to get nervous about dwindling funds, and he is currently well-off), he finally agrees, at Chookie's urging, to talk with Cathy. She tells McGee about Junior Allen, an ex-con who befriended her father while both were serving time in Leavenworth prison. After his release, Allen came to Candle Key, moved in with her family, and soon became her lover. He often spoke about her father, displaying an almost obsessive curiosity about him. Then one day, the driveway markers in front of the house were torn down and Junior Allen was gone. Three weeks later he returned to town with expensive new clothes, a forty-foot yacht, and no interest in Cathy. She now realizes that he was only using her to get information about the location of the hidden treasure she recalls her father mentioning when she was a child. She wants McGee's help in retrieving whatever it was Junior Allen stole from her family.

McGee agrees to help Cathy because he feels the stirrings of "that shameful need to clamber aboard my spavined white steed, knock the rust off the armor, tilt the crooked old lance and shout huzzah." His decision to ride to the rescue of the damsel in distress is, however, also prompted by his uneasiness over a one-night affair he has with a Texas redhead named Molly Bea Archer, whose shallowness makes him appreciate the seriousness of Cathy Kerr's plight; his unsatisfactory experience with Molly Bea also reminds him of the Junior Allen side of his own nature, that heedless use of another for his own pleasure. Thus motivated by both altruism and self-disgust, he sets out to learn what he can about Junior Allen.

He begins by locating Lois Atkinson, the woman Allen moved in with when he returned to Candle Key with his new yacht. McGee is shocked when he arrives at her apartment and finds a wreck of a woman in the throes of a deep emotional trauma. For the next nine days he plays nursemaid to the distraught woman and gradually learns, as he nurses her back to health, the sordid details about her debauchery and degradation at the hands of Junior Allen. Angered and humiliated by Lois's rejection of his advances, he had returned to town with the intention of destroying and debasing her. A shy, sensitive woman, she was unable to withstand the shock of the sexual adventures Allen led her into (culminating in a ménage à trois Allen arranged with a Haitian whore); consumed by self-disgust and humiliation, she began drinking heavily to blot out the memory of her actions. It was at this point that McGee found her.

Lois is (barely) living proof of the devastation wreaked by such characters as Junior Allen. Although he has yet to meet him, McGee recognizes that Allen is of that breed of men who "are compelled to destroy the most fragile and valuable thing they can find, the same way rowdy children will ravage a beautiful home." Like many of MacDonald's villains, Allen is more animal than human, a frightening personification of evil which McGee describes as "the pustular bequest from the beast, as inexplicable as Belsen." Allen and those of his ilk embody MacDonald's contention that there exists in the world an evil that cannot be adequately explained:

> There exists in the world a kind of evil which defies the Freudian explanations of the psychologists, and the environmental explanations of the sociologists. It is an evil existing for the sake of itself, for the sake of the satisfactions of its own exercise. In our real world we have, for example, a two hundred and thirty pound teenager who roams the streets, mugging children for the pleasure of gouging out their eyes. For me it is less satisfying to say that this is the action of a sad, limited, tormented, unbalanced child than it is to see that this is a primordial blackness reaching up again through a dark and vulnerable soul, showing us all the horror that has always been with mankind, frustrating all rational analyses.

McGee's desire to recover Cathy's missing treasure thus also becomes a personal crusade to put an end to Junior Allen's debasement of vulnerable victims.

McGee solves the mystery of what Allen stole from underneath Cathy's driveway markers when he locates an army buddy of her father, now living in Texas, and learns that while stationed in India during World War II he made a considerable amount of money smuggling gold into China. Before returning to the States, he converted the money into precious gems, which he buried under the driveway gate. However, he was arrested for committing a murder and sentenced to prison, where he died before he could cash the gems in; in prison, Allen learned about the existence of the gems and his persistent nosiness paid off when he finally figured out their location.

McGee locates Allen's yacht and enlists Lois's aid in luring him away long enough to allow McGee to search for the hidden jewels. However, the plan backfires when Allen returns unexpectedly, finds McGee, and knocks him out; when McGee recovers consciousness, he hears the screams of a young woman Allen is raping. He rescues her and the two escape by jumping overboard and swimming to safety. Then he borrows a boat and chases after Allen, finally catching up with him in the middle of the Atlantic at night. In the ensuing struggle, Allen is sent to his "deep blue good-by" when an anchor McGee throws overboard catches him in the throat. But there is no celebrating for McGee, for he learns that while he lay unconscious, Allen brought Lois aboard and beat her brutally. Critically injured with a head wound, she dies three days later.

McGee is successful in terminating Junior Allen's evil campaign against women and retrieving five of the stolen jewels (although he is so disappointed at his failure to do better that he keeps only $1,000 as a fee, giving the rest, some $20,000 worth, to Cathy). He is also left with a heavy burden of guilt over Lois's death, for it was the trust she placed in him that led her to take part in his plan to stop Allen, a decision that cost her her life. On one level, her death solves MacDonald's continuing problem of how to extricate his hero from a relationship that might restrict his freedom for the next adventure. But more importantly, Lois's death serves to remind McGee (and the reader) that life is risky, and that he is engaged in a potentially deadly line of work. In his essay, "How to Live With a Hero," MacDonald acknowledged that one of the conventions he sought to avoid was the notion that the hero should always win, and Lois Atkinson's death serves to diminish McGee's sense of accomplishment at the end of the novel; indeed it humbles and humanizes him. Thanks to the tenderness and understanding of Cathy Kerr, however, his pride and self-confidence are restored before he returns to *The Busted Flush* at the end of the book.

It is clear from *Blue* that MacDonald intends to use the mystery format as a vehicle for presenting a hero of many dimensions. To this end, he includes a number of scenes that are not crucial to the plot but that reveal McGee's personality. For example, his nursing of Lois Atkinson back to health after he first finds her shows his patience and sensitivity; his tracking down of Cathy's father's army buddy reveals his ingenuity and dogged persistence; his bloody battle with Junior Allen demonstrates his strength and courage. What contributes most to the delineation of his character are those scenes that reveal him as a morally sensitive individual, and nothing shows this better than his relationships with women. A handsome man like McGee, surrounded by an unlimited supply of beautiful (and frequently amoral) young women looking for a good time, could easily lose himself in the fleshly pleasures of the sybaritic life. But while McGee has chosen to remain unmarried, he has not opted for hedonism or, for that matter, for any relationship that does not include some measure of emotional involvement. McGee admits to being "an incurable romantic who thinks the man-woman thing shouldn't be a contest on the rabbit level." In one of his ruminations—a mini-essay of the kind that will become a staple in the series—McGee reflects upon the sexual climate in which he lives:

> These are the playmate years, and they are demonstrably fraudulent. The scene is reputed to be acrawl with adorably amoral bunnies to whom sex is a pleasant social favor. The new culture. And they are indeed present and available, in exhausting quantity, but there is a curious tastelessness about them. A woman who does not guard and treasure herself cannot be of very much value to anyone else. They become a pretty little convenience, like a guest towel. And the cute little things they say, and their dainty little squeals of pleasure and release are as contrived as the embroidered initials on the guest towels. Only a woman of pride, complexity and emotional tension is genuinely worth the act of love, and there are only two ways to get yourself one of them. Either you lie, and stain the relationship with your own sense of guile, or you accept the involvement, the emotional responsibility, the permanence she must by nature crave. I love you can be said only two ways.

This explains his rejection of friend Chookie McCall's advances on the grounds, as he tells her, that, "You are just not trivial enough for purely recreational sex," as well as his refusal of both the obvious come-on from a stewardess he meets on a flight to Texas and the easy availablity of one of the playmates aboard Junior Allen's yacht. He even debates at some length the morality of sleeping with Lois Atkinson, deciding to do so only when he is convinced he is acting with the proper motivation. Sexual morality, i.e., proper behavior toward the opposite sex, has been an important feature of MacDonald's male protagonists throughout the many novels that preceded this one, and it is clear that MacDonald wishes it to be one of the prominent features of his new hero.

McGee's morality, however, encompasses far more than merely his bedroom behavior. For example, although he finds it necessary to use physical violence to get information from the army buddy of Cathy's father, resorting to such measures against a weak and pitiful individual disturbs him:

> He was a semi-ridiculous banty rooster of a man, vain, cocky, running as hard as he could to stay in the same place, but he had a dignity of existence which I had violated. A bird, a horse, a dog, a man, a girl or a cat—you knock them about and diminish yourself because all you do is prove yourself equally vulnerable. All his anxieties lay there locked in his sleeping skull, his system adjusting itself to sudden shock, keeping him alive. He had pulled at the breast, done homework, dreamed of knighthood, written poems to a girl. One day they would tumble him in and cash his insurance. In the meanwhile it did all human dignity a disservice for him to be used as a puppet by a stranger.

On the other hand, MacDonald is careful not to allow McGee to take himself too seriously in his role as hero. As previously noted, he rejected his first version of McGee because he was too somber and serious. He strikes just the right note in *Blue*, and despite some notable lapses (for example, when he cautions Chookie about her attitude toward sex with him, he is downright fatuous) MacDonald manages to keep the moralistic McGee from becoming too preachy and pompous. After debating at some length the merits of taking Lois to bed, he is honest enough to remark at the end of his worrying: "All the little gods of irony must whoop and weep and roll on the floors of

Olympus when they tune in on the night thoughts of a truly fatuous male." Then he adds, "And I hold several international records." Although MacDonald clearly wants his hero to be taken seriously by the reader, he doesn't want McGee to take *himself* too seriously.

Friendship rousts McGee from *The Busted Flush* again in *Nightmare in Pink* (1964) when he receives a call from Mike Gibson, a war buddy of his who has lain crippled and blind in a North Carolina veterans hospital ever since being wounded in Korea. McGee cannot refuse Gibson's request to help his little sister, Nina, whose fiancé, Howard Plummer, was recently killed. After his death she discovered $10,000 in cash among his possessions and, feeling betrayed by the suspicion that he was stealing from his employer, she has become embittered toward his memory. Gibson wants his old friend to go to New York (where Nina works in an advertising agency) and find out the truth about Howard Plummer.

Soon McGee is doing more than that; quickly shedding his brotherly attitude, he falls in love with her. Eventually, he gets around to the business at hand and with the help of Terry Drummond, sister-in-law of Charles Armister, head of the investment corporation where Plummer worked, he finds what he was looking for. He uncovers evidence of a massive plot, masterminded by Armister's lawyer, Bayard Mulligan, to steal $20,000,000 from Armister, a feat made possible by rendering him pliable through a combination of experimental hallucinogenic drugs and a lobotomy. When Howard Plummer became suspicious about Mulligan's activities, he was asked to resign from the firm; he agreed in return for $10,000 in cash, which he intended to take to the authorities as evidence that something fishy was going on. Ironically, he was killed as a result of a mugging that had nothing to do with the swindle (thus conveniently removing him from the novel and freeing Nina to fall in love with McGee). When McGee gets too close to Mulligan, he is drugged and spirited off to a nearby mental institution, where he finds himself scheduled for a lobotomy, the same fate that befell Armister. McGee escapes by killing an attendant and then spiking the cafeteria coffee with an hallucinogenic drug that kills four people and causes dozens of injuries and traumas. Back in New York, he informs the authorities, who begin closing in on Mulligan and his henchmen.

This second McGee adventure is decidedly inferior to *Blue*. For one thing, the plot is overly melodramatic, with McGee getting himself involved with demented doctors and their crazy experiments in personality modification. McGee is also noticeably out of his element among the sophisticates of New York café society, personified by such characters as doyenne Constance Trimble Thatcher and Armister's jet-setter sister-in-law, Terry Drummond. Furthermore, where there was a strong element of the personal crusade in his pursuit of Junior Allen in *Blue*, here McGee's only emotional involvement is with Nina Gibson, who is completely detached from the main action of the novel, and after clearing her fiancé's name there is no compelling need for him to continue investigating Mulligan's activities. His reasons for doing so are never made clear.

Another weakness in the novel is the character of McGee himself, or at least the emphasis placed on it in the novel. It is obvious that MacDonald intends to further clarify the personality of his protagonist; one effect of this, however, is a tiresome propensity for self-dramatization on McGee's part. The plot is also arranged in such a way as to make it inevitable that he fall in love with Nina, thus affording him ample opportunity to explain the foundation of his sexual philosophy: "If the spirit is involved, if there is tenderness and respect and awareness of need, that's all the morality I care about." So much time, however, is devoted to his relationship with Nina and to frequent espousals of his philosophy that the novel becomes bogged down in talk and sometimes silly romantic interludes. McGee's smarmy fatuousness is also allowed to run unchecked by saving doses of self-deprecation. For example, he is straight-faced when he applauds himself for his salutary effect on Nina: "I felt a fatuous satisfaction in having done so much for her." His later remark that "Every weary lover can, with just a little trouble, turn himself into an insufferable horse's ass" all too pointedly sums up his problem in *Pink*.

At the end of the novel, McGee and Nina travel to North Carolina to visit her brother before his latest operation, from which he does not recover. Before the operation he makes McGee promise that he will take care of Nina but that he won't marry her simply as a memorial to their friendship. The two leave for several months of amatory bliss sailing the waters off the Florida coast, but as it inevitably happens in these books, Nina, her confidence restored, gets the itch to return to her work in New York. McGee is left alone but with no regrets, for both he and Nina have been mutually enriched by their experience together.

Pink lacks the pace and excitement of *Blue*. Certain scenes, such as McGee's terrifying drug-induced hallucinations and his perilous escape from the nightmarish world of the asylum, are tributes to MacDonald's descriptive skills, but they remain set pieces detached from the overall texture of the novel, which suffers from a static quality and an overdose of talkiness. In *Blue*, MacDonald created an interesting character who was given an exciting task to perform; in his second outing, MacDonald devoted so much time to refining his hero's attitudes and philosophy (especially as it relates to women) that he failed to provide an effective vehicle for his actions.

Still experimenting to find the proper formula, MacDonald sends McGee to the desert Southwest in his third adventure, *A Purple Place for Dying* (1964) (although, according to MacDonald's account, fifth in order of composition). McGee is called upon to act more like a private eye than he has in his previous adventures, and the result is an exciting whodunit with an emphasis on mystery and suspense. In the process, the character of McGee is brought into sharper focus, his narrative becomes leaner, his commentary less self-indulgent.

Running perilously low on funds, McGee agrees to accept Mona Yeoman's invitation to fly to the western town of Esmerelda to discuss a possible job. The attractive young wife of a wealthy businessman, Mona tells McGee she has fallen in love with John Webb, a philosophy professor at a nearby college. She intends to leave her husband and run away with Webb, but first needs McGee's help in finding out what happened to her inheritance. She tells McGee she suspects her husband, Jass, her father's closest friend and executor of his estate, of defrauding her by completely depleting her trust fund and using it for his own interests. She claims that over $2,000,000 has vanished and Yeoman refuses to give her an accurate accounting, insisting only that the estate money has been used up. Suddenly Mona pitches forward, dead of a gunshot wound to the head. McGee scrambles for cover and eventually locates a phone and calls the sheriff. When the authorities arrive, however, they find no body and no evidence of any killing. In a variation on a situation used in several of MacDonald's early novels, where the hero was forced to prove he did *not* kill the woman whose body was found with him, McGee has to prove the opposite, that the woman with him *was* killed. What makes his task more difficult is considerable evidence suggesting that Mona Yeoman might have actually eloped with her lover: Webb's apartment has been cleaned out; his car was found at the local airport; a couple matching their description was seen on a flight to El Paso.

With Mona Yeoman's death, McGee loses any prospect of a job. The sensible thing for him to do would be to return to Ft. Lauderdale and pursue another job possibility. However, he can't rid himself of a feeling of obligation to the woman, her sudden death forcefully reminding him of his own mortality. Furthermore, he would like to convince Sheriff Buckleberry that he is neither crazy nor a stooge hired to provide cover so that Mona could slip away with her lover. He knows the woman is dead and the thought that someone might get away with murder is distasteful to his very nature.

He searches Webb's apartment and discovers that, although a diabetic, Webb has inexplicably neglected to take his insulin with him. When he talks with the stewardess on duty during the flight Mona and Webb reportedly took to El Paso, the description of the couple she provides convinces him that the pair were imposters. (Incredibly, he later even spots the woman who impersonated Mona Yeoman walking along the street; he picks her up and gets her to admit that she was hired to take the flight.) McGee's suspicion of foul play is confirmed when the rock slide blocking the road to Mona's mountain cabin is cleared away and John Webb's body is found. Now there are two murders to solve and the prime suspect is Mona's husband, Jass.

Jass Yeoman is a good example of a type of character MacDonald creates very convincingly—the good-ole-boy wheeler-dealer whose homespun demeanor belies a poker player's shrewdness and nerves of steel. He is the kind of self-made man (like Elmo Bliss in *A Flash of Green* and Homer Galloway in *The Only Girl in the Game*) who can manage so many different affairs at the same time that he resembles the circus clown who can keep several dishes spinning atop skinny sticks. Yeoman is not without his faults—his attitude toward his wife is naive and simple-minded and he does admit to having used his wife's inheritance to see him through a rough period—but he is nonetheless presented sympathetically in the novel. Unlike those financial manipulators (like Bayard Mulligan in *Pink*) who will stop at nothing, including murder, in their mad pursuit of money, Yeoman cherishes other values, such as loyalty, friendship, trust, and the love of his wife. McGee likes Yeoman and concludes he would be incapable of killing either his wife or her lover. His faith in Yeoman's innocence is apparently well-placed, for he too is murdered, the victim of a fatal dose of strychnine slipped into his coffee.

MacDonald is especially adroit at sustaining the mystery of the identity of the killer or killers and their motivation for not only murdering Mona, Webb, and now Jass himself, but for the elaborate attempt to make it appear that Mona fled rather than was killed. McGee's speculation centers around money, with the impending tax investigation of Jass a possible factor. However, the denouement turns out to be disappointing. Recalling a remark Yeoman made that perhaps one of his many bastard children has returned to get revenge against him, McGee discusses the possibility with Sheriff Buckleberry, who sends him into the desert to find the Mexican woman Jass is known to have been involved with some twenty-five years earlier. As unlikely as locating a needle in a haystack, McGee not only finds the woman but also her two sons, who rather implausibly turn out to be the killers he is looking for. He and Isobel Webb (John Webb's sister, who has been accompanying him) flee for their lives and narrowly escape death in the purple light of dawn in the desert before McGee manages to kill both brothers and lead Isobel back to Esmerelda safely.

It turns out that, contrary to what McGee assumed, the motivation behind all the killings is hatred, not money, and the person responsible is Dolores Canario, the Yeoman family maid and Jass's daughter by the Mexican woman. Horrified when her drunken father took her to bed one night, she recruited her half brothers to kill Mona and Webb, then killed Jass herself. Her hatred is convincing, although the Perry Mason–like scene at the end when McGee tricks her into confessing her guilt isn't. Nor is the involvement of her two brothers; for one thing, there is no adequate explanation either for their actions in hiring the couple to impersonate Mona and Webb or for burying Webb's body beneath the rubble of the road leading to Mona's mountain cabin, where it would surely be found. What saves the novel from the improbabilities of its plot are MacDonald's outstanding skills in managing tension and suspense, creating exciting individual scenes (the Sosegado brothers' pursuit of McGee and Isobel Webb into the desert and their narrow escape from death when one of the men tosses a four-foot rattlesnake into the small cave where they are hiding is truly harrowing), and depicting interesting characters—including some interesting new shadings in the character of McGee himself.

McGee's role as a self-described "salvage expert" (or, as he also refers to himself in the novel, "Samaritan McGee, savior of doomed womanhood") is more effectively dramatized in *Purple* than it was in *Pink*. He can, of course, do nothing for Mona Yeoman, who dies before the end of chapter one. But he can, and does, do wonders for a woman in real need, Isobel Webb, John Webb's sexually repressed sister, a "twisted virgin, frightened by men, sex, pleasure, wanting— thinking it all a conspiracy of evil against her." Unhealthily attached to her brother, she feels rejected when he becomes romantically involved with Mona. When she learns that he is dead, rage turns to despair, and she tries to kill herself by taking an overdose of barbiturates. McGee finds her and nurses her back to consciousness, then ministers to her psyche, gradually restoring her self-confidence and sense of self-worth. With infinite patience and self-restraint, he permits her to discover her slumbering sexuality in due time. (He promises that whenever she says "No" he won't go any further in their lovemaking, thus allowing her to "find her own increments of exper- imental boldness" while discovering the previously unknown mysteries of sex.) Eventually she is transformed, as so many of MacDonald's female characters are when treated properly, from a frigid woman into something of a sexual tigress. The therapy continues unabated when the two travel to Isobel's family's cottage on an island in the Bahamas. Inevitably they part, Isobel now capable of making her own plans for the future thanks to McGee's success in allowing her to develop her independence.

McGee accomplishes all this with a minimum of self-analysis and without the windy discussions of sexual politics that weighed down the action in *Pink*. Thanks to MacDonald's decision to reveal McGee through action rather than words, there is a spareness in *Purple* that was lacking in its predecessors. One disadvantage of such economy, however, is the absence of the observations and comments about contemporary American life that were featured in the earlier entries. Although *Purple* is an improvement over *Pink* in pace and economy, it lacks the color and depth of *Blue* as MacDonald is still working to arrive at the most effective balance between the laconic and the verbose.

McGee's damsel in distress in *The Quick Red Fox* (1964) is movie star Lysa Dean, who tells McGee that she recently paid $120,000 in blackmail to obtain twelve negatives of pictures taken with a telephoto lens which show in graphic detail her participation in a seamy group-sex scene with her lover at the time, Carl Abelle, and nine others. Now she has received a new threat, this one not demanding money but instead promising that the "shameless whore of Babylon" will be "cut down by the sord [sic] of decency." Embarrassed at having been caught behaving "like a fifty-peso floozy in a back-room circus in Juarez," and worried about the effects of exposure on her career and her upcoming marriage to a wealthy individual, she offers McGee $50,000 to put an end to the threats and restore her privacy.

Accompanied by Dana Holzer, Lysa Dean's private secretary (whom she foists on him), McGee sets off on a trail that will take him to a treatment center for alcoholics in the Florida Keys, to a ski resort in the Adirondacks, and then west to San Francisco, Sausalito, Las Vegas, and finally Phoenix. Along the way, he tracks down the other participants in the orgy, searching among them for a likely candidate for blackmailer. He discovers that one of them, Vance M'Gruder, hired a photographer to take pictures depicting his wife, Patty, engaged in lesbian activities so he could obtain an annulment of his marriage, and thus avoid having to split his community property with her. The photographer, D. C. Ives, apparently then used the same photographs to blackmail Lysa Dean on his own. Ives was recently killed, and when M'Gruder's now ex-wife Patty is also brutally murdered, M'Gruder becomes a prime suspect in their deaths. But when he too is killed, McGee is forced to rebuild the structure of his speculations. He was correct in his assumption that Ives was blackmailing Lysa Dean, and that he also attempted to blackmail M'Gruder when he decided to marry Ulka Atlund. What McGee is surprised to discover is that it was Ulka, a breathtakingly beautiful eighteen-year-old, who, fearing the financial consequences if her marriage to M'Gruder were to be prevented by her strict father, killed Ives and then Patty when she became suspicious about her. She was finally driven to murdering her own husband when he eventually figured out that he was married to a killer. But before McGee can deliver her to the authorities, she bashes him on the head and flees, only to die in the wreck of her speeding car (a convenient way of administering justice that MacDonald also used in an early novel, *April Evil*).

Like *Purple, Red* is an engrossing whodunit in which McGee, using a variety of investigative skills to locate each of the possible suspects, employs an assortment of clever methods to obtain the information he seeks. With pretty-boy ski instructor Carl Abelle, he uses physical intimidation to get information; with a character who "can't believe anything that doesn't sound crooked," he is convincingly shifty; with D. C. Ives's naive daughter, he is a softy, carefully preserving her illusions about her dead father by playing along with her impression that he was secretly involved in some high-level government spy operation. McGee is as subtle or as blatant as the situation requires.

But like *Purple, Red* is also marred by a less than satisfactory resolution of its mystery. For one thing, Ulka M'Gruder isn't a very convincing murderess. MacDonald's sensuous portrait of her Nordic beauty demonstrates his keen descriptive skills:

> She looked as if she had enough animal heat to keep her entirely comfortable at thirty below. Her body, under the touch of the fabric, was ripe, leggy and entirely perfect. Without makeup, her features were almost those of some heroic, dedicated young boy, a page from the time of King Arthur. Or an idealized Joan of Arc. Her tilted gray-green-blue Icelandic eyes were the cold of northern seas. Her hair was a rich, ripe, heavy spill of pale pale gold, curved across the high and placid brow. She had little to say, and a sleepy and disinterested way of saying it. Her eyes kept seeking out her husband. Over all that stalwart Viking loveliness there was such a haze of sensuality it was perceptible, like a strange matte finish. It was stamped into the slow and heavy curve of her smile, marked by the delicate violet shadows under her eyes, expressed by the cant of her high round hips in the way she stood. Though by far the youngest person there, she at the same time seemed far older. She had been bolted to the bowsprit of an ancient ship for a thousand years.

But there is nothing in this vivid word-portrait (nor anywhere else in the depiction of her character) that hints that she is a "psychotic bitch" who can coolly carry out three brutal murders, including that of her husband. Samuel Bogen, D. C. Ives's demented associate, is another problem. It turns out that he was the one who threatened Lysa Dean with punishment after he obtained Ives's incriminating photos of her. He is needed to get the action going by prompting Lysa Dean to seek McGee's help in putting an end to these new threats against her, but then he is all but forgotten while McGee investigates and solves the three murders in the book, none of which have anything to do with Lysa's current problem. After these matters are resolved, MacDonald is left with the bothersome problem of what to do with Bogen. He handles the matter in perfunctory fashion by having McGee offhandedly arrange for the L.A. police to nab Bogen when he attempts to shoot a stand-in for Lysa Dean.

Although the ending is a bit slipshod, there is nothing careless about MacDonald's portrayal of characters in the novel. Each one, major and minor, comes alive on the page. One of the most striking portraits is that of Lysa Dean, the vixen of the title. A star of the first magnitude and a persuasive actress, at least when it comes to men, she both attracts and repels McGee. Although he responds positively to her call for help, he is turned off by her calculated seductiveness. He gently rebuffs her advances, recognizing that going to bed with her, the fantasy of millions of male admirers, would be "like getting taught to dance by your older sister. She would keep trying to lead, and giving irritable little instructions, and counting out loud and spoiling the music. Then she would give you a patronizing pat and say you did just fine." The "quick red fox" reveals her true colors when, after McGee successfully ends all threats of exposure of her careless escapade, she gives him only $10,000 of the $50,000 she promised, reminding him that, "Darling, you don't exactly have a contract, you know. And a frightened person can make some *very* rash promises." To make it up to him, she again offers herself, confident that such a generous gift ought to be worth at least $40,000 to McGee. Again he declines, this time far less gently than before: "It wouldn't mean one damn thing to you," he tells her, "and it would mean just a little less than that to me."

The most interesting character in the novel is Dana Holzer, Lysa Dean's secretary. Initially put off by her prim, officious, and disapproving manner (especially when she spots the oversized bed in *The Busted Flush*), McGee is not at all enthusiastic about having her tag along on his investigation. However, the usually infallible McGee (at least in matters feminine) turns out to be dead wrong, for what he thought was an uptight virgin turns out to be a mature woman with considerably more character and depth than he first surmised. He learns that she has been cruelly victimized by misfortune: her son, severely retarded, is institutionalized; her husband, an epileptic who was shot and critically wounded by a trigger-happy policeman who thought him a dangerous drunk, now lies permanently comatose in a hospital. Dana keeps her high-paying job with Lysa Dean only to pay the bills to support her damaged family. Despite the soap-opera quality of her tragic experiences, McGee is deeply moved by her courage, her toughness, her stoic dignity. Here is no coy girl in need of McGee's therapy; here is a mature woman of immense inner strength whose no-nonsense manner toward others is simply a measure of her impatience with the frivolous and superficial.

Soon, despite Lysa Dean's warning that some of the greatest experts in the industry have attempted to seduce Dana and have "wandered glassily away with icicles forming on their whatsis," the two end up in bed. Sex with Dana inspires more than "goaty self-esteem," it produces "a feeling of achieving and establishing identities, hers and mine." Dana was self-sufficient before she met McGee and thus doesn't need his assistance in developing strength or establishing self-confidence, as his wounded women usually do. So it is not surprising (although it is a matter of some disappointment) when she decides to leave him. She thanks McGee for everything, but reminds him that she is in fact still married and apologizes for giving him any false hopes. Once again McGee is saved from an entangling emotional involvement and is free to return to *The Busted Flush* alone. But for the first time, he feels a deep sense of loss at losing the woman he has become so close to.

His relationship with Dana offers much more than a handy romantic diversion to enliven the dull moments on the road. She performs the role soon to be assumed by Meyer of friend and confidant. In this respect she assists MacDonald (as Meyer will do) in delineating McGee's character. Too often in the previous three books, McGee was forced to define himself, to toot his own horn. And too often such reflections focused only on his sexual role. Now MacDonald has an opportunity to enlarge upon McGee's character by expanding into other areas. For example, one of the things about McGee that helped Dana to overcome her initial disapproval of him was his attitude toward his own sometimes brutal activities. Although he had to resort to physical violence to get information from Carl Abelle, he afterwards displayed deep displeasure at having stooped to such methods, a factor which Dana admits was an important consideration in her revised estimate of his character:

You could have stomped around, the hard-guy grin and all that.

But you felt bad about hurting and humiliating him. And he isn't much, certainly. So I figured out you don't go around proving you are a man because you are already sure you are. It isn't all faked up. And in the same way you didn't have to try to use me to prove what a hell of a fellow you are.

Dana provides an external perspective on McGee, one which reveals him to be a hero sensitive to the morality of his actions, and not just those which involve women.

Conversation with Dana also provokes an admission from McGee that provides a clue to his motivation. Sure, he takes cases for the money, but he also acknowledges for the first time that behind everything else is his love for his work; "investigation can be a disease," he admits, for it can produce one of the supreme pleasures in his life:

So what if I am hooked on the hunt? All it does is make an orderly life untenable. You trade the kiddies and fireside and regular promotions and appointment to the house committee or the greens committee for a few, a very few, clear clean moments of a savage satisfaction akin to joy.

Thanks to the nature of his relationship with Dana, there is no need for preening on McGee's part, her maturity prompting a greater degree of maturity from him. This in turn affects his comments about other subjects, which take on a richer, more thoughtful quality in *Red*. Whether he is describing the decline in the attractiveness of San Francisco or bemoaning the creeping conformity that is invading suburbia, his comments reveal less glibness and more depth. McGee's character is gradually becoming more complex as MacDonald is no longer simply satisfied to define him primarily in sexual terms. Whatever its faults as a mystery novel, *Red* is the most successful entry in the series to date as far as depiction of character is concerned.

As is often the case in MacDonald's fiction, the obligations of friendship provide the initial motivation in *A Deadly Shade of Gold* (1965), the fifth novel in the series (although the fourth in order of composition), when Sam Taggart phones McGee for help. Taggart abruptly left Ft. Lauderdale three years earlier, abandoning the woman he loved, Nora Gardino, and all his friends without any explanation. Now just as suddenly he has returned and wants McGee's help. He invites his old friend to his run-down motel room, where he shows him a solid gold, pre-Columbian statuette and admits that his original plan was to ask his help in recovering twenty-seven others which he claims were stolen from him—total value: over $300,000. He has changed his mind, however; the possibility of patching things up with Nora (who apparently still loves him) has prompted him to decide to sell his statuette for $12,500 to the current holder of the rest of the collection. As he explains to McGee, "Twelve-five plus Nora is better than three hundred without her." McGee, delighted at playing the role of Cupid, prepares Nora for her reunion with the prodigal Taggart. However, when he brings her to Taggart's motel room, they are treated to the gory sight of his bloody body, hacked to death. The brutal killing of Taggart, a "fellow refugee from a plastic structured culture, uninsured, unadjusted, unconvinced," like himself, rouses McGee to seek revenge against whoever is responsible for the deed.

A helpful local professor suggests that McGee might be able to obtain information about Taggart's statuettes from the Borlika galleries in New York. McGee flies to New York and soon befriends Betty Borlika, widow of one of the gallery's owners. Despite his oft-repeated arguments against casual or purely recreational sex, McGee is not above using sex for professional reasons—in this case, as a way of getting information from Betty. She gives him the name of Carlos Menterez, a wealthy Cuban who had purchased a number of statuettes from her in the past. From a friend in the Cuban community in Miami, Raoul Tenero, McGee learns that Menterez is a "barracuda," a crafty politician who "screwed millions out of Cuba" and left with it all when Batista was overthrown. His current whereabouts are unknown.

McGee recruits Nora Gardino's help and the two trace Taggart's trail to the small Mexican fishing village of Puerto Altamura, where Sam moved after leaving Florida. (MacDonald frequently vacations in Mexico, and Mexican settings are common in his early fiction. One of the special pleasures of *Gold* is the loving detail with which MacDonald portrays the sights and sounds of the town and its colorful inhabitants.) McGee learns that Taggart was employed by a wealthy Cuban named Garcia, but when McGee sneaks into his villa, he discovers that Garcia is actually the notorious Menterez, now almost totally incapacitated by a stroke. He is being nursed by a beautiful blonde, Almah Hichin, whom McGee overhears imploring Menterez to sign a document giving her power of attorney over his affairs (in order, he later learns, to get her hands on $600,000 Menterez has stashed in a Mexican bank). McGee kidnaps the woman and frightens her into confessing all she knows about Sam Taggart. She reveals that Menterez paid her to use her sexual charms to persuade Taggart to kill the three Cubans who had made an unsuccessful attempt on his life (for which he promised to pay Taggart $100,000). Taggart agreed, but while he and Miguel Alconedo, Menterez's hired man, were carrying out the murders on the Cubans' boat, they unexpectedly discovered a woman, whom they were also forced to kill. Before Menterez could pay Taggart for his work, he suffered a stroke, so Taggart took the twenty-eight gold statuettes from Menterez and tried to sell them to Cal Tomberlin, a wealthy Puerto Altamura neighbor of Menterez who had earlier attempted unsuccessfully to purchase them. McGee concludes that Tomberlin managed to steal all but one of the statuettes from Taggart and surmises that it was Tomberlin with whom Taggart was negotiating to sell the remaining statuette when he was murdered.

But before McGee can figure out his next move, tragedy strikes. When Miguel Alconedo attempts to start the ignition on Menterez's boat, it explodes and the blast drives a sharp piece of mahogany railing into Nora's neck as she is standing nearby, killing her instantly. This freak accident frees McGee once again from the woman with whom he was becoming romantically involved, but it also serves to make a dramatic statement about the precariousness of human existence. And it gives McGee a strong personal incentive for finding the person responsible for her death.

McGee concludes that the man "who lit the fuse" that precipitated everything from Taggart's original involvement in the murder of the three Cubans to the blast which killed Miguel and Nora is Cal Tomberlin. He heads to Los Angeles and contacts a Cuban-exile friend of Raoul Tenero's now living in Long Beach, Paul Dominguez, who introduces him to Connie Melgar, a beautiful Venezuelan widow. She gets McGee invited to a party at Tomberlin's luxurious canyon home, where he is unfortunately recognized by one of Tomberlin's Puerto Altamura agents. McGee escapes with Tomberlin's collection of gold statuettes (which now number thirty-four), but is wounded in the process. Connie takes him to the safety of a lonely mountain hideout where he can be treated by a Cuban doctor.

During his recuperation he is visited by yet another Cuban exile, Ramon Talavera, who confesses that it was he who killed Taggart because the woman Taggart killed on the boat was his sister. Now all the mysteries are solved: Taggart was killed as a matter of family honor; Tomberlin ordered Miguel to silence Almah Hichin by killing her, then had Miguel himself silenced by arranging for the boat explosion which killed him. McGee takes his "bloody spoils," the thirty-four statuettes, to New York, and sells them to Betty Borlika for $162,500. However, he is so dispirited by events that he loses all interest in the money: he gives $125,000 to Shaja Dobrak, Nora's friend and business partner, so she can purchase her husband's release from the Hungarian prison where he has been languishing since his arrest for revolutionary activities; the rest he sends to Felicia Novaro, Taggart's Puerto Altamuran mistress.

The plot of *Gold* is so complicated that it is a real challenge to keep track of the separate elements, especially the confusing political affiliations of the various feuding Cuban groups. There are so many murderers (Taggart, Miguel, Talavera, and Tomberlin) and so much political intrigue that the novel staggers under the excess weight. Although *Gold* is over a hundred pages longer than each of the three previous McGee adventures, the extra length results only in a confused and uncertain plot. There are too many extraneous matters: Almah Hichin's plan to steal $600,000 from Menterez, Tomberlin's curious association with Doctor Girdon Face and his right-wing American Crusade, McGee's irrelevant involvement with Junebug, an L.A. woman who arranges for him to borrow her friend's apartment and car—and too many subplots that begin promisingly yet end anticlimactically (the lengthy search for the notorious Menterez disappointingly leads only to the bed of a sickly old man and Taggart's murder turns out to have nothing to do with the quest for the gold statuettes). MacDonald's plots are usually streamlined affairs, fast-paced arrangements of action. There is ample action in *Gold;* the problem is that its diffuse organization produces a plot that falls short of MacDonald's usual standards.

As well as being the most confusing entry in the series, *Gold* is also the most violent thus far, with ten murders bloodying its pages. And the killings are especially gruesome: Taggart is slowly and methodically sliced to death; Almah Hichin is virtually beheaded by a knife; Miguel is blown to bits in an explosion. McGee himself is personally responsible for two of the bloodiest: in escaping from Tomberlin's he kills one man by smashing his skull against another's and then blows the top of a woman's head off. McGee's own description of all the action provides an apt summary of the novel's deficiencies: "Too much blood. Too much gold and intrigue. Too much fumbling and bumbling."

Nevertheless, the violence is not entirely without purpose. The novel opens with a kind of overture to blood which evokes an appropriate atmosphere for the carnage which follows:

> A smear of fresh blood has a metallic smell. It smells like freshly sheared copper. It is a clean and impersonal smell, quite astonishing the first time you smell it. It changes quickly, to a fetid, fudgier smell, as the cells die and thicken.

The pervasive violence not only lends a darker hue to the novel, it also provokes a variety of significant emotional responses from McGee: personal loss upon discovering Taggart's bloody body; disillusionment when he later learns that his old friend committed equally bloody murders for pay; guilt for having placed Nora in a location that proves fatal when the railing fragment lodges in her throat; finally, after killing two people himself, one of them a woman, the painful awareness that he "was going to wear it for a long long time." These incidents combine to portray McGee as a suffering hero, as one whose triumph (recovering the gold statuettes) pales in comparison to the damage done to his pride and self-image. In *Red* McGee described the "clear clean moments of a savage satisfaction akin to joy" that often accompany his investigation. In *Gold* there are no such moments, only painful ones. It isn't accidental that McGee also experiences his first serious injury, a bullet wound in the back—a symbol perhaps of the inner anguish he is suffering.

Even his well-intentioned actions produce guilt. He takes it upon himself to shatter the irritatingly casual air of indifference with which Almah Hichin recounts how she recruited Taggart to become a hired killer. In order to make a lasting impression on her, he announces that he is going to kill her. The ruse works: she starts blubbering and even loses control over her bodily functions. McGee succeeds in teaching her the lesson he himself has known for a long time (and that he will be painfully reminded of again shortly with the death of Nora), that life is fragile and can be mercilessly snuffed out at any moment by the ugly finality of death. But delivering the message proves to be as unsettling as learning it, for after leaving Almah he heads immediately for a bar to drown his sorrows. After getting suitably drunk, he stumbles off to the bed of Taggart's whore, Felicia Novaro, to spend the rest of his dark night of the soul.

McGee's sexual relationships also generate guilt. For example, sleeping with Betty Borlika is such a coldly calculated plan to get information that it leaves him with a sourness that can't be explained away as simple postcoital depression:

> The physical act, when undertaken for any motive other than love and need, is a fragmenting experience. The spirit wanders. There is a mild feeling of distaste for one's self. She was certainly attractive, mature, totally eager, but we were still strangers. She wanted to use me as a weapon against her own lonely demons. I wanted information from her. We were more adversaries than lovers. The comments of old Sam'l Johnson about the pursuit of women kept drifting into my mind. The expense is damnable, the position ridiculous, the pleasure fleeting.

He sneaks away early the next morning in what he appropriately describes as "the first grey of a tomcat dawn." And even though his relationship with Nora is mutually enriching, he is nonetheless bothered by the idea of sleeping with the woman who was planning to marry a good friend of his.

Gold is the first novel in which McGee is not called upon to apply either emotional or sexual therapy to a woman in need. The women he meets are either well in control of their lives—Shaja Dobrak stoically and confidentally awaits the release of her husband from prison, and Nora Gardino, who temporarily needs McGee's help in recovering from the shock of Taggart's death, is an emotionally mature and self-sufficient woman—or are themselves the ones who minister to McGee: Taggart's whore, Felicia Novaro, worldly-wise beyond her young years, comforts him in his period of despair, and Connie Melgar, whose steely self-sufficiency actually frightens McGee, nurses him through his recuperation from the wound he receives at Tomberlin's. Sadly, the only woman with whom he shares any degree of emotional involvement, Nora Gardino, is abruptly snatched from him before anything serious develops.

Despite its plot weaknesses and diffuse structure, *Gold* represents a significant development in the series, for in it MacDonald discloses his intention to strive for something other than entertaining storytelling. McGee as usual is the central character in the novel, but for the first time his inner self is the focus of attention. By dramatizing his fears, vulnerabilities, and uncertainties, MacDonald humanizes McGee, reduces the swaggering, swashbuckling elements that prevailed in the earlier books, and emphasizes the reflective qualities that will become increasingly important as the series continues.

4

Perfecting the Formula
(*Orange, Amber,*
Yellow, Gray)

Following the burst of creative energy that produced five McGee novels in a single year (seven, if one includes the two discarded efforts), MacDonald settled down to a more leisurely pace (for him) which nonetheless saw the publication of seven more McGee books during the next six years. The first novel he wrote after determining there was sufficient compatibility between himself and his new hero to continue, *Bright Orange for the Shroud* (1965), is the most successful of the novels to date. After sending McGee all over the United States and Mexico in the first five books, MacDonald keeps him in Florida in *Orange*, which gives the book a unity several of the earlier novels lacked and also allows MacDonald an opportunity to describe some of the natural beauty of his state. Also, the crime that prompts McGee's involvement is the type MacDonald knows best; anybody can write about simple theft or blackmail, but it takes a writer with MacDonald's business training to devise the financial shenanigans in *Orange*. MacDonald used the first five books to establish the character of McGee in some depth; now with *Orange* he begins to develop other elements—specifically the Florida setting and the clever intricacies of financial skulduggery—that will become standard features of his successful formula.

Old friend Arthur Wilkinson shows up one day in wretched physical and emotional shape (McGee notes that "I had never seen a

man so changed by one year of life"). His heart set on spending a
"slob summer," McGee casts about for someone to foist Arthur off on
and, recalling that he had at one time been romantically involved with
Chookie McCall, settles on her; it is a perfect opportunity, he decides,
not only to get rid of Arthur but also to pry Chookie away from her
unhealthy attachment to no-good Frank Durkin, currently serving a
prison sentence for felonious assault. However, his plan backfires:
Chookie is so upset by Arthur's whipped condition that she demands
that McGee help him. McGee has little choice but to see what he can
do for Arthur.

Arthur is universally liked, everybody's friend, the kind of good-
hearted pal who

> was the gatherer of driftwood for the beach picnics, the one who
> drove drunks home, the one who didn't forget the beer, the
> understanding listener who gets girl-tears on his beach coat, the
> pigeon good for the small loan, the patsy who comes calling and
> ends up painting the fence.

Only someone like Arthur could have gotten himself into the mess he
did. He tells McGee that thanks to the persistence of his new bride,
Wilma, he was accepted as a partner in a land-development syndicate
that purchased an option to buy a large tract of prime Florida land.
Lured by the promise of a handsome return on his money, he agreed
to invest $200,000 in the partnership headed by Tampa businessman
Cal Stebber. But he is such a babe in the woods that he didn't even
bother to read the contract before signing it. Before long, he was
required to pay another $33,333 as his share of an "additional
assessment"; a month later another $33,333 was demanded. When he
finally did read the contract, he learned to his dismay that it contained
a provision stipulating that all monies invested by any partner would
be forfeited if that partner defaulted on any payment. Arthur was
being systematically stripped clean of everything, including over $5,000
he raised by writing to all his friends. As he was about to go under,
he discovered that his wife was actually a "bird dog" who set him up
for the financial kill; to make matters worse, when he went to confront
Boo Waxwell, one of his partners, he spotted his wife, naked in
Waxwell's bed, watching approvingly as Waxwell beat him senseless.

After several months of hard work, Arthur managed to save $700,
enough to enable him to go after Cal Stebber. However, he is such a

natural-born victim that he is burned again. He gets only as far as Stebber's secretary, who drugs his drink, which results in his arrest for public drunkenness by a policeman who assumed he was intoxicated. He spends the next thirty days working on a roadside detail. When he is finally released, with $1.30 to his name and his tail between his legs, he heads for Ft. Lauderdale and his friend Travis McGee.

The reluctant McGee, with Chookie and Arthur in tow, sets off on *The Busted Flush* for Naples, a trip that will, he hopes, allow enough time for him to get himself into shape physically while Chookie does what she can to get Arthur's chin off the floor. In Naples, McGee begins tracking down Arthur's "partners" and soon becomes acquainted with one, Crane Watts, whom Arthur had identified as the lawyer for the syndicate. When McGee, who is posing as an agent for a wealthy financier interested in investing in a land-development deal, confides to Watts that he would like to make considerably more than the finder's fee he is being paid, Watts tells him about the shady deal that defrauded Arthur and sends him to Boo Waxwell, the partner who reportedly ended up with Arthur's wife.

McGee finds Waxwell at his isolated cabin and tells him he is looking for Wilma Wilkinson. Waxwell denies knowing her whereabouts and claims that Arthur was mistaken when he said he saw his wife with him. He must have confused her, Waxwell maintains, with a waitress who resembled her. However, Waxwell's widely known propensity for violence, coupled with about $25,000 worth of new purchases scattered around his property, convinces McGee that Waxwell is lying; he fears that Waxwell might have murdered Wilma to get his hands on her share of the take from the con.

McGee heads for Tampa and arranges a meeting with Stebber, who admits that Wilma has been his partner in a variety of scams over the past fifteen years (she has been married, it turns out, to eleven men, all victims of one con or another). He is unhappy to report, however, that she is missing along with $139,000 of Arthur's money, half of it Stebber's share of the take. Stebber reluctantly agrees that McGee's theory that Waxwell killed Wilma and took all the money is a good possibility, but Stebber firmly declines McGee's offer of ten percent of anything he recovers from Waxwell if Stebber will decoy him away from his place long enough so McGee can search the property. Stebber is so fearful of Waxwell that he wants nothing further to do with his former partner.

McGee speculates that there might be as much as $90,000 buried somewhere on Waxwell's property, but if Stebber won't help him distract Waxwell he has to find another decoy. He decides the best alternative would be Crane Watts's beautiful wife, Viv, about whom he has heard Waxwell express an interest. She hates Waxwell, but when McGee offers her $10,000 so she and her husband can move away and reestablish his faltering law practice, she agrees to consider his offer. However, when McGee returns to her home for an answer that evening, he spots Waxwell's car in the driveway; as he approaches the house, he is shot and wounded by Waxwell. After regaining consciousness and painfully crawling to the house, he sees Watts slumped in a chair, sound asleep in a drunken stupor; what he sees in the bedroom, however, horrifies him—Waxwell brutally raping Viv Watts. He is too weak from his wound to do anything but listen helplessly to her cries, which sound to him "as pretty as the raw sound of a throat being cut. Or the sound of the great caged carnivore at feeding time."

With Arthur's help (he returned after fleeing at the first sound of shots), McGee gets to a hospital for quick treatment of his head wound, then returns to the Watts home, where he finds Watts dead in the chair where he slept, a bullet in his head. His wife, dressed in the floor-length orange housecoat that has become her shroud, also lies dead of a bullet wound. McGee finds a suicide note and reconstructs what happened; devastated by her brutalization at the hands of Waxwell and disgusted by her drunken husband's failure to save her, she shot him where he slept and then in desperation turned the gun on herself. But although Viv didn't live long enough to act as a decoy for Waxwell, McGee decides he can use her death for the same purpose. He rearranges things, removes all evidence of suicide, and then phones the police anonymously to report the sound of screams and a shot at the Watts residence. He also provides the license number of Waxwell's car. Soon Waxwell is forced to flee in order to escape arrest for the murders of the Watts. With Waxwell safely out of the way, McGee is finally free to search his property, where he finds $60,000 of Arthur's money buried in the backyard. Despite the terrible tragedy of the Wattses, things appear to have ended happily for Arthur: he has a portion of his money back; he has Chookie; and he has plans for a new career as a home builder.

But the happy ending is rudely interrupted by Waxwell's unexpected return. As MacDonald demonstrated in his early thriller, *Dead*

Low Tide, when the villain is not completely eliminated from the scene he has a nasty habit of returning to seek revenge. As McGee and his lovebird companions sail through the narrow channels of the Everglades at dusk, they are surprised by Waxwell, who suddenly emerges from the cover of a mangrove and boards *The Busted Flush*. He grabs Chookie and threatens to kill her if either McGee or Arthur makes a move. McGee's clever plan to make Waxwell a suspect in the Wattses' murders has turned Waxwell into a desperate fugitive with nothing to lose by killing all three of them. MacDonald's handling of the suspense and terror throughout the scene is masterful. There appears to be no escape until Chookie, seemingly dazed by Waxwell's rough handling of her, suddenly turns and throws a cup of boiling water at her captor. Arthur then picks up an ashtray and throws it at Waxwell, knocking the gun from his hand. Chookie grabs it and begins firing at Waxwell, who leaps overboard and, in a gruesomely appropriate death, impales himself on a submerged limb. With Waxwell eliminated, the novel can now end happily, as it does with the wedding of Chookie and Arthur.

Waxwell is one of MacDonald's most fascinating villains. Physically strong and brutally arrogant, he exercises control over others by intimidation and physical threats. In his propensity for corrupting and degrading women, he resembles Junior Allen in *Blue*. McGee, observing his "seedy, indolent brutality, a wisdom of the flesh," speculates that he attracts women even as he repels them: "women, sensing exactly what he was and knowing how easily they would be used, would yet accept him, saying yes on a basis so primitive they could neither identify it nor resist it." Like Allen, Waxwell is strongly attracted to those women who spurn him. He confesses to McGee that he intends to line up Viv Watts because she looks like she could use a real man, although he hints at his actual motive when he adds that "she look at ol Boo like he's a spitty place on the sidewalk." Waxwell is dedicated to proving his sexual prowess to as many women as possible (whether they agree to it or not) and then chalking up another notch on his bedpost.

What makes Waxwell a far more credible villain than Junior Allen, who is little more than an evil presence in *Blue*, is MacDonald's skill in creating a flesh-and-blood character. Among other things, Waxwell, an Everglades guide, is effectively individualized by his colorful backwoods dialect, with its quaint and charming expressions. For example, he describes an attorney as "a lawyer man crooked as a ball of baby snakes" and says of a prospective victim of a woman friend's highly developed sexual charms that "he's got as much chanct as a key lime pie in a school yard." But McGee is never fooled by the hayseed charm of his colorful expressions and mannerisms, for Waxwell is mean and ruthless. (All the Waxwells, according to a man who knows the family, are "pure mean as moccasin snakes.") Although he confesses he did not intend to kill Wilma Wilkinson, his roughhouse tactics with her burst something in her neck, causing her death. And although he did not actually pull the trigger of the gun that killed Crane and Viv Watts, he is as responsible for their deaths as if he had. Thus his appearance aboard *The Busted Flush* at the end of the book generates an atmosphere of acute terror because the reader is fully aware of his ruthlessness.

MacDonald achieves an added dimension in the novel by including a pair of contrasting relationships, neither of which, interestingly, involves McGee, who remains celibate throughout the book. The most significant is the one which develops between Chookie and Arthur. As noted earlier, McGee hoped to use Arthur to pry Chookie away from her unhealthful attachment to Frank Durkin. (Presumably he is the same Frank with whom Chookie was involved in *Blue* and whom she described there as "my Junior Allen.") Chookie is so vibrantly alive that McGee can barely contain his admiration for her: "There was so much of her, and it was so aesthetically assembled, so vivid, so a-churn with vitality, that she faded the people for ten tables around to frail flickering monochromatic images, like a late, late movie from a fringe station." However, he shies away from her; he previously spurned her advances in *Blue*, and when she comes to him all heated and aroused following a frustrating session in Arthur's bed and all but begs him to make love to her, he declines and cools her ardor by throwing her into the cold sea. His interest in her is purely avuncular, and his analysis of his wary attitude leads to some revealing insights. He wonders if he keeps his distance out of fear:

> Maybe she was a little too much. She created a certain awe in the standard-issue male. I had noted that fewer passes were made at her than she had a right to expect. All that robust, glowing, powerful vitality might actually have given me a subconscious block, a hidden suspicion that I might, in the long run, be unable to cope—an

alarming prospect for male vanity, of which I certainly had my share.

Or perhaps she is simply too stable for his taste:

> Maybe I could be stirred only by the wounded ducklings. Maybe I could respond best to the cripples I cut out of the pack, the ones who, by contrast, could give me a sense of inner strength and unity. And a whole woman might, conversely, serve to give me a less fictional image of the inner McGee, showing the fracture lines and the clumsy ways I had pasted myself back together, and too many tricks with mirrors. When you have learned control over your own dear little neuroses, you can have empathy with the ones who are shaking themselves apart, and get your jollies out of teaching them how to dampen the vibrations. But a sound and solid one can only make you aware of how frequently precarious your acquired controls can become. It could be that this wariness of the sound ones and the true ones was one of the hidden reasons why I had to be a roamer, a salvage expert, a gregarious loner, a seeker of a thousand tarnished grails, finding too many excuses for all the dragons along the way.

Whatever the reason, he is content to play the role of matchmaker between Chookie and Arthur.

Chookie is the one who performs the sexual therapy usually administered by McGee. She patiently restores Arthur's sexual confidence until he is able to assume the role of aggressor, then, after she has done all she can for his bedroom confidence, turns him over to McGee with the request that he make Arthur feel useful. Chookie is a bright woman, but it takes her a long time to realize that Arthur is far better suited to her than the undesirable Durkin. McGee is so delighted when they decide to get married that he forgoes his usual fifty-percent split of the $9,000 he finds among Waxwell's possessions and gives the entire amount to the couple as a wedding gift.

Things don't end so happily for the Wattses. After word gets around that Watts was involved in the shady deal that defrauded Arthur, his law practice declines rapidly. So does he, wasting his days drinking and gambling. As his professional life sours, so too does his personal life, his attractive young wife finding it increasingly difficult to remain loyal to him. Because he thinks Watts capable of redemption,

McGee offers his wife $10,000 of Arthur's money to decoy Waxwell
off his property. He convinces her that the money will allow them to
move away and start anew. But before Watts's rehabilitation can begin,
Waxwell intrudes and triggers the tragic chain of events that will leave
Watts and his wife dead. MacDonald makes no excuses for Watts's
involvement with Cal Stebber and his fraudulent scheme; he was
looking to make a fast buck by illegal means and his first foray into
the world of shady deals ruined his reputation, threatened his marriage,
and ultimately cost him his life. MacDonald's portrait of the Wattses
is not, however, designed to illustrate the moral that the wages of sin
is death; rather he traces, with compassion and understanding, the
dire consequences of one man's ill-fated mistake in judgment, and the
unfortunate repercussions of his ensuing guilt. The tragic story of the
Wattses forcefully reminds us that, for some, there are no happy
endings.

"Darker than amber" are the beautiful eyes of Vangie Bellemer, who
makes a dramatic entrance in the exciting opening scene of *Darker
Than Amber* (1966). Relaxing after an emotionally exhausting ten-day
session with one of his "wounded ducklings," McGee and friend Meyer
(more about him later) are quietly fishing one evening in a boat
underneath a bridge. Suddenly a car stops above them and a body is
dropped into the water five feet away from them. McGee dives in and
spots a woman in the dark chilly water, alive, her feet wired to a block
of cement. Lungs bursting, he struggles to free her feet, then drags
her to the boat, where Meyer takes over and gives her artificial
respiration until she regains consciousness.

Wary of the two, she will identify herself only as Jane Doe, and
her steely composure while McGee removes some fishhooks embedded
in her thigh confirms the suspicion that she is a tough cookie. She
eventually lowers her guard, identifies herself as Vangie Bellemer,
and tells her story. Born in Hawaii, orphaned at twelve, she soon
ended up in a vice ring, and was recently earning top dollar as a
hooker in Jacksonville. But for the past two years she has been involved
in a bigger and more dangerous game, which she hints has something
to do with the disposal of victims. Vangie is cautious in her remarks,
admitting only that she was marked for execution because she had
gone soft and had tried to warn a potential victim about what lay in
store for him. She refuses to say more, except that she has managed

to save $32,000 which she intends to retrieve from her apartment. She borrows $200 from McGee and promises to return for help if she cannot get her money.

McGee is disquieted by the woman. He has little difficulty turning her down when she arrives naked in his room and offers herself to him. But although he knows that her "twelve years on the track had coarsened her beyond any hope of salvation" and that it is "the utmost folly to sentimentalize or romanticize a whore," there are several things about Vangie that he cannot help but admire: she has a "certain toughness of spirit"; having saved her life, he feels a proprietary interest in her future; and as she talks about her past, she displays more and more remorse for her actions (in fact, it was just such a softening of attitude that led to her near-execution). McGee is torn between an open-eyed recognition of her hardness and unredeemability on the one hand and the stirrings of a romantic urge to dust off his rusty lance and involve himself in the woman's plight on the other.

The nudge he needs to prompt him into action comes unexpectedly: a radio newscast reporting a hit-and-run accident sends him to the Broward Beach morgue to confirm his fears—shortly after leaving *The Busted Flush*, Vangie was run down by an unidentified driver in a stolen car. This time her executioners didn't miss and McGee is angry. Spurred on by a thirst for justice, by a desire to right a wrong, by a hunger for revenge against those who so quickly canceled out his heroic deed in rescuing Vangie from the water (and reminded that he has already invested $200 in her), McGee sets off to find out what he can about the nasty business that led to Vangie's death.

McGee eventually locates Noreen Walker, the woman who used to clean Vangie's apartment. His encounter with her illustrates one of MacDonald's special talents as a novelist. At first, she appears to fit the stereotypical image of the black maid—hardworking, uneducated, wary of the inquisitive white man. However, the woman turns out to be as much a master of the charade as McGee is. When he mentions that he is from Ft. Lauderdale, she excuses herself and makes a phone call to a friend there, who vouches for McGee's trustworthiness; then she drops the darkie façade and identifies herself as the regional director of CORE (Congress of Racial Equality). A former teacher and graduate of the University of Michigan, she works as a maid because it provides a protective cover that allows her to carry on her work for racial equality in the South without undue harassment.

MacDonald frequently devotes as much care to the creation of his minor characters as he does to the major ones. (And since their appearance is usually so brief, he must be more effective in a limited space.) Anyone could have provided the information McGee is seeking about Vangie. But MacDonald is interested in the character of Noreen because he can use her to express his own views on the racial issue. The woman allows him to divide his usual mini-sermon into two sections; one part is expressed by McGee in his characteristic manner:

> If there were people around colored green or bright blue, I would
> have a continual primitive awareness of the difference between us,
> way down on that watchful animal level which is a caveman heritage.
> But I would cherish the ones who came through as solid folk, and
> avoid the slobs and fools and bores as diligently as I avoid white
> slobs and fools and bores.

The rest is delivered by Noreen and reflects MacDonald's opinion (circa 1966) about how intelligent, militant blacks view the question of equality:

> My boys are two and a half and four. What am I doing to their lives
> if I let them grow up here? . . . We want out, where the law is,
> where you prosper or you fail according to your own merits as a
> person. Is that so damned much? I don't want white friends. I don't
> want to socialize. . . . I don't want to integrate. I just don't want
> to feel segregated. We're after our share of the power structure of
> this civilization, Mr. McGee, because, when we get it, a crime will
> merit the same punishment whether the victim is black or white,
> and hoods will get the same share of municipal services, based on
> zoning, not color.

McGee follows up on a suggestion Noreen gives him about the location of Vangie's hidden loot, returns to her apartment, searches behind the kitchen light fixture, and finds the cash. As he leaves, however, he is accosted by Vangie's former boss, Griff, who has been watching her apartment. He forces McGee to a lonely stretch of beach, where he intends to kill him. Luckily McGee manages to pull a tiny pistol from his pocket and shoot Griff, who, as he is dying, utters a cryptic message: "Ans Terry. Him and the Whitney bitch. Monica Day."

McGee ought to be satisfied with his efforts. He has recovered Vangie's money, which, thanks to her death, he doesn't have to split with anyone. He has gained a measure of revenge by killing Griff, one of those probably responsible for her death. He tells himself he should return to *The Busted Flush* with the money, which will support his comfortable life-style for many months to come. Nevertheless, he cannot shed his sense of personal commitment to the case. McGee knows that if he walks away now, he will spend a lot of time "wondering at what moment they were knocking off what new pigeon, now that they'd cleaned up the operation by disposing of the one weak link." Thus motivated by a desire to spare the lives of future victims of the deadly game, he decides to seek out the remaining pieces of the puzzle.

After he figures out that "Monica Day" is actually *Monica D.*, the name of a cruise ship that sails the Caribbean, he and Meyer fly to Nassau and board the ship in hopes of locating the others Griff mentioned, Ans Terry and "the Whitney bitch." Aboard ship, McGee spots a woman who, thanks to his sure instincts, turns out to be Del Whitney, a friend and former partner of Vangie. McGee tells her about Vangie's death and warns her that her own life is in danger. Shaken by his account of Vangie's murder, she agrees to McGee's plan for her getaway, which involves pretending that she has committed suicide by jumping overboard. To make everything appear authentic, he persuades her to write a suicide note in which she confesses all the details about the murder scheme she and Vangie were involved in. (The two women would lure wealthy middle-aged men to the ship and then, with the aid of their partners, rob them, kill them, and toss their bodies overboard. The team of Del Whitney and Ans Terry was responsible for the deaths of fourteen men.)

While Terry lies in a drink-induced slumber, McGee retrieves the $26,000 he took from his most recent victim, then arranges for him to be arrested by the authorities when the ship docks in Florida. The police also arrest Del, whose detailed "confession" will enable them to round up the remaining members of the murder-for-profit ring.

Back aboard *The Busted Flush*, McGee's sense of satisfaction is soured somewhat by his recent experiences, from Vangie's death to his association with Del Whitney, whom he characterizes as a "dumb empty punchboard." Even his characteristically romantic gesture of sending the $26,000 he recovered from Ans Terry to the family of the victim from whom it was stolen fails to lift his spirits. Meyer, sensible investor that he is, takes the $10,000 of Vangie's money McGee gives him, banks it, and plans to use the interest to finance the first annual Meyer Fourth of July Festival devoted to "Booze, Broads, Beer, Bonhomie, Bach, Blues and Rhythm, Bombast, Blarney and Behavioral Psychology." But it will take more than a party to overcome McGee's depression. It requires something as stunning, yet as simple, as a shooting star to gladden his spirits, to remind him that despite his recent experiences, the world is good. "What the hell was the use," he asks himself, "of taking my retirement in segments whenever I could afford one if I was going to slop around and groan and finger the sad textures of my immortal soul?" His resurrection is completed when he receives an unexpected call from Merrimay Lane, the model he hired to decoy Ans Terry by posing as the dead Vangie. *Amber* thus ends on an upbeat note with McGee smiling in anticipation of an evening with Merrimay.

Among other things, *Amber* demonstrates MacDonald's capacity for surprise. One of the remarkable things about the forty-odd novels he wrote prior to the McGee books is how he managed to avoid repeating himself. With this, his seventh McGee adventure, he once again shows his versatility; just when it appeared he might be falling victim to a rigid pattern, MacDonald introduces something new. For the first time, McGee is involved in a case in which he defends no one, is hired to salvage nothing, ministers to no wounded duckling. McGee's motivation is entirely personal, his efforts aimed at solving a mystery in order to prevent future murders from occurring.

Although the pattern is new, there is nothing surprising about MacDonald's typically skillful handling of mystery and suspense. From the opening page, the reader's curiosity is piqued, his desire to know more about Vangie and her plight titillated. *Amber* demonstrates MacDonald's storytelling skills at their finest; information is revealed bit by bit and only gradually does the reader become fully aware of the nature and extent of the murder ring. Once this occurs, attention shifts to McGee's elaborate plan to expose the ring and deliver Del and Terry to the police. In a plot as well constructed as this, with all the elements neatly fitting into a fast-paced and exciting story, it is easy to overlook the skill with which everything has been carefully arranged.

MacDonald's characterization, especially his portrayal of the two prostitutes, is equally skillful. Vangie and Del are as physically attractive as any of MacDonald's vulnerable victims, but in their cold-bloodedness they are as deadly as his most evil villains. Vangie is partially redeemed by the stirrings of remorse that bear evidence of at least a trace of compassion, but Del shows no such softness. She is so devoid of normal human feeling that she can transfer her allegiance from Terry, her companion for seven years, to McGee as easily as switching brands of toothpaste. She is empty, shallow, trivial, with no interest in anything more important than her clothes or her hairdo. She believes McGee is saving her life, but can't even be bothered to remember his name. Any effort to shake her up, to teach her a lesson, as McGee did with Almah Hichin in *Gold*, would be wasted, for there is nothing of substance beneath Del's attractive surface.

Which is not to say she doesn't hold a certain attraction for McGee. He is surprised to discover in himself a "very real yen to take a hack" at the beautiful but murderous woman:

> I wanted to grab at this one. Maybe everybody at some time or another feels the strong attraction of something rotten-sweet enough to guarantee complete degradation. I wanted to pull her down and roll into that hot practiced trap which had clenched the life out of fourteen men. And there was a big shiny rationalization. It's the way to make her trust you, fella. Go right ahead, lull the broad. It'll take about nine minutes out of your life. You're a big boy. A broad is a broad is a broad, and who'll know the difference?
> You will, McGee. For a long long time.

As usual, Meyer is able to explain McGee's attraction to Del by comparing him to the little boy dressed in his finest clothes who always manages to find the sloppiest mud puddle in town. "There is sometimes a hypnotic deliciousness about dirt," he warns McGee. But thanks to his innate good sense, and well-established principles, McGee is able once more to tiptoe safely past the corruption he so frequently encounters.

The most notable feature of *Amber* is the expanded role given to Meyer (just Meyer: whether surname or given name is intended is not entirely clear, although in *Gray* he poses as G. Ludweg Meyer and in *Indigo* McGee introduces him as "my associate, Mr. Meyer"). First mentioned in *Purple,* the third McGee novel, Meyer also appeared briefly in *Red, Gold,* and *Orange.* But it isn't until *Amber* that his character is fully developed for the first time as he assumes what will become a continuing role as the most important influence in McGee's life.

Semi-retired like McGee, Meyer lives only seventy feet away from his friend aboard his cabin cruiser, appropriately named *John Maynard Keynes.* A large, shambling, hairy bear of a man, he combines enormous intelligence (an international expert in economics, he has a Ph.D.) with an abundance of personal charm. Saddled with what McGee jokingly calls in *Gray* "one of the ugliest faces of the Western world," Meyer is also blessed with the kind of beatific smile that magically transforms his imposing features into pure gentleness. McGee's description in *Scarlet* of Meyer in repose gives a good indication of his wide range of intellectual interests:

> He has those places to go, inside his head. He looks as if he was sitting and dozing, fingers laced across his middle. Actually he has walked back into his head, where there are libraries, concert halls, work rooms, experimental laboratories, game rooms. He can listen to a fine string quartet, solve chess problems, write an essay on Chilean inflation under Allende, or compose haiku.

Meyer is as comfortable with people as he is with bewildering corporation reports or complex tax problems, as bewitching to children as he is to the hordes of cute little lollipops who hover about him.

> He can walk a beach, go into any bar, cross any playground, and acquire people the way blue serge picks up lint, and the new friends believe they have known him forever. Perhaps it is because he actually listens, and actually cares, and can make you feel as if his day would have been worthless, an absolute nothing, had he not had the miraculous good fortune of meeting you. . . . He could have been one of the great con artists of all time. Or one of the great psychiatrists. Or the founder of a new religion. Meyerism.

But his most important feature is his relationship to McGee.

Meyer is companion, critic, confidant, and confessor to McGee. Although cast in the subservient role of Watson to McGee's Holmes, his brilliantly logical mind frequently reverses the relationship, with him assuming the Holmesian role. He is the one, for example, who detects the Hawaiian background in Vangie's speech pattern, who notices the labels in her clothing, who figures out how an extra passenger can be smuggled aboard the *Monica D.* Blessed with infinite understanding, he is, according to McGee, a "splendid listener" and "the best of company, because he knows when talk is better than silence." Meyer has enough sensitivity to know, for example, when to prod McGee out of his sullen funks and when, such as after his killing of Griff, to leave him alone. This Sancho Panza understands his Quixote well enough to know when he can joke with him about succumbing to Del Whitney's sleazy sexuality (because he knows McGee wouldn't) and when to remind his friend that despite his ironic postures, he is at heart a true romantic. Nowhere are his special qualities more succinctly expressed than in McGee's description of him in *Turquoise*: "Meyer is a transcendent warmth, the listening ear of a total understanding and forgiveness, a humble wisdom."

Meyer also frees MacDonald, to some degree, from the confining limits of the first-person narrator, thereby relieving McGee of some of the burden of commentary, both about himself and the passing scene. MacDonald describes the development of Meyer this way:

> During the first few books of the series, there was no Meyer. As I began to work ever harder to try to obviate the need for endless internal monologues on the part of McGee, I began to realize that there had to be some middle ground between achieving all exposition through show rather than tell, and achieving it through all tell. I invented Meyer out of fragments in the vast scrap basket in the back of my mind, vowing that I would not have a clown on scene, nor would I have someone dependent upon McGee emotionally, financially or socially.
>
> I worked with Meyer, throwing away paragraphs and pages and chapters until he finally emerged, nodding in hirsute satisfaction, little wise blue eyes gleaming with ironic amusement, amused at himself and at my efforts, proclaiming like the bottle genie that he had been there all along, waiting for someone to perform the magic spell of rubbing the right words together.

Once he realized that his Tonto-figure did not have to be a dummy, that he could in fact be smarter than McGee in certain ways, MacDonald began to use him to make comments and observations that might be out of character coming from McGee. For example, while reporting to McGee about what he learned during a search of Del Whitney's room, Meyer lapses into an extensive monologue in which he analyzes the psychological dimensions of her personality. McGee, anxious to learn what Meyer found, has to wait impatiently until his friend finishes explaining her behavior in terms of the opposing concepts of "I" and "Not-I." The conversation discloses Meyer's tendency toward pomposity (although he is also shown to have a quick and ready wit; referring to Vangie's dramatic plunge into the water, he chides McGee by remarking, "Damned handy, Travis. As soon as you run out, they drop you another one"). But more importantly, Meyer's comments also provide the best explanation for Vangie's behavior, and what would have been awkward coming from McGee sounds natural and convincing coming from the erudite Meyer, who offers MacDonald— as Noreen Walker also does—an alternative mouthpiece for his views. The intimate relationship between McGee and his hairy friend and the engaging byplay it produces are among the special pleasures the McGee series provides.

McGee forsakes the warmth and sunshine of his beloved Florida in *One Fearful Yellow Eye* (1966) for Chicago, a "huge damp cellar" of a place whose lake stinks and whose air is so foul that "when you swallowed you could taste the city." But an urgent S.O.S. from another friend from his past, Glory Geis, rouses him. Glory's husband, Dr. Fortner Geis, recently died and a family squabble has arisen between Glory and Geis's two children, Roger and Heidi. It has been learned that during the last year of his life, Geis converted all his assets to cash, totaling over $600,000, which has mysteriously disappeared. There is almost nothing left in his estate, and Geis's children suspect that Glory had something to do with the disappearance of her husband's money. Bewildered, she summons McGee to help her find out what happened to it.

McGee immediately suspects blackmail and even manages to turn up some skeletons in Geis's closet. Eighteen years earlier, as his first wife lay dying of a heart ailment, he succumbed to the seductive availability of Gretchen Ottlo, seventeen-year-old daughter of his housekeeper. She became pregnant and had a daughter, for whose support Geis assumed responsibility. He did not hide this past indiscretion from Glory, nor did he conceal his longtime affair with Janice Stanyard, his head nurse, a relationship that ended amicably prior to his marriage to Glory. However, McGee can find nothing to suggest blackmail in either situation.

He is puzzled, however, by a series of strange incidents that occurred nineteen months earlier: Geis's grandson was kidnapped, then released unharmed without any ransom ever being demanded; an intruder broke into Janice Stanyard's house and stabbed her cat to death; Heidi Trumbill, Geis's daughter, bit into a chocolate-covered cherry which someone had filled with Tabasco sauce and slipped into a box of candy in her home; a harmless smoke bomb was detonated in Glory's car. McGee concludes that someone was sending a warning to Geis, perhaps in an attempt to extort money from him by demonstrating how easily those he loved could be killed. McGee's puzzlement is compounded by a late-night encounter with two mysterious men, one with an English accent, who accost him outside Glory's house, question him about his activities, then release him without explanation.

The mysteries begin to unravel when Susan Kemmer, Geis's seventeen-year-old daughter by Gretchen Ottlo, arrives in Chicago, badly beaten and in terrible shape. She tells McGee that she ran away from the small Illinois town where she was living to escape the sexual assaults of her stepfather, Saul Gorba, and got in touch with Janice Stanyard, whose name her father once gave her as a person to call if she ever needed help. McGee wonders whether Gorba, an ex-con, might have had something to do with the disappearance of Geis's money, so he heads for rural Illinois, where he locates Gorba's ransacked house; inside a nearby shed, he finds Gorba, dead, his body bearing evidence of horrible torture. He searches carefully and eventually finds $178,650 in cash hidden underneath plastic filler Gorba used to cover dents in the body of his car. McGee concludes that Gorba was indeed involved in the extortion of Geis and surmises that he probably killed Gretchen—who, according to Susan Kemmer, has been missing for three weeks—when she became suspicious about his newfound wealth. But McGee is at a loss to explain who might have killed Gorba or where the rest of the $600,000 might be found. Nevertheless, for his success in recovering at least a portion of the money, Heidi rewards him with $18,750 and also agrees to accompany him to the Virgin Islands for as much sun, sea, and sexual therapy as it takes to thaw her frigid body.

Six weeks later, McGee's magic has transformed the sexually inhibited Heidi into a fully responsive, sensuous woman. But McGee isn't relaxed; something keeps nibbling at the edges of his consciousness. When Heidi casually mentions that Anna Ottlo, whom she knows as Gretchen's mother, said she was planning to spend the winter in Florida with a woman who has been dead for years, McGee's suspicions come into focus. He gets in touch with Glory, who tells him she recalls seeing a postcard of Anna's with a Florida address, something like Mark Bay or Macko Bay. McGee guesses it was probably Marco Bay, so he and Heidi head there to see if they can locate Anna. McGee finds her, sporting freshly dyed red hair and without any trace of her previously thick German accent, now living the life of a retired housewife. But before he can get any information from her, he is grabbed from behind and knocked unconscious.

What follows is the kind of tense, terrifying scene MacDonald often ends his novels with. McGee, tightly strapped to a chair, is helpless to do anything about the horrible screams coming from the next room where Heidi is being sexually assaulted by Anna's partner. Unable to endure her screams any longer, McGee in desperation lunges at Anna and knocks her through a glass door, a large section of which falls on her neck, killing her. Hearing the noise, her partner enters the room, sees what has happened, and raises his pistol to shoot McGee. Suddenly, he falls over, a bullet in his forehead. McGee's last-second rescuers turn out to be the same men who grabbed him outside Glory's Chicago home, a pair of Israeli Nazi-hunters who have been tracking down Anna and her partner, whom they identify as former Nazi interrogation experts.

Anna (actually Fredrika Gronwald) managed to slip out of Germany before the end of the war by posing as the mother of a young girl, Gretchen, whose real mother she had murdered. When she became suspicious that agents were on her trail, she schemed to finance her new getaway by extorting the money she needed from her employer, Dr. Geis. With the help of her former Nazi associate, Perry Hennigan, and Saul Gorba, she devised the whole plan. Gorba killed Gretchen when she became suspicious about his activities, and then was himself tortured to death by Hennigan after outliving his usefulness. The Israelis search the house and find what they were after—a code book containing valuable information about other Nazi exiles. They also find Geis's missing $420,000, which is returned to Chicago and distributed to Geis's heirs. McGee accepts $10,000 for his services and then takes Heidi back to St. Croix to try to undo the damage done by Hennigan's brutal assaults.

This is not the first time MacDonald has used elements of foreign intrigue in his fiction. Communist spies, for example, figure significantly in two of his early works, *Murder for the Bride* and *Area of Suspicion*, and Cuban political exiles are intimately involved in the action in *Gold*. Although the Nazi material is not directly related to the extortion of Geis and the subsequent mysteries surrounding it, it does serve a useful purpose: on a simple plot level, it provides for the dramatic appearance of the two Nazi-hunters who come riding to McGee's rescue like the cavalry in the final reel of a Western film; and it introduces a broader context for an important theme in the novel, the relationship between past and present. The revelation of Anna's Nazi past prompts McGee to remark, "I had never thought that an ugliness of so long ago could ever reach into my life. I had thought it was all history-book stuff, and that all that Eichmann hooraw had been an anachronistic after-echo of it." Like the novels of Ross Macdonald, *Yellow* is concerned with the intrusion of the past into the present, and with the difficulty of escaping the effects of long-festering wounds.

The pages of the novel are strewn with casualties of the past. Gretchen Ottlo's unhappy life (four husbands, chronic alcoholism) can be traced to her early years, especially the five years she spent separated from her real mother in the Nazi concentration camp. Heidi Trumbill still bears the psychological scars inflicted when, as a child of seven, the shock of seeing Gretchen Ottlo naked in her father's bed was misperceived as rejection by her father. Even Glory Geis was almost destroyed by her own traumatic past: her first husband, insanely jealous and prone to violent outbursts, went beserk one day and killed their two children and himself. Consumed by guilt over the incident and on the verge of suicide, Glory was saved only by McGee's tender care after he found her on a Florida beach.

Interestingly, *Yellow* was published the same year in which the Beatles released one of their most popular songs, "Eleanor Rigby," a mournful tune whose oft-repeated refrain, "Ah, look at all the lonely people!"* might well serve as a subtitle for MacDonald's novel, which is a study in loneliness. One of the most moving of all the portraits of lonely people in the novel is that of Fortner Geis, whose character is

---

* From "Eleanor Rigby" by Lennon/McCartney, © 1966 by Northern Songs Limited.

thoroughly detailed even though he is dead before the action of the novel begins. Geis is an internationally known surgeon, a highly respected man whose professional skills are complemented by such personal virtues as sensitivity, warmth, and compassion. Tragically, his first wife died at a young age of a lingering heart ailment. Only the furtive encounters with the young Gretchen Ottlo managed to assuage his loneliness and pain during the final months of her confinement. Later, fearful at becoming so engrossed in his work that he was losing all human companionship, he entered into an affair with his nurse, Janice Stanyard, whose own life had been visited by tragedy: her husband had suffered a severe brain injury which would confine him to a hospital for the rest of his life. The relationship between Geis and Janice allowed the two of them to ward off the chronic loneliness that was souring their lives. Eventually Geis met Glory Doyle during a Florida vacation, and the two of them enjoyed four happy years until his untimely death. All of this sounds like the cheesiest kind of soap opera, but MacDonald manages to avoid mawkish sentimentality by creating believable characters who have no time for self-pity. These are people whose loneliness is prompted by tragic circumstance, not chronic disposition, and MacDonald treats them with the respect and dignity they deserve.

Even the minor characters long for an escape from the emptiness in their lives: Gretchen Ottlo marries four times in an unsuccessful search for a love denied her as a child; McGee rescues a drunken businessman whose desperate need for companionship has driven him to seek the favors of a prostitute who, McGee realizes, is planning to rob him; finally, there is Mildred Shottlehauster, Saul Gorba's neighbor. In a scene that might have come from the pages of *Winesburg, Ohio* (or, given *Yellow*'s Illinois setting, perhaps from *Spoon River Anthology*), McGee, seeking to question Mrs. Shottlehauster about Gorba, glances in the window and sees her sprawled on the kitchen counter making love with the bakery deliveryman. (His truck parked outside bears the company motto, "Fresh as a Stolen Kiss.") McGee quickly retreats and waits until the man leaves before approaching her. As they talk, McGee notices her eyes glaze and a sheen of perspiration appear above her lip; he suddenly realizes that she is searching for a way to show that she is also available to him if he wants her.

Unlike many of the women he has previously encountered in his travels, Mrs. Shottlehauster isn't brazen enough to express her desires openly. She offers only an indirect invitation: "Since my littlest one started school and Harry took to being away politicking here and there, these winter days do seem to get awful long for an outgoing-type person like me." The woman is lusty but not really promiscuous, McGee concludes, happily married yet lonely and sexually frustrated. Were it not for the incident he witnessed with the deliveryman he might have found himself in her bed (or on her counter), but instead he declines to acknowledge her offer. Later analyzing his motivation for spurning her tentatively made gesture, he comes up with a less than flattering image of himself:

> It had not been restraint after all, not a moral hesitation. It had been just my supercilious sense of my own dignity. McGee could not take over the morning chore where Darling Bread Boy had left off. Fastidiousness. A stuffy sense of social stratum, and of course no chance to exercise that jackassy masculine conviction that the lady would not have yielded to anyone less charming and persuasive.

Once again MacDonald demonstrates his economy by using minor characters to give depth and texture to his book while at the same time, through their interaction with McGee, revealing new dimensions to his character.

Poor McGee has remained celibate for the past two books and decides to do something about it, although the woman he finally chooses to bed, Heidi Trumbill, is something of a surprise. She is, in her ex-husband's words, an "ice queen," a sexually repressed "snow maiden" who makes a totally negative impression on McGee the first time they meet. Her icy arrogance so repels him that he childishly stoops to attacking her by criticizing the painting she is working on. Although she is abundantly attractive, McGee professes over and over a complete and total lack of interest in her.

But McGee doth protest too much, for his put-downs reveal a curious ambivalence. His critical comments notwithstanding, he finds himself inevitably attracted to her. When he tells her, "Maybe you're an example of conspicuous waste," he hints at his suspicion that rather than a useless neuter, Heidi is simply unfulfilled, incomplete, and therefore a likely candidate for his therapy. Doctor McGee accepts the challenge and proposes that the two of them go off together for a session in the sun. At first she refuses, but when McGee sings a paean to the pleasures of love and intimacy, she changes her mind.

Six weeks with McGee in St. Croix do the trick; Heidi's sexual hang-ups are successfully overcome and she learns to respond in a lusty and mature fashion. The bout with the sadistic Hennigan later nearly undermines McGee's work, but a renewed effort in St. Croix after the incident repairs the damage. However, his campaign to transform his latest wounded duckling into an independent woman proves to be *too* successful; Heidi thanks him for introducing her to the world of sensual pleasure, but tells him she must leave before becoming emotionally dependent on him. Ironically she gives him a dose of his own medicine, for she is simply repeating the advice he had given Glory Doyle four years earlier when, after helping her through the rough period following her husband's death, she became too emotionally attached to him. McGee is left at the end of the novel to find whatever comfort he can with the $28,750 he has received for his efforts.

Yellow contains scenes of intense excitement: McGee's dramatic encounter with Glory Geis, naked and suffering hallucinations, running in a frenzy along the frigid beach near her home (Anna Ottlo had put a dose of LSD into her orange juice in an attempt to get her out of the way by driving her to commit suicide); Heidi's sudden outburst of childlike terror upon seeing the naked body of Susan Kemmer in the half-light of her bedroom and flashing back to the traumatic incident when as a young girl she had seen Susan's mother, Gretchen Ottlo, naked in her father's bed; the excruciating agony of McGee's helpless realization that he can do nothing to stop the sounds of Heidi's screams as Perry Hennigan's sadistic sexual assault threatens to undo the emotional stability he has worked so hard to help her achieve. But the novel is also characterized by sensitivity and insight in its compassionate portrayal of human loneliness. *Yellow* is an excellent example of MacDonald's skill in combining the excitement of a good mystery with seriousness of purpose and subtlety of subject matter.

Pale Gray for Guilt (1968) opens with McGee testing out his new speedboat, *Muñequita*, which he recently purchased from the estate of a man named Kayd. (This creates an interesting connection with *The Last One Left*, published just prior to *Gray*. Bixby Kayd was a wealthy Texan murdered aboard his yacht in that novel, and the

Muñequita, which was being towed alongside, was the boat on which Leila Boylston drifted to shore, wrecking the carefully laid plans of Crissy Harkinson. *Muñequita* is also the name of a boat MacDonald used to own.) McGee's destination is Bannon's Boatel, a marina owned and operated by a friend and former football teammate, Tush Bannon, whom he hasn't seen in some time. Things aren't going well for Bannon; his business is falling off precipitously, thanks to a number of unfortunate factors: the local access road was closed for construction; a nearby bridge was relocated three miles upstream; pollution from a neighboring factory has been allowed to increase dramatically. McGee is sympathetic, but there seems to be little one can do but wait for the situation to improve.

However, when McGee bumps into Bannon a few months later in Miami he learns that, in fact, things have gotten worse. Bannon tells McGee that a local real estate figure, Preston LaFrance, has been pressuring him to sell his ten-acre property, which is smack in the middle of a valuable parcel of land LaFrance wants. He has refused all offers and now finds himself being driven (by LaFrance, he suspects) into bankruptcy: several valued customers have been pressured into taking their business elsewhere; county inspectors have revoked his license for trumped-up "violations"; and the bank has given him thirty days to pay off his entire mortgage or face foreclosure. McGee becomes worried when, a few days later, he is unable to reach Bannon by phone. He returns to the Boatel and finds it all but deserted; the only person around, a serviceman who has come to disconnect the telephone, tells McGee the sad news—the day before, apparently distraught over his financial problems, Bannon lay under an elevated engine block and dropped it on his head, killing himself.

Bannon's wife, Jan, who had left with their three young children the day before the tragedy, is apparently unaware of her husband's death, so McGee tracks her down in Frostproof, Florida, where she is staying at the home of a friend, Connie Alvarez, and breaks the news to her. A few days later, accompanied by Connie and her lawyer, Judge Rufus Wellington, McGee and Jan return to Sunnydale to rescue the marina by paying off the delinquent charges. The bank officer is reluctant to allow this (having already made a deal to sell the property to Press LaFrance, the man who unsuccessfully attempted to buy it from Bannon), but Judge Wellington reminds him of the law, and he concludes he has no choice but to return the title to Jan.

She in turn transfers the property to McGee, thus effectively finessing LaFrance by snatching the property out from under his nose.

McGee soon learns the reason for all the interest in Bannon's property: a large corporation desires to purchase the 480 acres surrounding it for a new facility. Prominent Florida wheeler-dealer Gary Santo owns half the acreage and has offered LaFrance a good price if he can deliver the rest. The only stumbling block to the deal is Bannon's property, which sits "like a June bug in the birthday cake." It isn't long before LaFrance comes calling. "I thought it might be time to see if we can eat out of the same dish or spill the dinner," he tells McGee. Drawing upon his knowledge of LaFrance's financial situation, his awareness of the value of Bannon's property, and Meyer's financial wizardry, McGee devises a beauty of a scheme: using a variation of the old pigeon-drop con, he aims to bilk as much money from LaFrance as he can; at the same time, posing as a stock market expert (his reputation certified by phony records supplied by Meyer), he will attempt to con Santo into investing heavily in a stock Meyer has found that is attractive on the surface but rotten at the core. If McGee's schemes work, both LaFrance and Santo will pay heavily for their conspiracy to force Bannon out of business.

His plans are temporarily interrupted, however, when he is arrested for the murder of Tush Bannon. McGee had earlier learned, after talking a pathologist friend into examining the body, that Bannon was probably a victim of murder rather than suicide. Now he finds himself accused of the deed by Arlene Dunn, one of Bannon's tenants, who claims to have witnessed the whole incident. The only thing wrong with her story is that McGee has an airtight alibi. Under questioning, the young woman breaks down and confesses that she was pressured into making the false charge against McGee by Deputy Freddy Hazzard, who, she now reveals, was the actual murderer. Hazzard arrested her during a drug bust and, while high, she made the mistake of telling him she saw him kill Bannon. Threatening her with prosecution on the drug charge, Hazzard coerced her into making the false statement. McGee is promptly released and the police set out after Hazzard, who slipped away when he overheard the woman changing her story.

Hazzard is Press LaFrance's nephew, and the possibility that LaFrance might also have been involved in Bannon's murder gives McGee an added incentive for revenge. McGee persuades LaFrance to become his partner in a joint venture to sell their combined acreage to another corporation seeking to purchase land in the area. Its representative, Dr. G. Ludweg Meyer (our Meyer), however, is demanding $75,000 in cash for securing an attractive price for their acreage. McGee cons LaFrance into putting up $40,000 (he puts in the other $35,000), which he seals in an envelope and places in his hotel safe, each of the three men receiving a portion of the claim check. Later, having surreptiously switched checks, McGee retrieves the envelope. He now has LaFrance's $40,000. To inflict further damage, he then phones LaFrance and tells him that he has given his share of the claim check to Meyer, who is willing to sell LaFrance both portions for only $60,000. LaFrance jumps at the opportunity to get $75,000 for only $60,000, but when he opens the envelope all he finds inside is a greeting card from Meyer. Trapped by his greed, LaFrance discovers that his involvement in Bannon's tragedy has wiped him out.

Meanwhile, Meyer is carefully monitoring the movement of Fletcher Industries stock; he waits for the right moment, then unloads his shares just before the SEC suspends all trading pending an investigation into the company's financial condition. Santo is trapped, having invested over a million dollars in a stock that is now virtually worthless. Meyer gives McGee half the profits he made by investing some of his own money in the stock, thus providing his friend with a tidy fee to go along with his satisfaction at having gained revenge over the two men who conspired to drive Bannon out of business.

Gray gives MacDonald an opportunity to show off his intimate knowledge of such things as the intricacies of land deals, option agreements, stock market manipulations, balance sheets, floats, investment strategies, and the like. He also gets a chance to demonstrate how such information can be put to devious ends, in this case the financial ruin of those who made the mistake of trying to put the squeeze on a friend of his. However, such shenanigans are both a strength and a weakness in the novel, for while they provide *Gray* with ingenious plot material, they also result in a diminishment of physical action. To remedy this weakness, MacDonald is forced to take the awkward step of creating a physical antagonist in the person of Freddy Hazzard.

Tush Bannon, it turns out, was killed accidentally when Hazzard punched him too hard in the face; to conceal his guilt, Hazzard arranged things to make Bannon's death appear to be a suicide. Actually the novel would be more effective if, in fact, Bannon had been driven to kill himself as a result of the economic squeeze put on him by Santo and LaFrance. McGee's revenge would be even sweeter if they, rather than Hazzard, were shown to be the ones responsible for his death. Santo and LaFrance make suitable targets for McGee's con-man artistry, but to test his physical mettle (and to introduce more action), MacDonald needs Hazzard who, like Boo Waxwell in *Orange*, unexpectedly shows up aboard *The Busted Flush* at the end of the novel and threatens to kill McGee and Jan Bannon. Only her quick thinking saves their lives when she bashes him in the head with a fire extinguisher, killing him.

However, in order to end the novel with one of his typically exciting confrontations, MacDonald is forced to rely on some clumsy ploys. First, he had to place Arlene Lunn in a location where she could surreptitiously witness Bannon's death; then, she is later arrested by the same man who happened to be the killer; following this we have the improbable situation of her confessing to Hazzard that she saw him kill Bannon; finally, Hazzard is turned into a fugitive when he conveniently overhears Arlene Dunn recant her false testimony. All in all, the situation is more contrived than usual in a MacDonald novel.

MacDonald's careful attention to the financial intricacies of his plot also seems to have distracted him from his usually effective use of minor characters. Potentially interesting characters, such as Connie Alvarez and Judge Rufus Wellington, are summarily dropped from the novel after they serve their brief function, which is assisting McGee in retrieving the title to Jan's property. More puzzling is the sudden disappearance of Puss Killian, the luscious redhead with whom McGee is romantically involved at the beginning of the novel. She too abruptly exits, leaving behind only a brief note announcing her departure. It isn't until the end of the novel, when McGee receives a letter from her, that we learn the reason for her leaving: dying of a brain tumor, she decided to return to her husband and live out her remaining days with him. (McGee knew nothing about the illness or the husband.) She also adds that she has instructed her husband to contact Jan Bannon after her death. The reader might have wondered why McGee never showed any romantic interest in the attractive widow who could have benefited from his attentions, but the existence of her three children would have made such involvement rather clumsy. Thanks to Puss's matchmaking effort, however, McGee is freed of any obligation to provide for Jan's emotional happiness, for there now exists the possibility that she will find a secure future with Puss's widower.

Despite such flaws, *Gray* successfully continues the pattern begun in *Yellow* of combining mystery elements with an exploration of human emotion, in this case the title hinting at its thematic intention, namely an examination of the varieties of human guilt. McGee's plan for gaining revenge against Santo and LaFrance requires that both men become fully aware of his motive for defrauding them. McGee takes great delight when, after bilking LaFrance out of $100,000, he is able to watch his reaction when he reveals for the first time that Bannon was a good friend of his: "I watched the gray appear. That gray was like a wet stone. Gray for fright. Gray for guilt. Gray for despair." Santo is a tougher cookie, but McGee notices enough of that telltale tinge of gray appear under his "barbered, lotioned, international complexion" to satisfy him. It isn't enough that both men be cleaned out, they must also make the connection between what McGee does to them and what they did to Bannon. Relentless in their single-minded pursuit of monetary gain, both have lost sight of what it means to be human. Only a crippling blow to their most vulnerable area—the pocketbook—can shake them enough to squeeze the guilt from them.

The other type of guilt examined in the novel is far healthier, for it arises from within and attests to the moral sensitivity of the individual who experiences it. There are numerous examples of this variety: Puss Killian's regret at leaving her husband eventually prompts her to return to him; Jan Bannon feels shame at having struck her young child for asking too many questions after she damaged her car in a minor accident; Connie Alvarez still agonizes over having spoken harsh words to her husband shortly before he was killed in an auto accident; Meyer regrets the angry outburst in which he uncharacteristically advises LaFrance to go out and kill himself; McGee feels bad about delivering Mary Smith, Gary Santo's private secretary, into the satyric hands of a local stud named Hero. In each instance guilt is a sign of moral health, a measure of human sensitivity and ethical awareness. Meyer acknowledges that, like McGee, he sometimes does things that "hurt him in the way he thinks of himself," but without such feelings, the world would fast become overpopulated with the likes of Santo and LaFrance.

5

McGee's Maturity
(*Brown, Indigo,*
Lavender, Tan, Scarlet)

Just when the reader thinks he knows what to expect next in a McGee novel, MacDonald surprises him with one that does not fit neatly into the pattern of the previous books, that introduces something new and unexpected. *The Girl in the Plain Brown Wrapper* (1968), for example, combines elements of detection from the conventional private-eye novel with features borrowed from the gothic horror story, the psychological thriller, and the suburban love story to produce one of the most interesting of all the McGee adventures.

The novel opens with McGee in a nostalgic mood. While engaged in a salvage effort off the Florida Keys (a *real* salvage effort), his thoughts drift back to a period five years earlier when he offered comfort to Helena Pearson, widow of a friend. That she was eleven years his senior did nothing to inhibit the development or intensity of their affair. Thanks to his ministrations, she regained the sexuality she temporarily lost following the death of her husband, to whom she had been married for twenty-one years. But in one of those unsettling coincidences of life which are impossible to explain, when he returns to Ft. Lauderdale he discovers that his happy remembrance of Helena occurred on the very day she died of cancer. He learns the sad news from her attorney, who sends him a check for $25,000 along with her final request of him—that he do what he can to prevent her twenty-five-year-old daughter, Maurie, from killing herself (she has already made three unsuccessful attempts).

In the past, McGee has received an interesting variety of requests for help from friends, but this is the first to come from beyond the grave, as it were, and he is hesitant about acting upon it. Nevertheless, to honor Helena's last request, he flies to the small town of Ft. Courtney, calls Maurie's sister, Biddy (who lives with Maurie and her husband, Tom Pike), and learns what he can about the woman's situation. Biddy tells him her sister is subject to frequent bouts of memory loss and fits of unpredictable behavior. The doctors have suggested many possible causes—manic depression, schizophrenia, Korsakoff's syndrome, virus infection, a tumor, calcium deposits restricting the flow of blood to the brain—but nothing adequately explains her odd behavior. McGee is saddened by the plight of the young woman and the suffering her condition is causing her husband and sister but, despite his impressive record of past therapeutic successes, he wisely concludes that this is no job for an amateur. He considers his obligation to Helena to be concluded.

As he is preparing to check out of his motel, however, he notices something that causes him to change his mind: the toothbrush in his toilet kit, always carefully placed in the same position, has been moved, signaling that someone has been in his room. His curiosity whetted, he decides to remain in town a little longer. That evening he meets a woman in the motel bar and, one thing leading to another, they retire to his room for a nightcap. The always cautious McGee detects that his gin has been doctored, so he plays along by pretending to pass out; as soon as she thinks he is unconscious, the woman summons her partner. McGee surprises him when he arrives and demands to know what the two are after. The man identifies himself as Rick Holton, a former assistant state attorney, who, with the help of the woman, Penny Voeltz (also his lover), is investigating the death three months earlier of Dr. Stewart Sherman, for whom Penny worked as a nurse. Sherman was found dead in his office of a massive morphine overdose; the official verdict was suicide, but Holton and Penny are convinced he was murdered. A tall, tanned man was seen leaving Sherman's office the night he died and was later observed receiving a bundle of cash from Tom Pike. After McGee was spotted at the Pike house earlier in the day, Holton wanted to investigate to see whether he was the mysterious unidentified man.

McGee sends Holton packing, but Penny, angry at him for being so quick to believe McGee's phony story that he made love to her before she called him, decides to stay, and before the night is over the two of them end up in McGee's bed. The following day, the memory of the previous night still fresh in his mind, McGee finds himself anticipating with pleasure the prospect of spending another night with the attractive woman. Instead he spends it with a pair of local policemen who come to question him about the murder of Penny Voeltz, stabbed to death in her kitchen some time after leaving McGee earlier in the day.

Mysteries are rapidly piling up all around McGee: What is causing Maurie Pike's odd behavior? Why all the interest in the late Dr. Sherman? If he was murdered, who did it? and why? Why was McGee's room searched? Who killed Penny Voeltz? and why? What does any of this have to do with Tom Pike? Gradually, from several different sources, McGee pieces together enough information about Pike to cast serious doubt on the general impression of him as a loving and devoted husband and brilliant financial whiz kid. He learns, for example, that Pike is having an affair with Holton's wife, Janice; that he was quietly eased out of his former job because of serious irregularities in his performance; that he is subject to sudden outbreaks of violent behavior.

When McGee hears from a neurologist friend that there is a substance called puromycin that can destroy memory, and learns that Dr. Sherman was reportedly experimenting with such a drug, he decides to search Pike's house to see if he can turn up anything. Telltale dust spots in a locked medicine cabinet indicate that several bottles of medication have recently been removed. Worried that this might mean that they will no longer be needed to treat (or to control) Maurie, he hurries to the reception she is attending with her husband, arriving just in time to hear a sickening thud on the roof above the parking garage. When he investigates, he finds the mangled body of Maurie Pike.

Although her fall is designed to look like suicide, McGee is now convinced that Pike murdered her after carefully planning it to appear that she was finally successful in her grim determination to kill herself. To thwart Pike's scheme, he wraps Maurie's body in the large sheet of heavy brown packing paper on which she had fallen and hides "the girl in the brown paper wrapper." Then he recruits local police officer Al Stanger and state attorney Ben Gaffner to help him trap the crafty Pike. He convinces them that Pike is a dangerous sociopath who killed his wife and intends to marry her sister in order to gain control over both their inheritances. To this end, he also murdered Dr. Sherman, who was supplying him with the drugs to control his wife, and Penny Voeltz, who was becoming overly suspicious about Sherman's "suicide."

Thanks to a hastily installed phone tap, they learn that Pike is due to meet with his accomplice, Dave Broon, special investigator in the sheriff's department, whose skill in uncovering dirt has given him control over half the population in town. From a safe distance, McGee hears Broon demand more money from Pike. Suddenly a fight breaks out and Broon grabs a rope, ties it around Pike's neck, and begins hauling him up a tree. When McGee attempts to intercede, Stanger stops him, warning, "Don't go messing with the evidence, boy." The police wait patiently until Pike is dead, then arrest Broon for his murder. In this chillingly appropriate manner, justice is crudely served, with Pike executed and his partner arrested for murder.

Although it contains elements borrowed from the Gothic thriller (the beautiful but erratic wife kept a virtual prisoner in her own home, controlled by exotic drugs and a mysterious electrosleep machine) and the suburban romance (the devoted husband romantically involved with another man's wife while his sister-in-law quietly burns with secret passion for him), *Brown* owes its success to its mystery ingredients. MacDonald has produced one of his most baffling and suspenseful stories, a real page-turner in which the reader is kept genuinely mystified about the characters and their relationship to the puzzling incidents in the book. To solve the mystery—the key to which is the gradually unfolding character of Tom Pike—McGee must exercise his wits rather than his sexual expertise or brute strength. In his efforts to uncover the truth, he resembles Ross Macdonald's Lew Archer in that he acts as a catalytic agent, his presence in Ft. Courtney the impetus for the action. The murder of Dr. Sherman is the incident from the past that refuses to lie buried. When McGee is spotted with Peggy Voeltz, Tom Pike becomes so worried about exposure that he kills her, thus providing McGee with the motivation he needs to get to the bottom of the mystery.

Brown is also unique in the series to this point in that its action is restricted to a single locale, the town of Ft. Courtney, which affords MacDonald an opportunity to explore, as he did in such early novels as *The Crossroads* and *The Neon Jungle*, the social, political, and financial structure of a community. Ft. Courtney is a prosperous little town set amidst the rolling hills, citrus groves, and ranches of northern Florida. Only the right kind of clean, quiet industry is allowed: "No boomland this. No pageants, gator farms, Africa-lands, shell factories, orchid jungles. Solid, cautious growth, based on third- and fourth-generation money and control—which in Florida is akin to a heritage going back to the fourteenth century." The town is populated largely by professional men whose booming voices speak of "confidence, optimism, low handicaps, capital gains." And one of its brightest stars is Tom Pike, whose syndicate is apparently making all his many local investors a nice little profit.

But the tidy financial structure Pike erects for his investors will come tumbling down as dramatically as his wife's body did when he pushed her out the window of his new office building, for the bright young entrepreneur is a fraud. Among other things, he uses newly invested capital to pay his previous investors, calling it a distribution of capital gains. Furthermore, it turns out that many of his investors have been pressured into investing by the blackmailing efforts of Dave Broon, who spent the past seven years as a special investigator in the Sheriff's Department accumulating dirt against local figures. According to Deputy Al Stanger, "this whole city and county is a big piece of truck garden to Dave Broon. He goes around plowing and planting and fertilizing, and harvesting everything ripe." It was Broon who uncovered evidence that Dr. Sherman had murdered his wife, which gave him the leverage he needed to pressure him into investing in Pike's syndicate and also into providing the drugs Pike used to manipulate his wife. For his services, Broon received a fat payoff from Pike. Their corrupt partnership eventually comes unraveled over a money dispute, leading to the dramatic scene in which Broon murders his partner in full view of the police and seals his own doom.

MacDonald employs an interesting stratagem to introduce another important element of Ft. Courtney's population. McGee forgets to remove the bottle of doctored gin from his motel room. When one of the maids passes out after sneaking a sip of it, he recruits one of her fellow workers to help him treat her. This allows him to meet Lorette Walker, who is able to provide him with important information about the blacks who live in the less visible, less prosperous section of Ft. Courtney known as Southtown. Among other things, she tells him about the curious arrangement that allows a powerful political figure like Dave Broon to own forty homes in the black neighborhood, each one in disrepair, each one with rising rent, but, thanks to his influence, each with taxes that mysteriously never increase. Information is also revealed about the strained relations between the Southtown blacks and the white police, despised for their brutal treatment of black offenders. Even Al Stanger knows how inequitable the situation really is: "I try to level with them, but shit, they know as well as I do there's two kinds of law here, two kinds of law practically everyplace. One of them kills a white man, they open the book to a different place from where a white man kills a Negra." McGee offers no solution to the problem, only a brief commentary in which he expresses hope that in the future things will improve:

> And so, Mrs. Lorette Walker, no solutions for me or thee, not from your leaders be they passive or militant, or from the politicians or the liberals or the head-knockers or the educators. No answer but time. And if the law and the courts can be induced to become color-blind, we'll have a good answer, after both of us are dead. And a bloody answer otherwise.

It is material like this which, while not integral to the plot, combines so effectively with the mystery and suspense elements to produce such an uncommonly good novel.

Harl Bowie is an old friend of Meyer's, a "poor sick sorry rich and sad son of a bitch" whose life has been distinguished by both enormous financial success and terrible personal tragedy: his wife died of a brain tumor; he has recently been paralyzed in an automobile accident; and he has just been informed that his only child, Bix, was killed when the car she was driving plummeted off a winding mountain road in Mexico where she was living. Distraught over her death, his feelings intensified by guilt over having always been too busy to be a good father to his daughter while she was growing up, he now wants at least to learn what the last six months of her life were like. What has especially alarmed him is an anonymous note he received written prior to her death, which warned: "You want Bix to come back ever, or ever want to come back even, you better come after her or send somebody pretty quick because she doesn't have any idea what's happening to her lately." Crippled as he is, he is unable to go to Mexico himself, so he calls for help from Meyer, who was a kind of unofficial godfather to the girl when she was young. McGee, seeing how troubled Meyer is by Bowie's story, offers his assistance. Soon the two are headed for Mexico, and thus begins *Dress Her in Indigo* (1969), McGee's eleventh adventure.

From a number of contacts he makes (most of them expatriate Americans like Bix) McGee gathers enough information to construct a gruesome picture of the final weeks of Bix's life. She and four friends came to Oaxaca in order to get in on the profitable drug trade; with her were Walter Rockland, by all accounts a nasty character, whose present whereabouts are unknown, Minda McLeen, whose father has been searching fruitlessly for her, Carl Sessions, recently found dead of a drug overdose, and Jerry Nesta, whose Mexican girlfriend and the American couple they were living with have just been found beaten to death. According to Nesta, Rockland used drugs, sex, and violence to keep the others in line; among other things, he introduced Bix to heroin and even once forced her to have sex in a cornfield with several men for two pesos a trick. McGee has no choice but to agree with Nesta's grim assessment that Bix "was dead before she was dead."

The most obvious person to try to find is Rockland, but McGee gets a real shock when he stumbles upon his decomposing body in the back of his abandoned camper, the corpse bearing evidence of terrible torture wounds. The only suspect in his death is a most unlikely one—the portly, garrulous, slightly ridiculous figure of Wally McLeen, Minda's father. McGee arranges to meet him at the site of some ancient ruins outside of town and is surprised when he readily confesses to murdering Rockland as well as Nesta's three friends. Suddenly, he produces a bolo-like weapon and knocks Meyer unconscious. When he fails in an attempt to do the same to McGee, he turns and runs, but while fleeing slips on the steps of the temple ruins and falls to his death on the rocks below. Thus in this single brief scene, MacDonald has both solved the mystery of all the deaths in the novel and brought the killer to an abrupt reckoning.

Never one to leave a loose string unpulled, McGee is curious about who gave Wally McLeen the information about his daughter that turned him into a mad killer. The only other person with any connection to all the characters is Eva Vitrier, a wealthy Frenchwoman with whom Bix and Minda were living at the time of Bix's accident (and the one who provided identification of her mangled body). McGee traces her to a luxury hotel in Mexico City and discovers that the

missing Minda McLeen is living with her. However, when he slips
into her bedroom at night, the woman he sees making love with Eva
is not Minda but the supposedly dead Bix Bowie. When McGee
confronts Eva, she confesses the whole story, beginning with the
admission that it was Minda, not Bix, who died in the automobile
accident. In order to give Bix a fresh start, she switched the girls'
papers and falsely identified Minda's body as Bix's. Using a substitute
drug, she has gotten Bix off heroin and back to a state of semi-
normalcy, although her drug-damaged mind will never allow her to
function in the real world. Eva has also become the girl's lover.

McGee is faced with a difficult decision: should he allow Bix to
stay with Eva, who loves Bix deeply—and who has offered him
$200,000 if he will let the girl stay—or return her to her father, whose
lack of love during her formative years probably contributed to her
later problems? He concludes that his primary obligation is to her
father, so he brings Bix back to Miami with him.

For the first time in the series, McGee's disposition of the case
unsettles him, for he is far from convinced that he did the right thing.
Is he more concerned with *his* sense of obligation than with the welfare
of the girl? His uneasiness isn't helped any by the reunion scene, for
when Bix is at last reunited with her father, the spaced-out girl
complains petulantly that this isn't the special surprise McGee promised: "Is this the big treat, you rotten, dirty bastard? You bring me
back to this silly old fart? Where's Eva? What have you done to Eva?
Look, I've got to have a surprise. Honest to God, I've got to have a
surprise or I'm going to go up the walls screaming." McGee realizes
that his decision has brought happiness to no one: Eva is deprived of
her lover; Bix wants nothing to do with her "silly old fart" of a father;
and McGee worries that Bowie will quickly grow impatient with his
daughter's condition and have her institutionalized. McGee's action
only demonstrates the truth of Meyer's observation: "A grownup man
must make a lousy decision from time to time, knowing it is lousy,
because the only other choice is lousy in another dimension, and no
matter which way he jumps, he will not like it."

MacDonald rescues his usually confident hero from further
torments of self-doubt by delivering him into the voluptuous arms of
the lovely Guatemalan secretary who has been his bedmate throughout
the novel. Whenever he became upset or depressed after learning
about Bix's sordid experiences, Elena was conveniently handy to

relieve his misery. Now she comes to the rescue again, melting away all his cares in her life-affirming way. His doubts about his self-confidence and fears about the reliability of his judgment are swept away once he begins making love with Elena, his clouds of uncertainty dispersed by the sunshine of her sex.

MacDonald's portrayal of women in *Indigo* is uncharacteristically negative. They can be divided into three types: predator, sex object, and lesbian. Although McGee is sexually involved with two of the women, he is emotionally involved with neither. The first is Lady Rebecca Divin-Harrison, a legend in Oaxaca. McGee has encountered sexually aggressive women before (notably Lysa Dean in *Red* and Connie Melgar in *Gold*), but none with so much energy, persistence, dexterity, and muscle control as Becky, who describes herself as a "wicked old woman with a ravenous appetite for strong young men." Thanks to a careful diet, rigorous exercise, hormone injections, and endless practice, she has come close to realizing her goal of becoming "the jolly best piece of Anglo-Saxon ass in all Christendom." Once she sets her sights on McGee, he has little choice but to comply with her wishes, and following their first bout of lovemaking the only response he can muster is an awed, "Holy Mackerel." Combining the authority of a drill sergeant with the enthusiastic encouragement of a cheerleader, she orchestrates the whole procedure, but she is so insatiable in her demands that McGee is soon reduced to a quivering mass. The situation becomes so perilous that incredibly McGee confesses to Meyer that it will probably be two or three years before he'll want to see another woman: "From now on, buddy, every broad is going to look as enticing as a rubber duck. I would rather have one handful of cold mashed potato than two handsful of warm mammalian overdevelopment."

McGee's wobbling ego is bolstered thanks to the more sedate efforts of Elena, one of the "three little crumpets" McGee's friend Emelio Fuentes imports for his, McGee's, and Meyer's pleasure; their purpose, according to Emelio, is to help the men "lose the stink of death in the sweetness of girls." Elena is lively and sensual, and her "splendid earthiness spiced with innocent wonder" is a healthy antidote to Becky's practiced proficiency. "There are some things which practice does not enhance," McGee concludes. "Thunderstorms never practice. Surf does not take graduate lessons in hydraulics . . . That business of acquiring expertise in screwing turns it into something it wasn't meant to be." Whenever his mood needs elevating, the compliant Elena is handy to "turn some bad day to good things" for the handsome American visitor, although her halting command of English makes anything other than sexual communication difficult.

Besides Becky and the three crumpets, the only other woman of consequence in the novel is Eva Vitrier, the lesbian who is, at least indirectly, the cause of all the deaths in the book. When Minda McLeen became upset after discovering the sexual relationship between Eva and Bix (so much so that she was prompted to write the anonymous letter of warning to Bix's father), Eva hired Walter Rockland to take the girl away until she could get out of Oaxaca safely with Bix. Minda died trying to flee Rockland, however, so Eva took advantage of the situation to ensure that she could have Bix without interference. When Wally McLeen came looking for his daughter, she sent him after Rockland and Nesta by telling him exaggerated tales about their treatment of his daughter. Now safely ensconced with Bix in Mexico City, she promises McGee that if he will allow her to stay, she will care for her, take her to lovely secluded places, and dress her in indigo to highlight the deep violet in her eyes. (McGee asks sarcastically whether she will also "get her her distemper shots and keep her coat glossy.") McGee rejects her offer in rather crude fashion by knocking her out before returning Bix to her father in Florida. One wonders whether McGee's decision is prompted less by a desire to honor his obligation to her father and more by his displeasure at the nature of their homosexual relationship.

Indigo is not MacDonald's best McGee novel, nor is it his favorite (in a note about *Lavender,* he wrote: "It is better than *Indigo.* But what isn't?"), but it is not without its virtues. The playful banter between McGee and Meyer, and between McGee and Emelio Fuentes, is witty and good-natured. Becky and her insatiable demands on McGee provide humorous diversion, as does the at first comic figure of Wally McLeen, outfitted in his blue beret and burgundy shorts, sporting a new goatee and a multitude of bruises as a result of his unsuccessful encounters with a new motorcycle, and sounding like an Ohio businessman (which he is) trying to bridge the generation gap by acting like a middle-aged hippie. However, the novel abruptly shifts from comedy to stark seriousness when the three bodies are found at Nesta's place (an incident that does not occur until well past the halfway point in the novel). It's as if MacDonald suddenly decided that the novel was too frivolous and needed a jolt to get it on a more serious track. From this point on, the humor fades and the pace picks up as McGee closes in on a solution to the mysteries in the book.

One weakness in *Indigo* is the choice of Wally McLeen as murderer, especially in light of the comic manner with which he has been presented to the reader. There is inadequate explanation for his surprising behavior, only the simple statement that he went mad after learning about his daughter's treatment by Rockland. As if embarrassed at having so abruptly transformed the slightly ridiculous McLeen into a homicidal maniac, MacDonald just as quickly disposes of him by tumbling him off the temple steps and onto the rocks below.

Another problem is the setting. MacDonald has been infatuated with Mexico ever since 1948, when, after reading Malcolm Lowry's *Under the Volcano*, he and Dorothy moved to Cuernavaca for several months; since then, they have become frequent visitors to Mexico, and even lived in Oaxaca prior to the writing of *Indigo*. MacDonald lovingly celebrates the Mexican people and the picturesque beauty of the landscape in several of his early novels (*The Damned, The Empty Trap, Please Write for Details*). However, the Mexican setting, colorful as it is in *Indigo*, is simply inappropriate for what is, to a large extent, a study of disaffiliated American youths. Beginning as early as *The Neon Jungle* and continuing in such later novels as *Death Trap* and *The End of the Night*, MacDonald has been fascinated by the problem of the rebelliousness of the young. In *Indigo*, he is specifically interested in the hippie phenomenon of the late sixties. The choice of Mexico, however, instead of, say, San Francisco is clearly a mistake, for placing American youths south of the border and then using them as a vehicle for commentary on such issues as the harshness of American drug laws and the alienation of the young from the establishment strikes a hollow note with the objects of his scrutiny so far removed from the center of the phenomenon.

The final comment about the novel is MacDonald's. To a reader who complained that McGee should never have left home, he could only agree: "It's just about the way I feel about the book."

The Long Lavender Look (1970) opens with McGee and Meyer driving along a deserted Florida highway one night when a scantily clad woman materializes out of the darkness and dashes across the road right in front of McGee's pickup. He narrowly misses her, but while struggling to control his pickup, a tire blows, sending trusty *Miss Agnes* off the road and into a drainage canal. Meyer quickly pulls McGee from the water and, after failing to find any trace of the woman, the two head off to the nearest service station, Meyer good-naturedly chiding his friend for the alarming regularity with which he attracts women in the most unlikely ways: "McGee, have you ever wondered if you don't emit some sort of subliminal aroma, a veritable dog whistle among scents?"

As they continue along the lonely highway, a man in a truck, apparently mistaking them for a pair he calls Orville and Hutch, drives by and begins shooting at them. Luckily they escape injury, but when they finally reach the service station, the highway patrolman investigating their accident is instructed by radio to hold the two of them for questioning by the Cypress City sheriff. When the sheriff arrives, he arrests them both for murder. Thus in the space of a few short but action-filled pages, McGee nearly kills a woman, almost drowns, is shot at, and then is arrested for murdering a man he never heard of.

In a rare switch, McGee is the one forced to summon an old friend for help, Miami lawyer Leonard Sibelius, who is able to learn that the murdered man, Frank Baither, is suspected of having been involved in a robbery of $900,000 from a Miami racetrack four years earlier. McGee and Meyer were arrested not only because they fit the descriptions of two of Baither's suspected accomplices, but an envelope bearing McGee's address and his handwriting was found near Baither's body. Sibelius eventually secures their release, in return for which he requests that, as long as McGee has to remain in town for *Miss Agnes* to be repaired (and to be available if the sheriff wishes to question him further), he act as his representative. Sibelius figures that whoever killed Baither and planted McGee's letter near his body is probably connected to the missing $900,000 and should anyone be arrested in the case, McGee ought to be around to encourage him to hire an excellent high-priced criminal lawyer like Sibelius.

McGee decides to attend to some personal business first: he wants revenge against Lew Arnstead, the deputy who savagely beat Meyer while he was being held in custody. Arnstead isn't at home when McGee comes calling, but his cooperative and garrulous mother is very helpful; admitting that her son has been acting very strangely lately, she invites McGee to search his bedroom, where he finds several bottles of amphetamines (which might explain his erratic behavior) and a collection of Polaroid photographs of over a dozen women, all naked. Four of the shots are of special interest to McGee, for they feature the same woman he nearly ran over the previous night.

McGee soon meets another of the photographic subjects when he locates Betsy Kapp, Arnstead's ex-girlfriend. He immediately sizes her up as the type of woman who habitually transforms everything into a romantic fantasy:

> Her smile, as she stood up, was the distillation of several hundred motion pictures, refined in the loneliness of the bathroom mirror, born of a hunger for romance, for magic, for tremulous, yearning love. This was the meet-cute episode, immortalized by all the Doris Days, unexpected treasure for a thirty-summers blonde with something childish-girlish about her mouth, something that would never tighten into maturity. It would always yearn, always hope, always pretend—and it would always be used.

After agreeing to join McGee for a drink, she deliberately manages to get her hair soaked, thus ensuring that the two of them spend the evening in her apartment. Impatient at her Doris Day games, McGee decides he isn't going to get anything useful from her unless he adopts a direct approach, so he asks her point-blank about Arnstead, characterizing him bluntly as a "brutal, sadistic, degenerate stud animal." If he wanted to shake her up, he succeeds, for she goes storming off in tears to the bathroom, leaving him to reevaluate (and to regret) his actions:

> You are a dandy fellow, T. McGee. All the lonely, wasted, wistful ones of the world have some set of illusions which sustains them, which builds a warm shelter in the wasteland of the heart. It does them no good to see themselves as they really are, once you kick the shelter down. This one was easy bed-game for any traveling man who wanted to indulge her fantasies by playing the role of sentimental romanticism, with a little spice of soap-opera drama.
>
> So, while you are digging up whatever might be useful out of the little ruin you have created, at least have the grace to try to put the make-believe garden back in order. If you get the chance.

Upset and frightened by McGee's account of Arnstead's brutal attack on Meyer, she pleads with him to spend the night with her for protection. Feeling mousetrapped by her coy techniques, he fears he has no choice but to play his assigned role in her romantic game. Nevertheless, his haughty attitude toward Betsy undergoes an interesting transformation, for although he expected a "lot of elfin fluttering" from the woman acting out her "bigger-than-both-of-us-game," he finds her hearty lovemaking a genuine and unexpected pleasure. When he later takes a closer look at the Polaroid shot of her, what had originally seemed only "an insipid leer and comedy breasts" is now dramatically transformed into something more substantial, the leer becoming "a troubled and uncertain smile" and the oversized breasts "oddly wistful, vulnerable." All of this leads him to the conclusion that his judgment was faulty and prompts the candid admission that he too has been game-playing, rationalizing his own actions into one of his wounded-duckling dramas.

Tragically, Betsy also provides something else—intensified personal commitment on McGee's part. Sometime during the night he spent with her, Lew Arnstead is murdered and his body dumped in McGee's car. Reluctant to call the police (having made no secret of his desire to get even with Arnstead for what he did to Meyer), McGee and Betsy haul the body to a deserted area and drop it down a deep sinkhole. Later, when Betsy fails to show up for a meeting with McGee, he assumes she is off playing another fantasy game, following a "new script patterned on the late late movies, suspense, perhaps, with elegant quips and handsome sets, and she was maybe Myrna Loy tracing down one of those fragments of female intuition which would clear up the case which had William Powell baffled." But when he eventually makes his way to an isolated cabin owned by Arnstead outside of town, he discovers, sadly, that whatever game Betsy was playing has led to murder: he finds her body tied to a tree, fence wire tightened around her neck, her face a "bulging clown-face in a long lavender look."

It is time, McGee decides, to find Lilo Perris, the woman whose sudden dash in front of his pickup caused his involvement in the case in the first place. Although he has yet to meet her, he already knows a great deal about her, all of it bad. In a letter he found among the items in Arnstead's bedroom, he read Betsy Kapp's warning to Lew to "LEAVE LILO ALONE!!!! She is bad news for one and all"; Arnstead's mother described Lilo as "wild as any swamp critter"; Betsy warned McGee that Lilo is "loud and mean and hard as nails"; and when he shows her picture to Dori Severiss, a former colleague in the girl-for-hire ring McGee discovers Arnstead was running, she gags, turns cold and sweaty, and admits that Lilo once tortured her to keep her in line for Arnstead: "She's as strong as a man, and she knows every way there is to hurt a girl. She's absolutely insane, Trav."

Expecting some kind of subhuman monster, McGee is in for a real surprise when he finally meets her face-to-face. The first thing he notices is "the extraordinary impact of a total, driving sexuality," an arrogant posture that challenges while it entices: "Here it is, baby, if you're man enough, and I don't think you are, because nobody has been man enough yet." In contrast to Betsy Kapp, there is nothing vulnerable about Lilo, nor anything subtle about her approach; where Betsy manipulated McGee by transparent subterfuge, Lilo is blatantly obvious in her come-on. Instinctively sensing her effect on McGee, she walks over to her blue Opel, takes a deep breath, and lifts the front end off the ground. Then she turns, looks at McGee, and smiles provocatively. The effect is devastating: "I had felt an unexpectedly savage surge of absolutely simple and immediate sexual desire for her, a brute impulse to fell her where she stood and mount her. And she knew it, and had deliberately caused it."

Lilo suggests that the two of them find a quiet place and "try us out." Taking him to a friend's trailer, she promptly strips, rolls over on her back, and announces, "As any jackass can plainly see, I am all the way ready." But all the dreadful stories McGee has heard about the woman make him wary and his instincts warn him that something is wrong with the situation. Instead of bedding the woman, he punches her as hard as he has ever hit anyone before, knocking her cold. Sure enough, crouched outside waiting for the right moment to attack McGee is Lilo's stepfather, Henry Perris, an accomplice of hers in the racetrack heist, the murder of their other partners, Orville, Hutch, and Frank Baither, and the planting of McGee's envelope (taken from his disabled pickup). Perris tells McGee that only Lilo knows where the $900,000 is buried, having extracted the information about its hiding place from Baither before plunging an icepick into his heart. He offers to make a deal if McGee will deliver Lilo to him. McGee declines and, thanks to a skill once taught him by a friend, succeeds in killing Perris by throwing an oyster knife into his chest. He leaves Lilo safely tied up and returns to town to report to the sheriff.

Just when he thinks he has everything solved, a new mystery arises: while McGee is telling his story to the sheriff, Deputy King Sturnevan calls in to report that he has just found the bodies of Perris and Lilo. Although she was alive when he left her, someone has finished her off by holding her head in a bucket of water. McGee, on a hunch that Baither buried the money on his place, goes there to see if anyone was able to learn the location of the money from Lilo before killing her. He is shocked when he discovers who the culprit is—King Sturnevan himself. Sturnevan confesses that he killed Arnstead in an attempt to find out where the money was, killed Betsy when she surprised him at Arnstead's place, and then killed Lilo after extracting from her the location of the money. Now he's going to have to kill McGee. Two punches from the ex-heavyweight boxer send McGee sprawling, but before passing out he manages to shoot Sturnevan, who later dies in the hospital.

Although McGee has had more than his share of surprises in the novel, the final two are pleasant ones. First, Meyer informs him that he will soon receive a check for $22,000, his share of the $900,000 recovered from Baither's place. Then comes the unexpected appearance of Heidi Trumbill (with whom he was involved in *Yellow*), summoned by Meyer to nurse McGee through his recuperation from his injuries. The novel thus ends on a happy note, with McGee, Heidi, and Raoul—Betsy Kapp's cat—comprising a contented domestic trio.

Lavender avoids many of the problems that weakened *Indigo*. Instead of proceeding at the sluggish pace that *Indigo* did, *Lavender* begins in dramatic fashion; where *Indigo* languished from lack of action, *Lavender* is filled with it; instead of paper-thin stereotypes (like *Indigo*'s Guatemalan "crumpets"), *Lavender* is populated by credible and convincing characters. The novel is not without its flaws: there is no real need for the subplot involving Sheriff Hyzer's secret relationship to the town tramp; King Sturnevan's motivation for the murders is unconvincing (he wanted to get his hands on the money because he felt cheated out of millions by bad managers during his fight career); and the explanation for Lilo's dash in front of McGee's pickup is never made entirely clear. However, these are far overshadowed by MacDonald's considerable success in combining action, suspense, and effective characterization to produce an exciting murder thriller.

As he had done in several of the previous books, MacDonald

organizes his material around a single underlying motif; *Lavender*, as the title suggests, is about looking and not looking, seeing and not seeing. Ranging from Cora Arnstead, whose vision is severely impaired by cataracts, to her son, whose drug dependency has induced a paranoiac tendency to see things that aren't even there, and from Betsy Kapp, who distorts things to fit the requirements of her Doris Day world, to Sheriff Hyzer, who averts his eyes so as not to see the involvement of one of his deputies in a lucrative prostitution ring (his blindness is caused by Arnstead's leverage after discovering that Hyzer is really Lilo Perris's father), MacDonald plays interesting variations on the theme of blindness and sight. A remark Dori Severiss makes to McGee capsulizes the theme: "Things aren't like what you always think they're like." How true, as MacDonald demonstrates by including several examples of how first impressions are often faulty and require modification in light of subsequent evidence and experience. For example, McGee's initial impressions of both Betsy Kapp and Lilo Perris undergo significant revision: Betsy reveals greater depth and substance than he first guessed, Lilo is more complex and alluring than he first assumed. His attitude toward Sheriff Hyzer also changes: at first dubious about his professionalism, he gradually comes to respect and admire him, and finally even to sympathize with him over his private torment concerning the hidden relationship to Lilo Perris. An almost fatal misperception involves McGee's judgment about King Sturnevan. His trust in Sturnevan almost costs him his life, for in his blindness to the man's true character he carelessly drops his guard when Sturnevan unexpectedly appears while he is waiting at Baither's place for Lilo's murderer to show up. Finally, his erroneous assumption that Arnstead's pictures were trophy shots blinded him to what they really were, i.e., evidence of an extensive prostitution ring. It takes a long time before McGee learns the lesson his experiences seem designed to teach him: it's like the way scientists discovered one of the planets, McGee explains to Hyzer; until they corrected their vision, they couldn't detect its existence.

Characters who lie, dissemble, and otherwise attempt to deceive are a convention of most mystery and detective fiction, and writers frequently emphasize the point in order to highlight the distinction between appearance and reality. In *Lavender*, however, the problem is not intentional deceit; for the most part, no one lies to McGee. The real issues are misperceptions, erroneous assumptions, and faulty interpretations. It would be a mistake to attach too much metaphysical significance to MacDonald's treatment of the subject. His concern, as usual, is with the concrete rather than the abstract. Nevertheless, he effectively continues a pattern begun in *Indigo* of introducing McGee to the murky world of uncertainty, fallibility, and self-doubt. McGee's admission, following a candid review of his many misperceptions, that "Maybe a very useful talent was fading, my ability to sense what people were after" attests to his grudging acknowledgment of imperfection and signifies his heightened awareness that he shares a common plight with the rest of flawed humanity.

In *A Tan and Sandy Silence* (1971), MacDonald extends this pattern by focusing on some of McGee's other vulnerabilities. This, his thirteenth adventure, proves to be one of his unluckiest, as he barely survives three narrow brushes with death. But in many ways it also proves to be one of his most fortunate, for in the process of almost losing his life, he gains considerably in maturity and self-knowledge.

The novel begins with McGee's encounter with Harry Broll, a man he isn't particularly happy to see, having become involved in a fistfight with him over his wife the last time they met. This time, however, Broll appears friendly and in need of help. His wife, Mary, has been missing for over two months and, knowing that she was romantically involved with McGee before their marriage, he has come looking for her aboard *The Busted Flush*. McGee insists he hasn't seen her in three years, but Broll refuses to believe him. Suddenly he pulls a gun and fires at McGee, miraculously missing him. Then he calms down and explains the reason for his desperation: he needs his wife's signature on an important document within the next two weeks or he will lose his entire financial investment in SeaGate, a large-scale residential community nearing completion. McGee promises that if Mary turns up, he will tell her that Broll is looking for her.

McGee does a little digging and learns from a close friend of Mary's that, upset after discovering her husband was having an affair with another woman, she took off for the Caribbean island of Grenada to sort things out. Satisfied that Mary is safe, McGee relaxes his efforts, for he feels no obligation to ease Broll's worries over his missing wife. However, the more McGee thinks about the situation, the more it bothers him. Mary Broll is too frugal to have left her car parked at the airport for two months as she has done, running up an enormous bill. Besides, if he could discover her whereabouts so quickly, why couldn't Broll? McGee phones the inn where she is reportedly staying and is told that Mary is indeed registered but that she will accept no calls. So, to satisfy his curiosity once and for all, he decides to fly to Grenada to speak with her in person. But the woman he sees coming out of Mary Broll's cottage is not Mary Broll, although she identifies herself by that name.

When McGee confronts her with the fact that he knows she is an imposter, she admits that she is really Lisa Dissat, Harry Broll's mistress, and confesses the whole story. She and her cousin, Paul Dissat, have been running a successful little con game in which they would extort money from wealthy businessmen Dissat set her up with. Their latest pigeon is Harry Broll, but unfortunately their scheme turned deadly when Mary Broll accidentally died during a struggle with Dissat. Because Broll needs his wife's approval of a $300,000 loan from her account to protect his investment in SeaGate (and to pay off Dissat), he is cooperating in an elaborate ruse in which Lisa has agreed to pose as Mary until her OK is needed for the loan. Then she will conveniently "die" in some sort of accident.

Once McGee convinces Lisa that she will become expendable as soon as the loan is approved and that Dissat will likely kill her when she returns to Florida, she agrees to help him get revenge against Dissat and Broll. McGee wants to convince the trio that, "if given a choice, they would elect retroactive birth control. I want them so eager to be out of it they'd dig their own graves with a bent spoon and their fingernails." But he doesn't act quickly enough; Dissat arrives in Grenada unexpectedly, sneaks into McGee's cottage, and knocks him out as he prepares to shower. Then he obtains all the information he wants about McGee in one of the most horrifying scenes MacDonald has ever devised: Dissat buries Lisa in the sand up to her neck, places a basket over her head, and listens to her confession as the tide slowly comes in. Once he has all he wants, he calmly allows her to drown. McGee's hands are tightly bound, but the length of rope securing his feet allows him enough mobility to run toward the water when Dissat is momentarily distracted. As a riptide carries him out to sea, he catches a final glimpse of Lisa: "Her black hair was fanned out, and in that instant of sharpened, memorable vision I saw the spume of sand drifting out of her open mouth, like a strange cartoon balloon, a message without sound. A sandy, tan farewell."

He is rescued at sea and eventually returns to Florida, where he learns that Broll, accompanied by Dissat, has already withdrawn the $300,000 from Mary's account. McGee arranges a meeting with Dissat's employer at a construction warehouse to tell him about Dissat, but when he and Meyer arrive at the agreed-upon location, they are surprised to find Dissat, who had learned about the meeting, waiting for them. After securing both of them, he confesses that he has already killed Broll and stashed his body in a large chunk of asphalt, the same fate he has planned for them. This time it looks like curtains for McGee, but with a final desperate burst of strength and determination, he lunges at Dissat, catches him off guard, and then watches in horror as he is buried under tons of hot asphalt.

Tan is a pivotal book in the series in that for the first time McGee himself is the primary focus of the action. In the previous two adventures, MacDonald began to introduce his hero to doubts and uncertainty: in *Indigo*, for example, McGee was left to debate with himself the wisdom of his decision to return Bix Bowie to her father; in *Lavender* he was dangerously misled by his mistaken impressions of characters and false interpretations of events. In *Tan*, everything seems designed to undermine his self-confidence. MacDonald is, of course, too canny to abandon his successful formula entirely and thus creates his usual action-filled story, although the action revolves around McGee to a greater extent than heretofore. McGee, for example, is not hired to perform a task for anyone; his motivation initially is simply to satisfy his own curiosity about Mary Broll's whereabouts. When he learns that she is dead, he decides to seek revenge against those responsible, again to satisfy himself. As a result of his decision, he twice has to resort to desperate measures simply to keep himself alive. The action of *Tan* is thus structured so as to place McGee in the kind of life-threatening situations that will lead him to important new insights about himself.

The first of these occurs when Broll comes looking for his wife and, enraged at McGee's denial that she is aboard *The Busted Flush*, shoots at and nearly kills him. The attack dramatically exposes McGee's vulnerability, worrying him above all because it seems to bespeak a potentially deadly deterioration of his reflexes. He can offer no satisfactory response to Meyer's concern that, "If Harry Broll can damned near kill you, Travis, what about somebody with a more professional attitude and background?" Perhaps Meyer is right when he advises, "Maybe it's time to give the whole thing up. What good is a way of life if it turns out to be fatal?" Incidents in *Indigo* and *Lavender* threatened to undermine confidence in his judgment; now he is forced to worry about possible deterioration of his physical abilities as well.

In the second incident, McGee is knocked out when Dissat unexpectedly shows up in Grenada. Having settled on a plan to use Lisa as bait to snare Dissat, McGee carelessly relaxes his guard, failing to allow for the possibility that Dissat might not simply sit around and wait to be snared. His mistake costs Lisa her life and him nearly his own; only his desperate dash into the ocean saves him. However, his terrifying encounter with Dissat so unnerves him, so undermines his confidence, that for the first time he is forced to acknowledge fear born of almost total helplessness; even the memory of the incident can later produce "the sudden and humiliating sting" of tears when he tries to describe the scene to Meyer, although the tears signal less a diminution of his macho image than a healthy awareness of his vulnerability, a faint but salutary whiff of his own mortality.

What McGee needs to rescue him from his funk is an opportunity to prove himself, which he soon gets in his third near-brush with death in the novel. While preparing him and Meyer for their hot asphalt bath, Dissat casually remarks that Harry Broll was an expert marksman who missed McGee intentionally when he fired at him, intending only to mislead him into thinking he was distraught over his wife's disappearance. McGee, suddenly realizing that perhaps his reflexes aren't as bad as he feared, begins to feel his confidence returning. Roused from his torpor, his whipped-dog lethargy giving way to angry determination, he lunges at Dissat, knocks him over, and watches the asphalt bury him, thus saving his and Meyer's lives and in the process regaining for himself a measure of self-esteem.

What intensifies McGee's self-doubts and uncertainties so much is the powerful urge he feels to chuck it all and accept the tempting offer of Lady Jillian Brent-Archer to join her—as husband, lover, houseguest, whatever role he wishes—on her estate in St. Kitts. Widow of an old friend, Jillian is, to quote McGee, "a lively, sexy, lovely, sexy, well-dressed, sexy, amusing, sexy, wealthy, sexy widow lady," who is quite willing and able to support him in the beach-bum

life-style to which he has become accustomed. And on the evidence
of his recent experience, perhaps the domestic life wouldn't be such
a bad idea:

> One life to live, so pop through the escape hatch, McGee. Try the
> islands. Damned few people can escape the smudge and sludge,
> the acids and stenches, the choking and weeping. You have to take
> care of yourself, man. Nobody else is going to. And the deft morsel,
> curled sleeping against you, is a first-class ticket for all the voyage
> · you have left. Suppose you *do* have to do some bowing and scraping
> and fetching. Will it kill you? Think of what most people have to
> do for a living. You've been taking your retirement in small
> installments whenever you could afford it. So here's the rest of it
> in her lovely sleep. The ultimate social security.

He worries a little about surrendering some of his freedom, but Meyer
wryly assures him that "a ring in the nose bothers you for the first
week or so and then you never notice it again." Even an unpleasant
taste of what domesticated life entails (he and Jillian end up arguing
like husband and wife over whether or not he agreed to take her to a
cocktail party) fails to dissuade him completely.

The combination of his doubts about himself and the temptation
to escape with Jillian makes McGee more introspective than ever, and
his internal debate is not easily resolved. He struggles to convince
himself that lovemaking is as good a way as any to spend the rest of
his life. Moreover, he reasons, "If I don't grasp the opportunity,
somebody will find some quick and dirty way to let the sea air through
my skull." Ultimately, however, he decides that only his "spavined
sense of mission, galumphing out to face the dragon's fiery breath,"
adequately justifies his pleasure-filled installment-plan retirement, and
he concludes that the illusion that he is doing something to clean up
at least a tiny patch of the grimy world is the only thing that allows
him to live comfortably with the sybaritic side of his nature. Accepting
Jillian's invitation to become her housepet and bedmate would only
turn him into something he isn't yet, but which he has an uncomfortable
tendency to become—a complete and total beach bum.

Obviously if the series is to continue, McGee cannot surrender
to his doubts or become immobilized by his fears. On the other hand,
although he rescues his hero, so to speak, by boosting his self-esteem
in the final encounter with Dissat, MacDonald doesn't let McGee off

scot-free. There remains a lasting residue from all the doubts and fears, a permanent impression on his escutcheon. For one thing, he suffers a recurring nightmare in which he buys a shirt to which the salesgirl affixes a white skull, one he realizes is Lisa's, signifying the guilt he feels over his role in her death. Also, there is the surprising admission to Meyer that he is tiring of his own philosophy, especially as it relates to women. Not that he no longer finds the female sex attractive; far from it. It's just that his standard statements about women are beginning to sound hollow to him: "I can't stand the thought of ever again hearing my own sincere, manly, loving, crap-eating voice saying those stale words about how I won't ever hurt you, baby, I just want to screw you and make you a more sincere and emotionally healthy woman."

McGee's spirits rise slightly when Jeannie Dolan, whom we first met when he began investigating Mary Broll's disappearance, shows up at *The Busted Flush*. With McGee's best interests in mind, Meyer rushes forward to question the woman about her current emotional state: "Miss Dolan, do you feel like a pathetic little bird with a busted wing who has fluttered aboard, looking for patience, understanding, and gentleness and love which will make you well and whole again?" Only after being assured that she is not a wounded duckling will he allow her near McGee. After all, one wounded duckling aboard ship is enough.

Although in *Tan* he focuses greater attention on McGee and his personal problems than heretofore, MacDonald displays no lessening of interest in his other characters. In the figure of Lisa Dissat, for example, he paints a fascinating portrait of a woman who is an interesting amalgam of two standard MacDonald types; combining the sexual aggressiveness of a woman like Lilo Perris with the vulnerability of a Betsy Kapp, Lisa is a villain with a potential for salvation. Almost from the first moment he meets her, she begins dipping into her repertoire, making all sorts of sexual advances toward him; she uses suggestion, innuendo, nakedness, even what he calls an "instant rape suit," and McGee is admittedly sorely tempted to sample the goods. All that inhibits him is the knowledge that she was involved in the scheme that cost Mary Broll her life, so he keeps rebuffing her, finally concocting a phony story about how he once shot the head off a former woman partner of his. This abruptly quells her ardor, but then a most interesting thing happens: forced to relate to McGee in a nonsexual way, the hussy image disappears and there begins to emerge a hurt and confused little girl.

Being with McGee, Lisa confesses, is "like being a kid again . . . and going out on a date. It's a feeling I haven't had in a long long time. It's sort of sweet, somehow." She drops her guard and confides to him a poignant story about her sexual initiation at the age of fourteen. Her convent school upbringing had so drummed virtue into her that when she was seduced by a teacher, she was torn apart by the conflict between her sense of obligation to report him and her desire to have him do it to her again. "Purity could not be regained," McGee speculates. "So she ran away and had spent a dozen years corrupting because she believed herself corrupt, debauching because she had been debauched, defiling because she was the virgin defiled." In an unguarded moment Lisa confesses to McGee her secret desire to enter a convent: "I don't ever want to be screwed again the rest of my life or be even touched by any man. I want to be a bride of Christ. Now laugh yourself sick." The tragedy of the book is that Lisa never gets a chance to act upon her secret wish. Her death also deprives McGee of one of the greatest challenges to his therapeutic talents: how far could he have rehabilitated her using methods other than sexual ones? Perhaps it is regret over this lost opportunity as much as guilt over her death that prompts the vivid nightmares he has about her.

Paul Dissat is another interesting variation on a standard type; cut from the same cloth as such sociopaths as Junior Allen in *Blue* and Boo Waxwell in *Orange*, Dissat differs from them in that he is not presented in the subhuman terms they were. He is handsome, bright (an accountant for SeaGate), athletic (a competitive skier), politically conservative, religiously devout—and deadly. Meyer diagnoses him as an "activated sociopathic sadist," whose violent proclivities have remained dormant until the incident that caused Mary Broll's death unleashed an unexpected and exhilarating response. Dissat admits that when he was compelled, as he puts it, to "amplify the pain" in order to get Mary to talk, he began to experience a strange new pleasure, "as if we were lovers." He gets a similar delight from torturing Lisa and announces that henceforth he intends to devote all his time to exploring the newly discovered pleasures of his galloping sadism. Only McGee's desperation move against him puts an end to Dissat's sick campaign for fresh new victims.

McGee is amply rewarded for all his close calls by ending up with the $300,000 Dissat stole from Broll, who won't be needing the money anymore. But his experiences pay an even greater dividend than this, for they lead him to valuable new insights, and a price tag cannot be placed on the worth of his advances in maturity and self-knowledge.

As if he didn't already have enough to worry about, what with his fears about his reflexes and his faulty judgments, McGee now faces eviction when he learns at the beginning of *The Scarlet Ruse* (1973) that the "Fort Lauderdamndale" city fathers have ruled that permanent habitation aboard all watercraft within the city limits will henceforth be prohibited. To make matters worse, McGee is also currently feeling financially pinched. To take his mind off his problems, and to replenish the larder, he accepts Meyer's invitation to talk with an old friend of his, Hirsh Fedderman, who is in need of the kind of services McGee provides.

Fedderman is a dealer in rare stamps who buys valuable items for a select number of investment accounts. Over the past eighteen months, he has purchased over $400,000 worth of stamps for a man named Frank Sprenger. He tells McGee that during his most recent transaction with Sprenger, he was horrified to discover that the stamps in his collection had been replaced with fakes. He hasn't yet informed Sprenger, but if he cannot locate the missing stamps he will have to come up with $400,000 to reimburse him. He assures McGee that all the transactions took place in the security of a nearby bank and involved only himself, Mary Alice McDermit, his clerk for the past five years, and Sprenger. The collection is kept in a locked box in the bank and no one but the three of them had access to it at any time, and a check of bank records shows that the only time the stamp album was examined was when all three were present.

McGee decides to take the case, which poses a real challenge to his problem-solving skills. He begins by uncovering information that Sprenger is a Miami bookkeeper and enforcer for the mob, a shrewd operator who was apparently laundering tainted money by investing it in a safe and legitimate commodity like stamps. But his trusted position within the crime syndicate makes it highly unlikely that he would attempt something as foolish as stealing his own stamps. Fedderman's unblemished record of honesty makes it equally inconceivable that he would try to defraud Sprenger by stealing from him. That leaves only Mary Alice McDermit, Hirsh's clerk, but when she learns that McGee considers her a possible suspect in the case she becomes outraged, angrily denying that she had anything to do with the theft. She convinces him that in view of the number of stamps in question, it would take someone over an hour to switch all the stamps in Sprenger's album, an impossibility given the brief time each transaction took.

Mary Alice's emphatic denial of guilt convinces McGee to give her a clean bill of health, although his judgment is largely instinctive, based as it is on the evidence presented to his gray eyes rather than to his gray matter. He is smitten by her beauty, her impressive stature (she is almost six feet tall), and a veritable catalogue of other features: "I liked the expression on her face"; "I liked the neat little creases at the corners of her mouth. I liked that tricky blue shade of her iris. I liked the genuine big-girl hunger with which she stashed away the medium-adequate meal"; and so on.

It isn't long before McGee becomes romantically involved with Mary Alice, and as usual he finds himself attracted to a woman with apparent problems. She admits that she is a refugee from a rotten marriage, the unhappy experience of which has made her wary of men. She rebuffs McGee's advances during a quiet cruise aboard *The Busted Flush* because, she confesses, her husband, from whom she has been separated for five years, is a "sick, murderous, tricky bastard" who has vowed to kill her if she ever makes love with any other man. He even sends someone to check up on her periodically. However, thanks to McGee's patience and the security of *The Busted Flush*, she overcomes her fears and surrenders to his charms. In return, McGee promises that at the first sign of trouble he will whisk her safely away on his boat for as long as necessary to escape her husband's wrath.

McGee's pleasure cruise is prematurely interrupted by the shocking news that Jane Lawson, Hirsh's other clerk, has just been found murdered in her home. Although at first it appears that she was killed when she surprised a gang of youths ransacking her home, further evidence reveals that the trashing was a smokescreen. Despite her record of fifteen years' loyal service to Fedderman, it now appears that she was murdered by someone looking for something in her home, possibly the missing stamps. Incriminating evidence begins to accumulate when McGee identifies a package Mary Alice finds among

Jane's things at the store as a shoplifter's gaff, a wrapped package with a hidden spring opening that would allow one to slip a large item inside. Since Jane had responsibility for ordering and imprinting the albums Hirsh used for his customers' stamps, she could easily have managed to obtain a duplicate of Sprenger's album and fill it with phony stamps. The conclusive piece of evidence comes when Mary Alice recalls that she became ill after having lunch with Jane one day, which necessitated that Jane replace her when Hirsh made an addition to the Sprenger collection. Mary Alice now becomes convinced that Jane poisoned her so she could switch albums using the fake one she hid in her package.

Although the evidence against Jane seems overwhelming, McGee is still bothered. For one thing, he can discover no likely motive. If Jane needed money, she could have had all she wanted from her late husband's father, a wealthy man who tells McGee he had made several offers of financial assistance to Jane but was always turned down. Also, a former employee of Hirsh's who worked with Jane for ten years adamantly refuses to believe she could have stolen the stamps, describing her as the sort of person "who, if she were using a pay phone and found a quarter in the coin drop, would feel very uncomfortable about keeping it." This brings McGee back once more to Mary Alice, but because of his emotional attachment to her he wishes he didn't have to consider the possibility that he might have been mistaken in his judgment. To set his mind at ease, especially now that he has just agreed to take her on an extended cruise aboard *The Busted Flush*, he recruits Meyer to help him determine Mary Alice's guilt or innocence. He asks Meyer to pay a visit to Frank Sprenger and, posing as his disgruntled partner, tell him that McGee has run off with Mary Alice and offer to lead him to their location. McGee figures that if Sprenger is involved with Mary Alice in any sort of scam, he'll take the bait.

While waiting to hear from Meyer, McGee witnesses an interesting transformation in Mary Alice's personality take place before his very eyes: what he had formerly seen as perkiness now seems bitchiness; what was engaging naiveté now strikes him as childish petulance; what was cute now seems only evidence of her ignorance. Even their lovemaking is reduced to what McGee describes as "all rubbery fakery, smack and slap, grunt and huff, like a pair of third-rate wrestlers in some lunch-bucket town practicing for the evening's performance for the nitwits who think it quite real." The effect of his sudden disillusionment is dramatic—for the first time in his life (as far as we know) he becomes impotent, although embarrassment and shame over his problem quickly give way to relief once he realizes that his body is smarter than his mind, for it sensed the true character of the woman he had fallen in love with before his judgment did.

It isn't so much that Mary Alice does an abrupt about-face as that McGee, bewitched "by the blue eyes and the great body," allowed his physical infatuation with her lush beauty to cloud his perception of her. McGee has made mistakes in judgment before (and with increased frequency in his recent adventures), but never one so grievous as this, where his emotional involvement blinded him to what he should have seen clearly: that Mary Alice not only defrauded her kind and generous boss, she also killed Jane Lawson when she became suspicious about her and then fabricated evidence purporting to prove her guilt. McGee is chastened by the humiliating lesson he learns:

> I had seen somebody I had invented, not Mary Alice. I explained away her inconsistencies, overlooked her vulgarities, and believed her dramatics. And so it goes. It is humiliating, when you should know better, to become victim of the timeless story of the little brown dog running across the freight yard, crossing all the railroad tracks until a switch engine nipped off the end of his tail between wheel and rail. The little dog yelped, and he spun so quickly to check himself out that the next wheel chopped through his little brown neck. The moral is, of course, never lose your head over a piece of tail.

However, he now faces a more serious matter than regret over his mistakes in judgment, for Meyer sends a radio message confirming his suspicions and alerting him that Sprenger is on his way to get the two of them. Mary Alice now admits that she lied about her husband; he isn't crazy, but a powerful mob figure currently serving time in prison. He sent her to Miami and put her in the care of Sprenger. Bored with her confining existence, she seduced Sprenger and persuaded him to become her accomplice in the scheme to get $400,000 from Fedderman. Now Sprenger has no choice but to kill them both in order to cover up his involvement in the plan and protect his position with the mob.

What follows is a tense action-filled scene whose suspense recalls the exciting conclusion of *The Executioners* (1958), where the hero nervously awaited the murderous assault of the crazed Max Cady. Unlike Cady, Sprenger is no madman but a shrewd and deadly operator. And an expert marksman. In *Tan* the security of *The Busted Flush* was briefly violated by Harry Broll's unexpected attack, although it was later revealed as a masquerade designed to mislead McGee. This time there is no game-playing; Sprenger is out for blood and McGee's peaceful refuge is about to become a sitting target for his assaults: "The *Flush* felt like a ponderous toy, something in a foolish game for over-aged children. Meyer and I had been using it as a treehouse, hiding the secret words, the pacts, the membership list, the slingshots, and the Daisy Air Rifle. Now a real live man was going to come across the flats and blow the treehouse out of the water."

McGee concludes that his best chance against Sprenger would be to lure him aboard the houseboat by convincing him that someone has already killed him and Mary Alice. He smashes the windshields of the *Muñequita*, partially submerges it on a sandbar, then using Mary Alice's floppy scarlet hat and a hunk of her long hair, fashions a dummy of her body, which he places on a raft that he floats nearby. Then he hides aboard *The Busted Flush* and waits. The "scarlet ruse" works. From the cover of a mangrove tree, Sprenger fires several shots into the dummy. Apparently satisfied that Mary Alice is indeed dead, he and his partner come aboard, where McGee is ready for them. The bullets begin to fly and soon the deck of the boat is red with blood as McGee shoots Sprenger's partner (who bleeds to death), Sprenger then shoots Mary Alice (who failed to heed McGee's warning to stay hidden), and McGee finally shoots Sprenger.

McGee thus survives yet another close encounter with death, but not without suffering serious injury: before collapsing, Sprenger manages to break McGee's jaw in three places, crush his cheekbone, and knock him unconscious for two and a half months. Now that he is getting older, it takes McGee longer and longer to bounce back from his injuries. When he finally makes his way back to *The Busted Flush*, feeling "as if I was made of corn flakes, stale rubber bands, and old gnawed bones," he senses a noticeable strain in his homecoming, as if something had altered the nature of his relationship with his old boat. Although cheered by the news that he won't have to move (it turns out the city ordinance banning permanent habitation aboard boats does not apply to residents of Bahia Mar) and buoyed by the unexpected reunion with Cathy Kerr (the woman with whom he was involved in *Blue*), McGee is troubled by the unwelcome intrusion of violence and bloodshed into what had heretofore been a sacrosanct refuge from the uglier elements of his profession. The bloody encounter with Sprenger has exposed yet another of McGee's vulnerabilities.

Scarlet artfully combines several of the most effective ingredients of MacDonald's successful formula: a unique and imaginative scam; a fascinating and informative behind-the-scenes look at both the arcane world of rare stamp trading and the creative methods by which mob-tainted money is laundered through legitimate investments; interesting characters, including (much to McGee's dismay) an unexpected female villain; a puzzling mystery of locked-room dimensions; a suspenseful conclusion of edge-of-the-seat proportions; and, as usual, as far as his recent adventures are concerned, a continuing focus on McGee's personal crisis. Less introspective than he was in *Tan*, McGee nevertheless has to deal with additional threats to his judgment and self-confidence, although the pleasure of his reunion with Cathy Kerr and Hirsh's generous gift of a rare and valuable stamp serve as partial compensation for the buffeting his ego suffers.

6

Crisis and Beyond (*Turquoise, Lemon, Copper, Green, Crimson*)

As *The Turquoise Lament* (1973) opens, McGee, only a week into his current chunk of retirement, gets a distress call from Pidge Brindle summoning him to Hawaii. Despite his usual reluctance to work unless his financial situation demands it, he responds immediately to Pidge's call, for a list of those to whom he owes a special favor would have to include Pidge's late father, Professor Ted Lewellen. Several years earlier, McGee was involved in a successful marine treasure hunt with Lewellen, who earned his undying gratitude by saving him from serious injury during a fight. McGee hasn't seen Pidge in over a year, since she and her new husband, Howie Brindle, left for a round-the-world cruise aboard their yacht. But the joy of his reunion with her is diminished when she tells him either her husband is trying to kill her or she is going insane.

McGee locates Howie and listens to his side of the story. He confides to McGee that he is worried his wife is flipping out. During their cruise to Hawaii, Pidge accused him of sneaking aboard a young blonde they had met in St. Croix, but when Howie insisted that Pidge search the ship she could find no trace of any stowaway. Although she maintained that she heard the girls's voice several times and even claimed to have taken some photographs of her, when she examined the pictures after the film was developed she found no trace of the girl in any of the shots. Most disturbing of all to Howie, Pidge fell overboard during the cruise and accused him of changing course abruptly in order to dump her over the side and then of trying to run her over while she was in the water. Howie confesses he is puzzled and deeply worried about his wife's mental state.

McGee, slipping into the familiar role of therapist, attends to Pidge's emotional problems, gradually forcing her to the painful admission that her self-image is profoundly negative. He tells her that she exhibits the classic symptoms of anxiety neurosis, which he attributes to the pressures she felt as an only child trying to live up to the high demands of her parents. When her marriage to Howie failed to measure up to her expectations, she blamed herself for all the problems. Under emotional stress her neurosis became more serious, turning suspicions about her husband into paranoiac delusions. As she became more and more anxious about what she perceived as her failures, she began seeing a girl who wasn't there, hearing nonexistent voices, even suspecting her husband of trying to run her over in the water.

Understandably upset at McGee's analysis of her predicament, Pidge is also relieved to hear such a sensible explanation for her unsettling experiences. As thanks, however, she offers more than a kiss and a friendly handshake: she maneuvers McGee into bed, something she has longed to do, she admits, ever since she was seventeen and had "one of the great crushes of the western world" on him. Besides, she explains, going to bed with him is one way of firming her resolve not to return to her husband. To the more than willing McGee, Pidge was a "temptation out of the past, served up on some kind of eternal lazy Susan so that it had come by once again, and this time we had taken it." After three days of spirited lovemaking, McGee returns to Florida, confident that he has resolved Pidge's problems.

Back in Florida, however, McGee slips into a deep funk brought on in part by his worries about Meyer, who collapses from what appears to be a heart attack, although it is later diagnosed as only a virus infection. But his dissatisfaction is also personal, and in response to his sourness he begins hewing his way through a solid wall of women, though even this fails to do anything but produce more remorse.

I was an absolutely trivial, wasted, no-good son of a bitch. I wanted to moan, tear my hair out and gnaw my hands raw. This had really been one great December. Point with pride, you dumb horny old scavenger. You zapped Pidge just because you missed her the first time around, and you're trying to make a perfect score, right? And since you got back, there have been a half-dozen casual availables, and if you put your mind to it you can remember four out of six of their names and maybe three out of six of their faces.

Eventually McGee realizes what is really bothering him: like a moony adolescent, he is in love. When he finally screws up enough courage to ask himself the crucial question "Would I, Travis McGee, bring thee, Linda Lewellen Brindle, aboard this houseboat to live herein and hereon, with me, happily, so long as we shall all remain afloat," his answer is a resounding "Hell, yes!" A letter from Pidge declaring her love for him only confirms his happy conclusion that she is the "one lady I want for keeps."

His bliss is soon interrupted by Frank Hayes, a fellow veteran of Ted Lewellen's treasure hunts. Now owner of his own salvage outfit, he tells McGee he received a call from an unidentified party offering him a fifty-percent share in a treasure operation if he will simply furnish the men and equipment. Hayes is suspicious about the offer and tells McGee he thinks the research documents and maps might belong to Ted Lewellen, whose notes and plans (which by rights would belong to Pidge) were never found after his death. The only individuals with access to Lewellen's files were his lawyer, Tom Collier, and his banker, Lawton Hisp, coexecutors of his estate. A little snooping reveals that the man who contacted Hayes was acting on behalf of Collier. His suspicions aroused, McGee takes another look at the pictures Pidge gave him and notices for the first time that the three which she thought she had taken of the female stowaway have a slightly different color cast to them. A visit to photographer friend Gabe Marchman explains the discrepancy: the pictures came from a different roll and were probably substituted for the photographs Pidge took while the film was being developed.

Nervously concluding that he might have been premature in reassuring Pidge she was seeing things that weren't there, McGee now becomes uneasy about Howie. Six-four and "a McGee and a half wide," an ex-college football player at the University of Florida, Howie is a big overgrown kid, a simple, cheerful, well-liked, and helpful

friend to one and all. About the only criticism anyone can make about
him is that he isn't very bright:

> He was like a little house with a door in the front and a door in the
> back. One room. He'd let you in his house and it was fun. Chuckles
> and games. No pressure. So you wanted to know him better and
> so you went through the doorway into what was going to be the
> next room of his personal house, but you found yourself back out
> in the yard, and the little house looked just the same, back and
> front. One room.

But in tracing Howie's past back to Bradenton, where he grew up,
McGee is alarmed to find that there is considerably more than
intellectual limitation to be worried about: he discovers a lengthy trail
of dead bodies in Howie's wake, including his parents, two siblings,
the grandparents who raised him, a football teammate, an ex-girlfriend,
and a former employer. All the deaths were judged accidental at the
time, but the coincidences are too incriminating to suggest any other
conclusion than that Howie is an "amiable maniac," a classic sociopath
without a trace of conscience or human feeling, to whom murder is
the simplest and most effective way of dealing with people who irritate
him.

McGee's fears about Howie are confirmed by Tom Collier, from
whom he extracts a confession that, having learned about Howie's past
himself, he pressured him to marry Pidge and then try to convince
her she was going insane—by, among other things, smuggling a girl
aboard, whom Howie had to kill when he learned Pidge had taken
photographs of her. Once Pidge was institutionalized, Collier could
freely use all the records and research documents that, as coexecutor
of her father's estate, he was able to steal from his files immediately
after his death. Collier has not only defrauded Pidge of what is
rightfully hers, he has also endangered her life by putting her in the
hands of a conscience-less killer. McGee feels helpless to do anything;
Pidge is somewhere in the middle of the Pacific with Howie bound
for Pago Pago, where they have arranged to sell their boat.

McGee flies to Pago Pago and begins an anxious vigil. Each
morning he takes the tram across the harbor to the summit of Mt.
Alava and watches and waits. On the seventh day his efforts are
rewarded when he spots Pidge and Howie's boat anchored in the

harbor. After making his way to their yacht, he is informed that Pidge has been taken to the hospital with a severe case of depression. When he locates Howie, he confronts him with what he has learned about all the dead bodies in his past. Suddenly the friendly expression on Howie's smiling face undergoes a stark transformation, reminding McGee of a similar look he once saw on the face of a bear when he was a child: "It was something out of the blackness. It was night. It was evil. It colored that whole year of my life with a taste of despair." Without warning, Howie strikes him, knocks him out, drags his body to his room, and attempts to drown him by holding his head underwater in the bathtub (all the while humming "On, Wisconsin"). McGee regains consciousness while his head is being submerged and manages to hold his breath long enough to fool Howie into thinking he is dead.

In the thrilling conclusion to the novel, McGee follows Howie to the top of Mt. Alava, arriving just in time to prevent him from tossing Pidge, whom he had picked up on his way, off the mountain. McGee throws a wrench at Howie, knocking him off balance. With surprising agility, Howie grabs the overhead cable of the tram to keep himself from falling; however, as he is about to swing to safety, the tram operator suddenly applies the brakes to the system, sending him spinning to his death in the water below.

The novel concludes with an epilogue that takes place eight months later. We learn that McGee brought Pidge back to *The Busted Flush* and that the two of them—"totally, blissfully, blindly in love"—set up house together. But it turns out their happiness is short-lived, for Pidge has fallen in love with the handsome young psychiatrist who has been treating her. With increasing frequency in the last few novels McGee has been making domestic noises, freely admitting his desire to settle down. In *Tan*, he was tempted to retire to St. Kitts with Jillian Brent-Archer, but decided his heart wasn't in it; this time, however, it appears that he is ready for the real thing. Ironically, he is rejected in favor of a younger man and left at book's end to lick his emotional wounds, trying to forget this latest bruise to his ego.

As the title suggests, *Turquoise* is in many ways a lament, a lament for McGee's lost love and his lost youth. The novel, for example, is filled with incidents that remind him of death: Ted Lewellen and Joe Dellandrio (another veteran of Lewellen's treasure hunts) both die unexpectedly in separate traffic accidents; a couple of McGee's Ft. Lauderdale friends commit suicide; dying patients surround Meyer in the hospital where he is being treated; and his sudden collapse on the beach shocks McGee into a consideration of his own mortality. In previous cases, McGee was forced to come to terms with the risks and dangers of his job and with the inevitable fact of his own limitations. The many references to death in *Turquoise* forcefully remind him that even if his luck should hold out and he is fortunate enough to survive all the risky encounters associated with his dangerous profession, he will still die, a realization which attests to his having reached the stage in life where he must accept the fact that he is not immortal. It is no wonder he feels saddened (and a little sorry for himself) at the end of *Turquoise*, for not only has he been thrown over for a younger man, he has been greeted by intimations of his own mortality.

Although *Turquoise* opens quietly, with emphasis on McGee's calm resolution of Pidge's crisis, the pace quickens dramatically as the action shifts from personal drama to puzzling mystery, with McGee transformed from mooning lover into ardent sleuth, seeking the real explanation for what is happening to Pidge. Finally, the novel is swept up in an exciting crescendo, with McGee in a desperate race to save Pidge's life. Thus, tender drama, baffling intrigue, and thrilling action are all effectively and seamlessly combined in a carefully constructed plot around which are woven two other typical MacDonald features: the usual number of thoughtful reflections about life and a variety of barbed commentaries about the state of American culture. Everything is kept in perfect balance, earning for *Turquoise* a deserved place among the most successful of the McGee novels.

McGee is roused from sleep at four in the morning at the beginning of *The Dreadful Lemon Sky* (1975) by the unexpected arrival of Carrie Milligan, whom he hasn't seen in six years. She opens a package, takes out $10,000 in cash, and offers it to him if he will take care of the rest of the money in the package, some $94,000. If anything should happen to her within the next month, she wants McGee to send the money to her sister in New Jersey. She won't reveal anything else, only that the money is "sort of . . . my share of some action." The task seems simple enough, and $10,000 will purchase a lot of retirement. However, when he comes across a newspaper account two weeks later about Carrie's sudden death in a traffic accident, he immediately becomes suspicious and decides that since $2,000 would have been more than adequate payment for watching Carrie's money, she's got $8,000 worth of service coming.

McGee begins by visiting the building-supply business where Carrie worked and talking to Harry Hanscomb, the owner, about the money Carrie had in her possession. Hanscomb is upset by what McGee tells him because it confirms his suspicion that Carrie was in cahoots with his partner, Jack Omaha, in bleeding him dry. Omaha disappeared just two days before Carrie visited McGee, which leads Hanscomb to conclude that she was helping Omaha convert all the assets of their struggling business to cash, leaving him with all the debts.

McGee turns up enough evidence after examining the site of Carrie's fatal accident to convince him that she was killed intentionally. When Cal Birdsong, owner of the marina where he is staying, dies in the hospital while being treated for minor injuries suffered in a scuffle with McGee, his suspicions rise even more, for Birdsong often skippered a boat owned by Jack Omaha. Omaha is missing and Carrie and now Birdsong are dead. When an autopsy discloses that Birdsong died not from his injuries but from a wound caused by a sharp object plunged into his heart, McGee becomes convinced he is onto something big.

Piecing the puzzle together, McGee theorizes that Carrie was associated with Omaha and Birdsong in a marijuana-smuggling operation which involved picking up the grass at a rendezvous spot somewhere near Grand Bahama with Omaha's boat and then distributing it throughout the condominium where Carrie lived. He further speculates that the fourth partner in the operation, the one who transported the grass from Grand Bahama to the boat, is local attorney and rising political star, Fred Van Harn; he is attorney for all the others, owns his own plane, even has his own airstrip. As McGee and Meyer continue to sift through their facts and suppositions, Carrie's friend Joanna Freeler boards *The Busted Flush* carrying a package. As she begins to open it, it explodes, killing her and knocking McGee out for five days. At the end of *Turquoise*, McGee was saddened at having lost Pidge to a younger man, but already in *Lemon* he has lost two women, neither of them to another lover but to an unidentified killer. Before continuing any further, however, he needs to restore himself—which he does with Cindy Birdsong, Cal's beautiful widow. Meanwhile, her marina employees busy themselves repairing the damage to *The Busted Flush*, which, as it did in *Scarlet*, seems to be suffering in sympathy with its owner.

McGee is peremptorily summoned to a meeting with Judge Schermer, a local power broker, who offers him $25,000 to leave town and forget about Fred Van Harn, his political protégé (and future husband of his niece). The Judge doesn't want McGee doing anything to jeopardize Van Harn's chances for election to the State Senate. McGee, explaining that he considers Van Harn to be a "murderous, spooky fellow," declines the offer. The next day he finds himself face-to-face with Van Harn himself, who with disarming frankness confesses that McGee's suppositions are correct, he was involved in a little drug smuggling with his friends, a caper he went along with only to earn some quick and needed cash. But he denies killing anyone, theorizing instead that Omaha was probably scared off by some professionals who were angry that he was moving onto their turf. McGee, impressed by Van Harn's sincerity, is tempted to return to Ft. Lauderdale, but "the habit of involvement is not easily broken," and he still hasn't discovered who killed Carrie.

During a romantic interlude with Cindy Birdsong she makes a casual remark that triggers a fresh new suspicion in McGee. Shortly before his death, her husband awoke terrified from a nightmare in which an unidentified object was falling from the sky and heading right for him; he ordered Cindy never to mention it to anyone. Acting on a hunch, McGee decides to pay another visit to Van Harn. He locates him on his ranch, where he has just finished digging a large grave into which he is about to bury his dead horse. McGee confronts him with a new scenario, one in which he theorizes that as Van Harn dumped the heavy bags of grass from his plane to Omaha and Birdsong in the boat below, one of the bags accidentally struck and killed Omaha, whose body was then dumped over the side. He continues, accusing Van Harn of then murdering both Carrie and Birdsong, the only witnesses to the accident. Suddenly Van Harn aims his jeep at McGee and tries to shovel him into the open grave. The two men begin to scuffle and soon tumble into the freshly dug grave, where McGee notices for the first time a blue bicycle handlebar and a human hand sticking up out of the dirt. With a burst of strength, he overpowers Van Harn and ties him securely to the jeep.

In another of those scenes in which MacDonald dispenses crude and diabolical justice to his villains, Van Harn is attacked by an army of fire ants while McGee is off phoning the authorities. Before going into extreme allergic shock (which will prove fatal) he denies killing Carrie and Birdsong, although he admits to killing Jason Breen, whose wrist McGee saw in the grave. An employee at Birdsong's marina, Breen attempted to extort $20,000 from Van Harn by threatening to go to the police and tell them that, on orders from the attorney, he killed Birdsong. Breen had really killed Birdsong after becoming upset over the way he was treating his wife. For his efforts, Breen ends up in a crude grave with the horse Van Harn killed to give him an excuse to dig the hole.

Following Van Harn's death, Judge Schermer and his political cronies put a clamp on things and concoct an official version of events which, in the words of Harry Max Scorf, the wily local police investigator who has been working with McGee on the case, "adds up to a crock of shit." McGee, Meyer, and Scorf begin another round of speculation and come up with a brand-new suspect, Harry Hanscomb, Jack Omaha's business partner. According to this revised scenario, Hanscomb, having spotted Carrie taking her share of the profits from the smuggling operation out of the office safe where Omaha kept the cash, killed her in order to gain access to the safe. (McGee figures that only Omaha, who took care of the company finances, and Carrie, his secretary, knew the combination to the safe. With Omaha missing and Carrie dead, Hanscomb could arrange to have the safe drilled open.) After Joanna Freeler became suspicious about Carrie's death, Hanscomb sent her a package of wine and cheese that contained a bomb hidden inside. When McGee and Scorf confront Hanscomb with their suspicions, he pulls a gun and shoots Scorf dead on the spot. The killer's momentary shock at seeing the gory results of his action gives McGee enough time to grab Scorf's gun and disarm him.

The disclosure of Hanscomb's responsibility for the deaths of Carrie and Joanna, while tying up several loose ends, is a blot on the novel. MacDonald's best plots usually feature a single villain to whom all the evil can be traced. By creating three separate killers, he keeps the mystery going but at the expense of believability (a weakness *Lemon* shares with *Gold*, where there were four murderers). In a conversation with writer Rust Hills, MacDonald acknowledged that his intention was to conclude the novel open-endedly, with McGee, Meyer, and Scorf each devising an equally plausible hypothesis, thus leaving the final solution of the mystery up in the air. But neither his agent nor his editor found such a conclusion satisfactory, so MacDonald wrote a second ending, laying the blame for the murders of Carrie and Joanna on Hanscomb's shoulders. MacDonald's admission confirms the suspicion that Hanscomb was an afterthought, the only character who could resolve his plot difficulties. The new ending does, however, provide the book with its title; in describing the smoggy air McGee used the phrase "the dreadful lemon sky," which replaced the original title based on the color azure, which MacDonald confessed he never liked anyway.

Using Hanscomb to bail him out of his plot difficulties only creates new problems for MacDonald. It is one thing to expose a previously unsuspected character as the villain of the piece, but in this case credibility suffers because Hanscomb appeared in only one scene early in the novel, then disappeared for well over two hundred pages until pulled out of MacDonald's hat at the end. Also, Hanscomb's villainy only serves to reduce Van Harn's culpability; it turns out that Van Harn is guilty only of killing Omaha accidentally and of killing Breen, an action that can be explained as self-defense when Breen attacked him. (And it doesn't help any that Breen's attempt to extort money from Van Harn is totally out of character for him, for up to this point his entire motivation has been shown to be a simple chivalric desire to defend women against mistreatment at the hands of their men.) *Lemon* does not display MacDonald's plot-making skills at their finest.

It isn't only in plot effectiveness that *Lemon* is an aberration; the novel also abandons the pattern developed over the previous books in the series of spotlighting McGee's personal crisis. The only reference to his emotional predicament is a brief remark McGee makes to Joanna Freeler when she asks why Carrie didn't marry him instead of the man she did. "Weren't you available?" she asks. "Weren't. Aren't. Won't be," is his cryptic reply, although the evidence of the recent books strongly suggests the contrary. McGee's comment can be taken either as a reaction to the hurt he suffered at having been dumped by Pidge Brindle at the end of *Turquoise*, or as evidence that *Lemon* might have been written prior to the recent books but published after they were.

All the McGee books contain varying amounts of social commentary, usually in the form of observations scattered throughout the book, but in *Lemon* for the first time MacDonald uses plot as a vehicle for social commentary. Although it turns out that all the murders are committed for the usual reasons—greed, self-defense, a misguided sense of honor—all of them can be traced to a crime with specific contemporary relevance, i.e., the lucrative smuggling of illegal drugs into Florida. As Joanna Freeler tells McGee: "Everybody and his brother is hustling grass into Florida. There's absolute tons of it coming in all the time. It's about as risky as running a stop sign." In *Lemon* it is ordinary people, not criminals, who become involved in the illicit drug trade, and their motivations are easily understandable: for Omaha, cash to keep his faltering business afloat; for Van Harn, a way to keep from falling behind in payments due on his ranch; for Carrie, the hope that there's "more to living than sitting on your butt forty hours a week in an office and getting laid once in a while by the joker who signs your paycheck." But each of them tragically gets more than he bargained for: Omaha accidentally dies in the risky business of transferring the grass from Van Harn's plane to his boat; Carrie is murdered because Hanscomb wanted to get his hands on the large sums of cash she and Omaha were earning; Birdsong is killed when his heavy drinking (prompted by his guilt over having had to dispose of Omaha's body at sea) leads to increased mistreatment of his wife, which spurs Breen into action; and Van Harn ends up dying of ant bites.

McGee isn't necessarily opposed on principle to the casual use of drugs as long as people solve their own "risk-reward ratios." He even admits to having used grass himself on a few occasions, although he confesses he didn't enjoy it because "it gave me the uneasy feeling somebody could come up behind me and kill me and I would die distantly amused instead of scared witless." And he is on record (in *Indigo*) as opposing the harsh penalties attached to simple drug possession. But when a friend once tried to recruit him as a partner in a smuggling operation similar to the one Carrie was involved in, he declined:

> I didn't want to go down that particular road. If you make it with grass, you find out that hash and coke are more portable and profitable. You kid yourself into the next step, and by the time they pick you up, your picture in the paper looks like some kind of degenerate, fangs and all. And all you can say is, Gee, the other guys were doing it too.

Whether this would have been the eventual fate awaiting Carrie, Omaha, Birdsong, and Van Harn will never be known, for the action of *Lemon* only serves to confirm a grimmer contention, namely that, in the words of Judge Schermer, "these people that get into drugs, they've got the life expectancy of a mayfly."

Friends have arrived on McGee's doorstep with a variety of requests for help, but none with one quite like Van Harder's in *The Empty Copper Sea* (1978). Most people want McGee's help in recovering money or a valuable item of some sort; Harder wants McGee's help in restoring his good name. He explains that he was employed by Timber Bay businessman Hub Lawless as skipper of his yacht. On a recent cruise with Lawless and his associate John Tuckerman, and two young women, Harder unaccountably passed out after having his usual single drink; when he was awakened, he was shocked to learn that Lawless had fallen overboard and apparently drowned. Since Harder once had a reputation as a heavy drinker (before he got religion), he was accused of being drunk on duty and his irresponsibility was cited as the cause of Lawless's death. But he assures McGee he had only one drink; more important, there are persistent rumors that Lawless is alive in Mexico, which, if true, would exonerate him of blame in the incident. He figures his good name is worth $20,000, so he promises half that amount to McGee if he will help. Despite a halfhearted protest that he isn't in the business of "salvaging the reputations of broken-down fishermen," McGee begins making plans for a trip to Timber Bay.

Within the space of his first few hours in Timber Bay, McGee manages to accomplish a number of things, several of which he isn't very proud of. On his first night in town, for example, he ends up in bed with a local piano player, Billy Jean Bailey, an affair whose "locker-room drabness" leaves him with an unpleasant aftertaste. Following as it does on the heels of an earlier scuffle with Nicky Noyes, one of Lawless's former employees, it leads McGee to the unflattering conclusion that "by diligent effort I seemed to be prolonging my adolescence to total absurdity." His postcoital depression so sours him that he nearly becomes immobilized:

> I had a sudden wrenching urge to shed my own identity and be
> somebody else. Somehow I had managed to lock myself into this
> unlikely and unsatisfying self, this Travis McGee, shabby knight

errant, fighting for small, lost, unimportant causes, deluding himself with the belief that he is in some sense freer than your average fellow, and that it is a very good thing to have escaped the customary trap of regular hours, regular pay, home and kiddies, Christmas bonus, backyard bar-B-cue, hospitalization, and family burial plot.

All we have, I thought, is a trap of a slightly different size and shape. Just as the idea of an ancient hippie is gross and ludicrous, so is the idea of an elderly beach bum. I dreaded the shape of the gray years ahead and wished to hop out of myself.

Reminding himself that he had given Van Harder his word, he decides to stop moaning and get on with his work. He ascertains that Lawless was on the verge of bankruptcy and reportedly converted all his business assets to cash, withdrawing almost $700,000 shortly before his disappearance. He discovers that Lawless's girlfriend, Kristen Petersen, hasn't been seen since the day after the accident, and he learns from the local police that they received a slide, sent anonymously, that shows Lawless sitting at an outdoor café in Guadalajara sometime in April, although his accident occurred in March. One of the two women who were on the cruise that night also tells McGee that she and her friend were paid by John Tuckerman to join them for the evening, thus providing, McGee concludes, convenient witnesses for Lawless's tragic "accident."

Although making respectable progress in his investigation, McGee isn't happy; in fact he is downright morose, the malaise that has been nipping at his heels now erupting into a full-blown identity crisis. "Where has gone all the lazy mocking charm of yesteryear," Meyer wonders. "Where is the beach wanderer, the amiable oaf I used to know?" McGee's mood belcomes so woebegone that he edgily confesses to Meyer that, "I feel as if some absolutely unimaginable catastrophe was getting itself ready to happen. And I feel as if, for no reason in the world, I was going to suddenly—for God's sake—start *crying!*" For one thing, McGee has reached the stage where he realizes that his life is becoming predictable, that there aren't "any more forks in the road to take." Empathetic as ever, Meyer consoles his friend by reminding him that what he is experiencing is a normal stage in human development, i.e., the painful awareness of his own mortality: "You have felt that horrid rotten exhalation, Travis, that breath from the grave, that terminal sigh. You've been singing laments for yourself. Laments, regrets, remorses." Meyer assures him that it is only natural to question his own validity, as well as the meaning of life itself. There is nothing to worry or feel guilty about, counsels Meyer; all McGee needs to dispel his angst is some healthy emotional interchange, which requires only that he "be receptive and hope it comes along."

Come along it does, for as if in answer to his prayers McGee is delivered from the burden of his depression by the stunning woman he meets when he and Meyer pay a visit to Lawless's friend John Tuckerman. Although he mistakenly assumes the woman is Tuckerman's girlfriend, he is delighted to learn she is actually his sister, Gretel Howard, who has come to help nurse him through his current problems. (Following Lawless's disappearance, Tuckerman began drinking heavily and his excesses seem to have scrambled his brains.) Gretel confirms all McGee's suppositions about Lawless: that her brother conspired with him to fake the "accident"; that Van Harder was drugged to knock him out; that Lawless, despite suffering a minor heart attack brought on by his arduous swim to shore, left town the next day with Kristen Petersen. But McGee's curiosity about Lawless takes a backseat to his intense interest in Gretel, who turns out to be his ticket back to the land of the living. The effect she has on him is nothing short of spectacular:

> I felt as if I had shucked some kind of drab outer skin. It was old and brittle, and as I stretched and moved, it shattered and fell off. I could breathe more deeply. The Gulf was a sharper blue. There was wine in the air. I saw every grain of sand, every fragment of seashell, every movement of the beach grasses in the May breeze. It was an awakening. I was full of juices and thirsts, energies and hungers, and I wanted to laugh for no reason at all.

Refreshed, renewed, reinvigorated, McGee resumes his investigation and, after questioning what seems to be half the population of Timber Bay, concludes that Lawless is indeed somewhere in Mexico with Kristen Petersen. Thus it appears that his task is completed, for there will be no problem in securing the restoration of Harder's skipper's license now that it is clear he was the innocent victim of Lawless's scheme. However, despite his admission that the rest of the mystery is "none of my business," he can't give it up, principally because he is reluctant to leave town now that he has found Gretel (and she doesn't want to leave her brother). So, to keep busy, he shows Lawless's wife the slide purporting to document her husband's presence in Mexico. But when she produces the exact same shirt he is wearing in the photograph, McGee realizes that it had to have been taken *before* Lawless's disappearance. Under close questioning, the police officer who traveled to Mexico to investigate the rumors that Lawless was living there now admits that the evidence he uncovered is a bit shaky. (He confesses he might have been swayed in his conclusions by the representative of the company that insured Lawless's life and stood to lose over $2,000,000 if he was really dead.) Now the question is: Who sent the misleading picture to the Timber Bay police? And if Lawless isn't in Mexico, where is he?

When McGee returns to Gretel's beach home, he is stunned to see her lying facedown in the sand. As he rushes toward her, someone begins shooting at him from the cover of a nearby dune. He scrambles to safety, but when he approaches Gretel his heart sinks, for he sees blood caked on the back of her head. Suddenly everything turns deathly quiet, the birds stop their singing, the "empty copper sea" becomes hushed, "as if the world had paused between breaths." A great desolation overwhelms McGee as the love of his life appears to have been cruelly taken from him. With grim determination he makes his way toward the location of the shots, but as he moves closer he is shocked by the sight that greets him: John Tuckerman, naked, badly sunburned, and totally out of his mind, busily digging a jeep out of the sand while carrying on an animated conversation with its two occupants, Hub Lawless and Kristen Petersen, dead all this time. Tuckerman spots McGee and grabs his gun, but the sudden appearance of Gretel—who was stunned, not dead—distracts him long enough to allow McGee to toss a club at him, the rough barnacles at the end of which pierce his neck, opening an artery. He falls to the sand, fatally wounded.

McGee concludes that Lawless died of the heart attack he suffered while swimming to shore. Shocked and disoriented by his death, Tuckerman became enraged at Kristen when she decided to take Lawless's money and run after learning of his death. He killed her and buried both bodies in the sand. However, the combined effects of booze and drugs quickly turned Tuckerman's brains to mush, and when McGee found him he was digging up Lawless so he could resume his getaway to Mexico.

Who then misled the police into thinking Lawless was still alive

by sending the slide? Clumsily, this mystery is cleared up when the
woman who sent the slide suddenly discovers she made a mistake;
the picture was contained on a roll of film she shot on an earlier trip
to Mexico. Misled by the date on the slide (which refers to the date
of development, not the date the picture was taken), she apologizes
for any inconvenience she might have caused.

As a mystery, *Copper* is weakened by its awkward denouement
and its relative paucity of action. Because there is so little for McGee
to do, he spends an inordinate amount of time questioning local
townspeople, most of whom repeat the same information. Apparently
having learned his lesson in *Indigo*, MacDonald is at least never
tempted to send McGee to Mexico to look for Lawless himself. So to
provide McGee with some physical action, he introduces Nicky Noyes,
whose name echoes his function: he annoys McGee first by challenging
him to a fistfight and then later by attempting to shoot him and Meyer.
His task completed, he is clumsily whisked from the novel in a bloody
crash when he dashes in front of a speeding car while fleeing after his
attempted shooting of McGee. Ironically, despite McGee's tireless
sleuthing, the solution to the mystery of Lawless's disappearance
comes not as the result of his efforts but only when Tuckerman's mind
becomes unhinged enough to prompt him to dig up the bodies.

But as a portrait of McGee, *Copper* is a crucial volume in the
series, a kind of Sun Belt *Pilgrim's Progress* that documents his difficult
journey from the Slough of Despond to the Celestial City, personified
by the beatific figure of Gretel Howard. Interestingly, McGee's midlife
predicament parallels that of Hub Lawless, whose restlessness and
self-doubts prompted him to abandon his wife and two teenage
daughters for the younger Kristen Petersen. Lawless recently turned
forty and, in the words of a friend, "was ready for anything that was
going to change things around for him. Nothing tasted good to him
any more." McGee himself is approaching one of those significant
birthdays—probably, like Lawless, his fortieth. Although *Copper*
appeared over a decade after *Blue*, McGee has aged only a few years
in the interim. MacDonald wants McGee to age, but out of "enlightened
self-interest" he doesn't want him to age as fast as the rest of us. Thus,
though he was probably in his mid-thirties when the series began, he
is now only approaching forty:

Those birthday years that end in zero are loaded. A time of

reevaluation. Where the hell have I been and what have I been doing and how much is left for me, and what will I do with the rest of my short turn around the track? I had one of those zero years coming up, not too many birthdays from now. Maybe Hub Lawless had felt trapped in his own treadmill, hemmed in by his juggling act, tied fast to success. The most probable catalyst was the random female who had come along at the wrong time in his life.

Like Lawless, McGee is itching for a change, for something to give him the impetus needed to complete the rest of his "short turn around the track." Happily, unlike either John Tuckerman or Nicky Noyes, who retreat from their identity problems into booze and drugs, McGee, like Lawless, finds his salvation in a woman.

The appearance of Gretel is a godsend, a gift McGee describes as a "sudden shining in the midst of life." Interestingly he never even sleeps with her during the course of the novel; in fact, only a single kiss passes between them. It isn't that McGee doesn't find her physically attractive; it's just that in this case it isn't sex that is regenerative, it is love. His attraction for Gretel transcends the physical and she is immediately elevated to a prominent place on the list of things he cherishes most in life: "pound sweet apples, songs by Eydie, pine forests, spring water, old wool shirts, night silence, fresh Golden Bantam, first run of a hooked permit, Canadian geese, coral reefs, good leather, thunderstorms, wooden beams, beach walking."

Thus it is particularly painful when Gretel declines his offer of marriage. As much as she admits she loves McGee, she confesses she "can't be . . . somebody's remedy. Some kind of medicine for the soul." She is willing to move to Ft. Lauderdale to be near him and promises to continue loving him, but after a miserable seven-year marriage during which she remained loyal to a man who proved himself unworthy of it, she now insists on being loyal to no one but herself. The novel ends with the two of them embracing on the deck of *The Busted Flush* during a late-night thunderstorm, but whether the falling rain symbolizes the promise of a fresh new life together or the prospect of a gloomy future must await final determination until the next chapter of McGee's personal saga unfolds.

It appears on the evidence of the opening pages of *The Green Ripper* (1979) that the question posed at the end of *Copper* will be resolved negatively. It is a damp, dark, and windy December day, the weather matching the gloomy mood of the three people aboard *The Busted Flush*. Meyer, just back from an economics conference in Europe, is distressed over the perilous state of the world. Because of rampant overpopulation and a decline in productivity, he is convinced the world is on the brink of disaster: "There will be fear, hate, anger, death. The new barbarism. There will be plague and poison. And then the new Dark Ages." McGee is unhappy because Gretel Howard, with her "very irritating and compelling need for total—or almost total—independence," has after several months aboard *The Busted Flush* moved out to take up residence at her new place of employment, Bonnie Brae, a "combination fat farm, tennis club, and real estate development." And Gretel is upset after having suddenly remembered where she had previously seen the strange man she bumped into a few days earlier near the private airstrip at Bonnie Brae—he was Brother Titus, an elder of the Church of the Apocrypha in California, who once turned her and her husband away when they sought to speak with her sister-in-law, who had joined the bizarre cult. Meyer eventually nods off, finding comfort in sleep; McGee and Gretel then adjourn to his oversized bed, although the celebratory mood is chilled by McGee's ominous remark that neither of them could have known at the time that it was to be "the very last night."

Gretel phones the next morning from Bonnie Brae with the news that one of the owners, Herm Ladwigg, has just died, apparently in a fall from his bicycle. When McGee arrives later in the day, he discovers that Gretel (who had mentioned when she called that she was feeling "sort of blah") has been rushed to the hospital with a high fever brought on seemingly by an insect sting she received on the back of the neck. Her condition deteriorates rapidly, and two days later she is dead. McGee is devastated by the shock of her death, by the utter finality of losing the woman he had planned to spend the rest of his days with (significantly, he identified himself to Gretel's doctor as her "common-law husband") to the dreaded scythe of "the green ripper"—a child's distortion of "the grim reaper."

According to MacDonald, one way he has been able to illustrate McGee's emotional and psychological aging is by involving him deeply with people and then killing some of those people off. At Gretel's funeral service McGee is consoled by many of the friends with whom he has become involved—Gabe Marchman, Raoul Tenero, Merrimay

Lane, Chookie and Arthur Wilkinson—but he is also saddened when he recalls the many who have already passed away: Puss Killian, Mike Gibson, Nora Gardino . . . But no death touches him as deeply as does Gretel's. "A fictional hero has to be real," MacDonald remarked, "and in order to make [McGee] real, I have to apply to him those same jolts and shocks of reality I have felt myself." The jolt caused by Gretel's death leaves him with a "hollowness beyond belief" and plunges him right back into that soul-searching depression from which he had, thanks to her, appeared to recover in *Copper*.

In the midst of his lamentations, he is visited by two men who identify themselves as members of the staff of the Select Committee on Special Resources in the Senate Office Building. They are seeking information about Gretel and are especially curious whether she mentioned any recent suspicious incidents at Bonnie Brae. McGee, always cautious, decides not to say anything about Brother Titus. Curious about the duo, Meyer makes a few calls to Washington and discovers that there is no such committee as the one they claim to represent. Meyer begins to wonder whether the deaths of Ladwigg and Gretel might be related: as far as anyone knows, he argues, they were the only ones to have seen the mysterious Brother Titus; what if someone were upset at that and wanted them silenced? Meyer's theory is at least partially substantiated when two other men—these, legitimate U.S. Government agents—inform McGee that Gretel's death was caused by a tiny poison-filled ball imbedded in her neck, an assassination method used in the widely publicized murder of Bulgarian defector Georgi Markov in London. The question they are unable to answer is who might have done the deed. McGee had had great difficulty adjusting to the fact of Gretel's death; now he is faced with the ugly thought that her death was caused by *someone*. "From this moment on," he vows, "the only satisfying purpose in life would be to find out exactly, precisely, specifically who."

Despite McGee's fervent wish to get his hands on whoever is responsible for Gretel's murder, Meyer cautions him that the "professional" manner of her death makes it unlikely that he could ever trace the killer. Besides, Meyer counsels, "Being an adult means accepting those situations where no action is possible." But McGee will have none of that. Steadfastly refusing Meyer's offer of assistance, he vows to go it alone: "Now there was nothing left to save but myself. And he couldn't help me there." He empties *The Busted Flush* of all perishables, disconnects the phone, and leaves behind his keys and a note for Meyer in which he announces that if he doesn't return in six months, everything is his. Then he adds ominously: "I have this very strong feeling that I am never coming back here, that this part of my life is ending, or that all of my life is ending."

McGee heads for California and, posing as Tom McGraw, a Florida fisherman searching for his long-lost daughter, eventually locates the Apocrypha Church headquarters in a deserted area near Ukiah. But, instead of praying souls, he encounters an armed patrol on maneuvers. He is quickly spotted and brought to their leader, Mr. Persival, who explains that the group McGee saw was "the militant arm" of the church, composed of graduates of some of the leading guerrilla training centers in the world. McGee (as McGraw) tells his concocted story about searching for his missing daughter and expresses interest in joining Persival's group himself. As a test of his sincerity, he is given a pistol and ordered to shoot an errant church member in the head. Figuring the gun contains only blanks, he complies, but is horrified when the young man falls over dead with a bullet in his head.

Later that night he learns the full extent of the terrorists' nightmarish intentions when one of the cultist members, an ex-hooker named Stella, slips into his bed. Thanks to a sudden bout of impotence (McGee can't get Gretel out of his mind), they decide simply to talk, and she gives him a full account of their plans to blow up gas and oil pipelines, bomb bridges and tunnels, and destroy chemical plants and television stations—all with the purpose of goading the government into more and more repressive tactics, thus stirring up discontent among the populace. The usually apolitical McGee finds himself unwillingly being drawn into a world of evil unlike any he has previously encountered. Despite his assertion that "I know from nothing about terrorism, funny churches, and exotic murder weapons," he finds he is "in it now," and killing the young man seems to have unleashed a kind of blood lust ("Like letting some kind of bad spell out of the bottle," is how he describes it). Just as he was required to assume a new identity as Tom McGraw to infiltrate the cult, he finds he must now also abandon his usual knightly methods in favor of more drastic ones: "The old tin-can knight had too many compunctions, scruples, whatevers. For this caper, I am the iceman."

Anticipating that his cover is about to be blown, McGee decides it is time to escape, but two of the cultists try to stop him. He kills one by smashing him in the head with a rock, then takes the man's gun and shoots his partner. The bloodbath has begun, with McGee himself now cast in the role of the grim reaper, ushering in the apocalypse for the remaining eleven members of the Church of the Apocrypha. One by one he kills them all, including three who are eliminated when he tosses a grenade at their plane. McGee is worried about having to kill the two female members of the group, but MacDonald saves him from undue agony by having one conveniently kill herself when, in attempting to toss a grenade at McGee, she slips and the grenade explodes in the air above her head. The other dies as a result of a blow to the head McGee gave her, although his intention was only to knock her out.

McGee's reaction to all this carnage is uncharacteristic, and more than a little disturbing. MacDonald has taken great care throughout the series to portray McGee as an ethical man, morally sensitive to his actions and their consequences. His own violent acts were usually shown to be both unavoidable and damaging to his self-esteem. For example, in *Amber*, after being forced to kill a man, he remarked, "It numbs, always, even when you keep asking yourself what other choice you had," later adding that "the him or me rationalization is never totally satisfactory." Moreover, McGee's forays into violence usually cost him physically, this being MacDonald's way of making the violence believable and impressing upon McGee (and the reader) the painful reality of suffering. But in *Green*, instead of guilt McGee experiences exhilaration:

> With the ghastly toothy grin of the skull-head of death looking over my shoulder, I was intensely alive. I was alive in every thready little nerve fiber, every capillary. I was tuned to quickness, the world all sharp edges around me, my ears hearing every small sound in the world.

McGee alludes several times to having "a John Wayne day," and the whole episode is treated like a scene from a low-budget Hollywood movie: the good guy in the white hat standing off all those black-hatted bad guys. (It doesn't help any that the terrorists are barely distinguished from one another; MacDonald's usual skill in character-ization fails him here, perhaps intentionally, with the result that the cultists are portrayed as simple two-dimensional figures.) McGee's admission that he was enjoying the "high-riding pleasure of doing some difficult thing far better than [I] expected to be able to do it" only underscores the playacting element of the whole matter. Also adding to the unreal quality of the situation is the fact that McGee escapes unscathed. In his hand-to-hand combats, he usually paid dearly for his efforts; here he walks away from a scene of massive bloodletting without a scratch and with hardly a blemish on his usually sensitive soul.

MacDonald, acknowledging that McGee's recent weltschmerz was becoming a bit tiresome, admitted that his hero "could not have gone on in that vein without boring me. I had to shake him up." It was time, he added, to introduce his hero to some political realities:

> I am trying to open up his world a little bit, to what is going on. In the bright Florida sunshine it is difficult to believe that a flock of school teachers in Iran would pour gasoline around a movie house and incinerate 450 people, mostly children. I have indulged in a lot of social, pseudo-realism in the McGee books. Now I want to try a little bit of the taste of international political realities.

However, having brought McGee face-to-face with the loathsome world of the terrorists, he then has to rescue him from his perilous situation, which involves McGee in one of the bloodiest bloodbaths since Hammett's *Red Harvest*.

In the past it has been sex (and more recently love) which has been the prime regenerative force, the elixir for McGee's soul. Now violence appears to be the remedy and the change is disturbing. For one thing, his desire to avenge Gretel's death notwithstanding, McGee's hunger for revenge seems out of character. The cult members he wipes out, with the exception of Brother Titus, had nothing to do with Gretel's death, which was ordered by their European allies. Furthermore, although the cultists were admittedly planning to launch some despicable acts of terrorism in the future, they have as yet not broken any laws and are in fact already under the close scrutiny of the government, whose future efforts may have been compromised by McGee's actions—which transform him into one of those Avenger-Revenger-Destroyer-Executioner types who go around single-handedly mopping up nasty problems they judge the government too powerless to solve. McGee's previous adventures have shown him to be temperamentally (and ethically) unfit for such a role; his forte is snooping out financial conspiracies, ridding the world of unscrupulous wheeler-dealers and con men, and tending to damsels in distress, all of which demands courage, intelligence, and charm. All he needs in *Green* is a sense of vengeance, plenty of bullets, and loads of luck.

In the epilogue, set six months later, McGee seems to be his old self again: we find him in the attractive company of Lady Vivian Stanley-Tucker, sharing her bed, sailing her yacht, sipping his Boodles gin, and basking in the sunshine—which has been notably absent from the novel up to this point. It is certainly not accidental that McGee's baptism in blood occurred on New Year's Day, for it is clearly MacDonald's intention to show a new McGee emerging from the crucible of his experiences. And McGee himself does assert that he is a new man:

> There was a black, deep, dreadful ravine separating me from all my previous days. Over there on the other side were the pathetic and innocent little figures of world-that-once-was. McGee and his chums. McGee and Gretel. McGee and his toys and visions.
>
> I could not approach the edge of that ravine and look down. Far far below were the bodies of the dead.
>
> And here I was, on this side. This side was today. This side was the crystal taste of icy gin, the brute weight of tropic sun, the tiny beads of sweat on my forearm, the lovely lines of the Magnum Maltese, those white popcorn gulls way out there, afloat after feeding. Viv's glad little cries of love, the way the stars would shine tonight, the way the clams would taste, the way we would fit together as we slept.
>
> I tasted all the tastes of today and felt in me a rising joy that this could be true. I had raised myself up from many madnesses to be exactly what I am. It had become too constant a pain to try endlessly to be what I thought I should become.

If he means by this that he feels renewed at overcoming his grief over Gretel's loss, then the news is welcome. However, his final statement seems to suggest that he also intends to shed the shackles of conscience—which, if true, would be inconsistent with the McGee we have known, the McGee whom Meyer complimented in his previous adventure for genuinely suffering "if you do not live up to your own images of your various selves." If McGee no longer feels the obligation to measure up to what he thinks he should be, then this represents a significant change and a distressing one. The problem is that the change in McGee is asserted rather than fully explained or convincingly dramatized. As has been the case with the previous few books in the series, the reader is left at the end of *Green* to anticipate the next adventure, which, because of McGee's comments here, promises to be one of the most crucial chapters in his ongoing saga.

As interesting as the character of McGee intrinsically is, and as empathic as the reader becomes with the ordeal of his mid-life crisis, it must be admitted that his personal predicament *was* becoming a bit tiresome. In retrospect it is clear that both McGee and his creator needed a book like *Green,* where the orgy of violence and bloodshed could blow the dust off things. At the end of the novel, McGee was left in a state of emotional collapse, but unlike Humpty-Dumpty his fall isn't fatal and he is put back together again in fine shape in *Free Fall in Crimson* (1981). At the same time, MacDonald demonstrates that he too is in fine form, for the novel is one of the best of the McGee books.

Following the death of Gretel and the ensuing bloodbath at the terrorist camp, McGee needed some quiet time, which, surprisingly, has led him to do some un-McGee-type things, like ferrying boats and demonstrating marine equipment. He is even contemplating, of all things, trying to find a nine-to-five job. But when Ron Esterland arrives with a proposition, McGee is more than ready to listen. Esterland reports that almost two years earlier his dying father, a wealthy plastics tycoon, drew up a will leaving the bulk of his estate to his twenty-year-old daughter, Romola, Ron's half sister. The will stipulated that if she were to predecease him (an unlikely prospect), the estate would be used to establish a research foundation. Unexpectedly, Romola is critically injured in a fall from a bicycle and while she lies in a coma in California, Ellis Esterland is beaten to death in what appears to be a mugging at a highway rest stop near Citrus City, Florida. Because he dies shortly before Romola does, the estate, worth $3,500,000 after taxes, goes not to the foundation but to Romola's mother, actress Josie Laurant. That he himself has been denied any inheritance is not Ron Esterland's prime concern; as a successful artist, he doesn't need the money, but he does want answers, for he is bothered by the suspicion that someone might have murdered his dying father to get possession of the estate. He is willing to pay $10,000 for expenses if McGee will find out what really happened.

Esterland's proposition is exactly the tonic McGee needs, for deep inside he knows that the nine-to-five life is not for him, not even in light of the close calls he has recently had: "You can't cut your life back like some kind of ornamental shrub," he decides. "I couldn't put the old white horse out to pasture, hock the tin armor, stand the lance in a corner of the barn. For a little while, yes. For the healing time." And so he agrees to begin sniffing around to see if there is a trail to follow at the edge of the swamp, although he is admittedly a little nervous about having to go "in there, into the mud and the snakes and the gators" if he should find one.

Gradually, methodically, McGee accumulates enough bits and pieces of information—from Anne Renzetti, Ellis Esterland's former personal secretary; Rick Tate, the sheriff's deputy who investigated Esterland's death; Ted Blaylock, a crippled army buddy of McGee's who now runs a motorcycle shop; Dr. Prescott Mullen, Esterland's physician; and actress Lysa Dean, who still hasn't completely forgiven McGee for walking out on her at the end of *Red*—to enable him to conclude that Esterland was indeed murdered. He determines that Esterland went to Citrus City to purchase some hashish recommended by his physician as a way of easing the pain of his cancer. But the drug buy was a setup; Esterland was met, McGee believes, by a pair of bikers, known as Dirty Bob and the Senator, who had arranged to sell him the drugs but who beat him to death instead. The two bikers were once featured actors in a couple of low-budget films, *Chopper Heaven* and *Bike Park Ramble*, directed by Peter Kesner. Kesner, McGee is interested to learn, is Josie Laurant's boyfriend, and the inescapable conclusion is that Esterland was murdered so that Josie would inherit the money Kesner needed to finance his latest project, a movie about hot-air ballooning, currently being filmed on location in Iowa.

His investigative work completed, McGee now has to find a way to verify his suspicions. He pays a visit to Lysa Dean in her luxurious Beverly Hills home, makes his peace with her, and then, armed with a letter she provides identifying him as a consultant for a television series planning to take a backstage look at the entertainment industry, heads for Rosedale Station, Iowa. He meets Peter Kesner, listens to his windy proclamations about the artistic statement he is trying to make in his new film, entitled *Free Fall,* and is even pressed into emergency duty as a crew member of one of the balloons featured in the movie. His exquisite pleasure at the serene excitement of the balloon ride is abruptly shattered, however, when the pilot, Joya Murphy-Wheeler, apparently mistaking him for the FBI agent she was expecting, tells him some sordid details about the late-night activities on the set, in which unsuspecting local girls are lured into a trailer and forced to become starring actresses with biker Dirty Bob in pornographic videotapes. Up to now there has been no sense of urgency to McGee's mission; the solution to the murder of a dying man isn't a pressing matter, nor has he any personal stake in the case. Conditions have now changed dramatically, however, for he is no longer faced simply with a puzzle from the past but with the ongoing corruption of naive young girls, a situation reminiscent of his very first case, where he sought to end Junior Allen's debasement of vulnerable young females. McGee now understands the import of Lysa Dean's warning that Josie and Kesner are "what they mean when they talk about a bucket of worms."

But before McGee can make a move, the citizens of Rosedale Station become aroused. The fifteen-year-old girl whose experience prompted Joya's complaints to the FBI is killed in a traffic accident, following which a friend of hers confesses to the local authorities the details about what went on at night at the film site. On the morning of the final day of shooting, several carloads of angry local residents, armed with tire irons, ball bats, and two-by-fours, descend on the set and begin flailing at everyone in sight. McGee narrowly escapes by climbing into the basket of one of the balloons as it is about to take off with Kesner and Linda Harrigan, one of the stuntwomen, inside. As the balloon heads for some high-tension wires, McGee bails out. Linda isn't as lucky, for Kesner pushes her out and her seventy-foot free fall proves fatal. McGee then watches in horror as the basket of the balloon hits the wires and explodes into a ball of flame, Kesner's burning body floating to the ground like a dying cinder.

The carnage is extensive—four movie people and one local youth dead; one female balloonist crippled; twelve local high school seniors in custody. Ironically, the tragedy is soon transformed into legend, as Josie Laurant begins touring the country with a selection of scenes from Kesner's unfinished film, now being hailed by the critics as a cinematic masterpiece, a "rhapsody of form and motion." McGee, happy to be free of the whole bunch, is able to report to Esterland that his suspicions about his father's death were correct: he was murdered by Dirty Bob as a favor to Kesner for having made him a popular cult hero. Unfortunately, Dirty Bob's present whereabouts are unknown; the last time McGee saw him he was floating safely away from the free-for-all on the movie set in another of the hot-air balloons.

Readers of MacDonald's novels know that loose ends have a nasty habit of turning up to cause trouble again, and *Crimson* contains one of the most gruesome examples of that. First, Jean Norman, one of the performers featured in the after-hours tapings, whose testimony is crucial in the indictment of Dirty Bob, is kidnapped from the drug rehabilitation center where she was being treated, and is later found murdered. Then Joya Murphy-Wheeler, the woman who first contacted the FBI about the taping session, is raped and murdered. Finally, despite McGee's repeated warnings to her about Dirty Bob, Lysa Dean and the Korean couple who lived with her are also found brutally slain in her home. Dirty Bob has been a very busy man and the next name on his list is McGee's.

In his younger days, McGee would have tried, as he puts it, "to hero this thing myself," but now, wiser and more mature, he decides he would rather be safe than sorry, so he gets in touch with one of his biker contacts and recruits two of his best men. (Significantly, McGee earlier also confessed after being seduced into a brief fistfight with a biker that "I wanted no part of any OK Corral syndrome. I had long outgrown that kind of testicular lunacy.") The three of them wait patiently aboard *The Busted Flush* until eventually Dirty Bob shows up, but he surprises McGee by arriving with a gun pointed at Meyer's back. He disarms McGee and is about to kill him with a steak knife when one of McGee's backups, who has been hiding in a storage locker, emerges and throws a knife at Dirty Bob, killing him a split second before he is himself shot in the chest.

Possessed of one of MacDonald's most effective plots, *Crimson* deftly switches from detection, with McGee painstakingly digging up the clues that eventually solve the baffling crime, to dramatic action sequences (notably McGee's narrow escape from the rampaging mob), to spine-tingling terror as McGee awaits his turn in Dirty Bob's murderous campaign. Into this fabric MacDonald also weaves such interesting features as behind-the-scenes glimpses at the biker subculture, at the controlled chaos of location filmmaking, and at both the intricacies and simple pleasures of hot-air ballooning. Completing the rich variety of the novel is a full gallery of uniquely interesting characters.

What is so remarkable about MacDonald's talent for characterization is that while his novels typically feature a Villain and a Beautiful Woman, he manages to avoid duplication by each time creating fresh figures to play the standard roles. The villains in *Crimson* are a case in point. A product of broken homes and reformatories, Dirty Bob became an outlaw biker, finding in its brotherhood his first real family. Luck then smiled at him for the first time in his life when Peter Kesner hired him to play a featured role in his biker movies, and he soon became a cult figure. "He had been pulled up out of the great swamp of common folk and placed on a hilltop," explains Meyer, and he vowed that he would "never return to the wicked ways of his prior life." But when he saw the opportunity, he repaid Kesner the only way he knew how by killing Esterland after learning that this would enable Kesner to obtain the money he needed to finance his new film. With Kesner now dead and his newly acquired respectability in ruins, Dirty Bob vows revenge against all those he holds responsible for the destruction of his prosperous new life. Unlike some of MacDonald's previous avatars of inexplicable evil, Dirty Bob is presented as an all too credible villain, a dangerous loser whom fate first rewarded, then ruthlessly rejected.

Although Peter Kesner is not a villain in the conventional sense, there is an aura of amorality about him that is deeply disturbing. While he did not directly order Dirty Bob to kill Esterland, he countenanced it and was more than willing to profit by it. And while he isn't personally ravaging Iowa farmgirls in front of the cameras, he is encouraging Dirty Bob's efforts, for he needs the cash that sales of the tapes bring. What is so unnerving about Kesner is that the motive behind all his actions is not greed but art. He is so wrapped up in his theories of cinematic art that he becomes ethically blinded to the moral implications of his acts. When McGee attempts to discuss Esterland's death or Dirty Bob's late-night activities, Kesner dismisses the subject, brushing him off with the comment that "Nothing about this conversation is important." Kesner is a perverted example of the statement William Faulkner once made about the primacy of art: "If a writer has to rob his mother, he will not hesitate; the 'Ode on a

Grecian Urn' is worth any number of old ladies." Kesner will stop at nothing in the furtherance of his art, which in his case is nothing more than exploitation films. But in one of the ironies of our time, his films achieve legendary status, prompting Meyer's sardonic observation about "the artistic conundrum" we are faced with: "How, in these days of intensive communication on all levels, can you tell talent from bullshit?"

Fortunately, to balance his encounters with the likes of Dirty Bob and Kesner, there is the life-affirming presence of Anne Renzetti, the instrument of McGee's recovery from the severe emotional trauma inflicted by the death of Gretel Howard. Anne is the first woman after Gretel for whom he feels any attraction (although at five-foot-two she is not his usual type), but the feeling is not mutual, for she is romantically involved with Prescott Mullen, Ellis Esterland's physician. But as luck would have it, McGee happens to be with her in the lobby of the hotel she manages when the handsome young doctor arrives. McGee watches her joy at their reunion abruptly vanish when Mullen introduces her to his new bride. Hurt, humiliated, and "all a-hum with ready. She was up to the splash rails with electric ready," Anne turns to McGee as a consolation prize (Meyer refers to him as "the catcher in the awry"). This fluky and, from McGee's point of view, fortuitous incident marks the beginning of a deep and emotionally enriching relationship.

Anne is no wounded duckling; she is mature, independent, self-assured, confident in her sexuality, and rightfully proud of her accomplishments as manager of the Eden Beach Hotel in Naples, Florida. Thanks to her organizational skills, she has turned the operation into a model of well-run efficiency. Although she isn't coy with McGee, she is cautious, anxious to avoid doing anything that might jeopardize her authority or standing with her employees. She is, most importantly, not the type of woman who requires any of McGee's usual therapy and thus can herself be the instrument of his restoration, offering the kind of emotionally satisfying relationship he needs. And because she is neither killed nor goes off to seek her own happiness at the end, the possibility of a continuing relationship with McGee exists. (Given the fate of her predecessors, there is also an element of suspense as to what MacDonald might have in store for her.)

Crimson is a restorative book, both for McGee and for his creator. Thanks to Anne, McGee is able to put grief behind him and regain a measure of personal happiness; furthermore, his success in solving the murder of Ellis Esterland demonstrates that he has lost none of the old skills and also affirms Ted Blaylock's observation that McGee is "too used to conning the world, knocking heads, saving maidens" to retire to the quiet life permanently: "You could lose an arm and a foot and an ear," he tells McGee, but he had no doubts that "when they rang the bell, you'd still slide down the pole and hop onto the truck." Nor has MacDonald lost any of *his* own skills, *Crimson* displaying an assuredness and vigor lacking in some of the recent books. Whatever fears one might have had that MacDonald was tiring of the McGee books are soundly disproved by the zest and confidence that inform the novel.

Like many of the recent books in the series, *Crimson* ends with an unresolved situation that anticipates the future, but in this case the one whose future is uncertain is Meyer, not McGee. For a while, it looked as if McGee was going to have to make a radical accommodation and adjust to becoming a genuine businessman, having inherited half interest in Ted Blaylock's motorcycle shop following his death late in *Crimson*. But he managed to get rid of his share, thus preserving his beach-bum status. Meyer isn't so lucky, as the blows to his self-image are more serious and not so easily remedied. When Dirty Bob used him as a shield to gain access to McGee, Meyer became so immobilized by the ultimate fear that his life was about to end, and then so shamed by his failure to live up to the image he had fashioned for himself (an image, McGee observes, that was too closely patterned on Meyer's image of him), that McGee becomes deeply concerned about his friend's emotional state. He tells Anne that he'll have to look for a situation that will permit Meyer to regain his drooping self-confidence and reaffirm his self-worth. This augurs well for the continuation of the series, for not only is Meyer promised a chance to redeem himself, MacDonald's loyal readers are assured that the series will continue. And if *Crimson* is any indication, there should be no concern that MacDonald's mastery of the form that has made him one of the best known of all popular writers is in any danger of slackening.

7

The Character
of Travis McGee

Despite his longstanding reluctance to become tied down to a series character, MacDonald surely must have been pleased by at least one distinct advantage of the situation, namely the opportunity to create a character with the kind of depth, complexity, and credibility that comes only when one is dealing with a recurring hero. In a continuing series, the writer can put his protagonist through a wide range of adventures, thereby revealing dimensions of his character impossible to do in a single book. Furthermore, as the series extends over a period of time, the author also has an opportunity to trace the growth and development of his hero's personality. A simple approach would be to make the hero a carbon copy of himself in each successive adventure; instead, MacDonald has created a fictional character whose gradual evolution over the course of the series has made him so lifelike, so credible, that he seems to transcend the boundaries of the stories in which he appears.

MacDonald had an entire biography of McGee in mind when he began the series and intended to drop bits of information about his hero's background into the books as he went along. However, he quickly decided it didn't feel right to be specific about McGee's early years, family, education, and so on. Too much information about his background would, in his judgment, limit him and "too much depiction would corrode the magic." Nevertheless, alert readers can construct at least the bare outlines of McGee's early years. Of Irish descent (his mother's maiden name was Mary Catherine Devlin), McGee spent his childhood in Chicago, served in the army during the Korean war, and came home to discover that his older brother, with whom he planned to go into business, was driven to suicide by financial losses caused by unidentified individuals against whom McGee eventually gained revenge. Although his reasons for becoming a "salvage consultant" are never revealed, it is likely that avenging his brother's death played a key role in his choice of career. The only real job he has ever held, as far as we know, was a two-year stint as a professional football player, his career as a tight end prematurely cut short by an injury.

Despite the sketchiness of his background, there is plenty of information about him once the series begins. Readers interested in a catalogue of details about McGee are directed to "The Special Confidential Report," a thirty-four-page supplement to the *JDM Bibliophile* compiled in 1979 by longtime MacDonald fans Jean and Walter Shine. Contained therein is every relevant fact available about McGee, Meyer, and *The Busted Flush*. One can find information about each and every physical injury McGee has suffered, his personal habits (he carefully adds all restaurant tabs, always travels first-class in airplanes, never sits in the front row of ballets), his special talents (he can hold his breath underwater for three minutes, is an excellent mimic), all the places he has been since 1960, the names of his friends, the women he has slept with, and the men he has killed. There is virtually no detail about McGee mentioned in any of the novels in the series that is not included somewhere in the Shines' report.

Like all of us, however, McGee is much more than a summary of the statistics that can be gathered about him. What makes him such an appealing figure to his many readers is his complex personality, and to understand that one has to look beyond statistics. In *Pink*, McGee mentions "the three unholy McGees—the one I try not to be, and the one I wish I was, and the one I really am." In order to understand the real McGee, one must examine the tension between the other two McGees, between the opposing images of himself as hero ("the one I wish I was") on the one hand and as fallible and sometimes failed human being ("the one I try not to be") on the other. MacDonald once observed that "The man who is utterly certain of himself and his mission is fool, saint, or psychopath." McGee is none of these, just a man struggling to reconcile his human frailties and self-doubts with his idealistic self-image. The result is a hero with both larger-than-life dimensions as well as a realistic sense of his human imperfections, a hero whose vulnerabilities and uncertainties are every bit as important as his virtues.

In the first several books in the series McGee, struggling to define himself, leans heavily on self-advertisement, trumpeting himself in bold and brassy terms: "McGee, that pale-eyed, wire-haired, girl-finder, that big shambling brown boat-bum who walks beaches, slays small fierce fish, busts minor icons, argues, smiles and disbelieves, that knuckly scar-tissued reject from a structured society"; "shopworn beach bum, a marina gypsy, a big shambling sharpshooter without an IBM card to his name"; "beach-bum McGee, the big chopped-up, loose-jointed, pale-eyed, wire-haired, walnut-hided rebel—unregimented, unprogrammed, unimpressed"; "that big brown loose-jointed, wire-haired beach rambler, that lazy fish-catching, girl-watching, grey-eyed iconoclastic hustler"; and so on. After a while he begins to sound like a carnival barker touting one of nature's oddities. ("He walks, he talks, he crawls on his belly like a reptile!") His verbal excesses are enough to make a dust jacket blurb-writer blush.

At the same time, woven throughout these same books are an equal number of passages that express the idealistic rather than the hedonistic side of McGee; but where there is a puffed-chest sound to the descriptions of the fun-loving side of his nature, there is an embarrassed tone about the references to his idealism. When he talks about riding to the rescue of a damsel in distress, for example, he speaks in self-deprecating terms: his armor is always "rusty" and "tomato-can"; his sword "tinfoil"; his lance "crooked"; and, as a self-styled "tin-horn Gawain," he invariably describes himself as "ga-lumphing" off on his "spavined steed" to do battle with evil dragons. Although acknowledging that he sometimes behaves like Don Quixote, he is reluctant to invoke his patron saint directly, preferring instead such circumlocutions as "noble brave name Kay-Hoe-Tee." He admits to a desire to become a "true hero," then undercuts it by confessing that "whenever I hear that word, the only hero I can think of is Nelson Eddy, yelling into Jeanette's face. And wearing his Yogi Bear hat." Defensive about his heroic inclinations, perhaps embarrassed by the anachronistic flavor of his impulses, he seeks the safety of an ironic stance.

Gradually McGee's inflated self-advertisements disappear, although he continues to fret about his actions, both professional and
private, questioning why he needs "some cachet of importance in this
world of wall-to-wall flesh in the weekend livingroom where the
swingers courteously, diligently, skillfully, considerately hump one
another to the big acid beat of the hifi installation." Is it, he wonders,
because he is "still impaled upon some kind of weird Puritan dilemma,
writhing and thrashing about, wrestling with an outdated, old-time,
inhibiting and artificial sense of sin, guilt, and damnation"? The answer
of course is yes, he is indeed guided by an old-time sense of morality.
While acknowledging the occasional urge for dissipation, he recognizes
that beneath all his bluster there beats the heart of a true moralist
motivated by a desire to help others and guided by what some might
see as an incongruous sense of honor and duty. Meyer once observed
that if McGee could only overcome his "ditherings about emotional
responsibility" he would be a far happier man, but he would also be
a far less interesting one. McGee eventually accepts the fact that he
is "an ant with a grasshopper syndrome," untemperamentally suited
to a life of uninterrupted leisure. The more one knows about McGee,
the more obvious it becomes that retirement is the aberration, the
temporary hiatus in his quixotic mission, not, as he would have us
believe, the other way around.

By evoking Quixote, McGee identifies himself with the tradition
of the American private eye, at least as the figure has evolved ever
since Philip Marlowe self-consciously likened himself to the knight in
the stained-glass window on the opening page of *The Big Sleep*. In
his sense of mission, his willingness to risk life and limb for his clients,
his stalwart defense of the defenseless, and his faithful adherence to
a private code of honorable behavior, McGee resembles the conventional private eye, although certain of his personality traits, attitudes,
and patterns of behavior call to mind other fictional antecedents. His
crusades against the rich, for example, remind us of Robin Hood; his
semi-exotic life-style and romantic adventures have something of a
James Bond flavor to them; his successful awakening of a number of
Sleeping Beauties from their sexual torpor qualifies him as a kind of
modern Prince Charming. MacDonald has effectively combined the
essential qualities of the classic private eye with several of these other
heroic patterns to create a character of refreshingly unique dimensions.

Like most private eyes McGee is an outsider who lives on the fringes of society, although in his case it is a matter of choice rather than circumstance. He has willfully rejected middle-class conventions, forsaking wife, family, split-level home, the whole nine-to-five American way of life. "Nothing can slow the reflexes," he argues, "like the weight of mortgages, withholding, connubial contentment, estate program, regular checkups and puttering around your own lawn." Only an unencumbered individualist like McGee would be free to accept the kind of work he does, free to take the dangerous risks he does.

But unlike the Continental Op, Philip Marlowe, Lew Archer, and other traditional private eyes, McGee is not alienated from normal human relationships. At the conclusion of a case, all Philip Marlowe had to look forward to was a "blank wall in a meaningless room in a meaningless house." McGee, on the other hand, enjoys an enviable life in the Florida sunshine aboard his well-equipped houseboat. Moreover, his private life is far from empty, enriched as it is by his friendship with the inestimable Meyer and enlivened by his relationships with all those beautiful young women who are inevitably ready, willing, and able to jump into bed with him. (MacDonald once confessed that if he weren't able to figure out a way to get rid of McGee's women, *The Busted Flush* would sink under all the excess weight.) Despite the appearance of paradise, McGee's life-style does exact a stiff penalty. Although he admits to no regrets over refusing to "pull an oar in the flagship of life" by accepting a real job, McGee on occasion confesses to a longing for some of the simple pleasures of the structured life he is denied:

> I am apart. Always I have seen around me all the games and parades of life and have always envied the players and the marchers. I watch the cards they play and feel in my belly the hollowness as the big drums go by, and I smile and shrug and say, Who needs games? Who wants parades? The world seems to be masses of smiling people who hug each other and sway back and forth in front of a fire and sing old songs and laugh into each others faces, all truth and trust. And I kneel at the edge of the woods, too far to feel the heat of the fire.

Why, one might well ask, would anyone forsake this, as well as willingly put up with the staggering amount of physical abuse McGee does, just to earn an extra few months of early retirement? (During the course of the series, he is clubbed, knifed, shot at, almost run over, nearly drowned, attacked by lesbians and Doberman pinschers, and drugged with LSD, among other things.) Although he claims to be a businessman and insists he accepts jobs only when there is a good prospect of making a sizable fee—"I like to ride to the rescue when I think that's where the money is"—most of his adventures are motivated simply by a desire to help a friend in need. In fact, only once, in *Purple*, is he actually in the position of a man looking for work. Furthermore, a quick tally of the fees he has received since his first case reveals that he has earned in excess of half a million dollars, far more than enough to enable him to retire permanently aboard *The Busted Flush* for the rest of his life, especially if he would allow Meyer to invest his money for him. Money is obviously not McGee's primary motivation. The fact that he receives fees for his efforts allows him to preserve his self-respect as a con artist, but like much of his bluster it is only his way of rationalizing his romanticism.

Perhaps the simplest explanation for his motivation comes in a statement he makes early in the series that "people hurting people is the original sin." McGee is invariably roused from his retirement by indignation over one individual's mistreatment of another. Unlike many private eyes, he is not committed to the pursuit of truth as an end in itself nor obsessed with justice in the abstract; a self-styled salvage consultant, he is simply out to right a wrong done to someone on a personal level. His interests are restoration and restitution; prosecution and punishment he leaves to the authorities: "I just stand back of the foul line and when something happens that doesn't get called by the referees, I sometimes get into the game for a couple of minutes," is his disarming way of describing what he does. McGee is a crusader not against Injustice in the abstract but against those who have committed acts of injustice against individuals unable to fight back on their own. That he is usually amply rewarded for his efforts is a bonus, not his raison d'être.

His narratives are filled with incidents which demonstrate that McGee's quixotism is an integral part of his personality and is not limited solely to the interests of his clients: in *Red*, for example, he goes out of his way to preserve Jocelyn Ives's illusions that her blackmailing father was involved in important government work; in *Gold* he gives away the bulk of the money he receives from the sale of the gold statuettes to Shaja Dobrak so she can purchase her husband's release from prison in Hungary; in *Brown* he spares Bridget Pike from full disclosure about the extent of her husband's evil activities; in *Yellow* he rescues a drunk from the prostitute who is about to rob him; in *Lemon* he defends Carrie Milligan's sister from what he considers to be unjust and inflated mortuary expenses; in *Turquoise* he gets into a fight with a man who is bullying one of his employees; and so on. Although McGee may at times worry about being an anachronism, it is clear from such examples that as long as he is around, the spirit of Don Quixote lives on.

McGee is realistic enough, of course, to know he cannot be a redeemer and rid the world of evil. If protest-marching could accomplish that he would gladly parade around with a placard proclaiming his own personal Commandments:

UP WITH LIFE. STAMP OUT ALL SMALL AND LARGE INDIGNITIES. LEAVE EVERYONE ALONE TO MAKE IT WITHOUT HURTING. LOWER THE STANDARD OF LIVING. DO WITHOUT PLASTICS. SMASH THE SERVOMECHA-NISMS. STOP GRABBING. SNUFF THE BREEZE AND HUG THE KIDS. LOVE ALL LOVE. HATE ALL HATE.

But he is too pragmatic for such a meaningless gesture. "Am I," he then wonders, "supposed to go out with my brush and yellow soap and scrub clean the wide grimy world?" This too is clearly impractical. Well, then, he asks himself, "If you can't change everything, why try to change any part of it?" This is the key question, the answer to which reveals the essence of his character: "Because, you dumbass, when you stop scrubbing away at that tiny area you can reach, when you give up the illusion you are doing any good at all, then you start feeling like this." In other words, while acknowledging that he can do nothing about Evil with a capital *E*, he nevertheless feels an obligation to do what he can to combat evil with a small *e*—evil on a personal scale. As long as he can accomplish something beneficial for those who have been injured, misused, or taken advantage of, he is able to satisfy his romantic compulsions and justify his stretches of early retirement.

Although McGee isn't as addicted to his work as, say, Hammett's Continental Op (who says of his job: "I don't know anything else, don't enjoy anything else, don't want to know or enjoy anything else"),

he does admit to being hooked on the particular pleasures associated
with his dangerous endeavors: "I'm hooked on the smell, taste, and
feel of the nearness of death and on the way I feel when I make my
move to keep it from happening. If I *knew* I could keep it from
happening, there'd be no taste to it at all." Following an incident in
Copper in which he narrowly escapes being shot, he stops to analyze
his situation as he makes his way toward the place from which the
shots were fired:

> The initial panic had settled into a reliable flow of adrenaline. It is
> my fate and my flaw to have learned too long ago that this is what
> I am about. This is when I am alive and know it most completely.
> Every sense is honed by the knowledge of the imminence of death.
> The juices flow. In the back of my mind I tried to tell myself that
> I had been turned into a murderous machine by the sight of Gretel.
> But it was rationalization. There was a hard joy in this acceptance
> of total risk.

Overcoming the odds against him, cheating death by surviving yet
another close encounter with "the green ripper," performing well in
the presence of the "ghastly toothy grin of the skull-head of death
looking over my shoulder"—these are what produce the intense
personal satisfaction that even righting a wrong cannot do, for these
are the things he does solely for himself.

Ross Macdonald once noted that Lew Archer's character is "so
narrow that when he turns sideways he almost disappears"—Macdonald's intention being to prevent an excessive development of his hero
from detracting from the other elements of plot and theme he regards
as the primary focus of his books. MacDonald's approach is the
opposite. Not that he considers plot, theme, and other characters
unimportant; far from it. But Travis McGee is clearly the main focus
in the novels. MacDonald's intention is to create a strong central
figure around whom the action in each book revolves, and to accomplish
this he has, among other things, striven to give McGee a substantial
private life, a major component of which is the relationship he develops
with a wide variety of women during the course of the novels.

Unlike Philip Marlowe and Lew Archer, for example, who often
appear starved for female companionship, McGee is almost always
involved with a woman (in fact, with over a dozen of them). No paragon

of virtue or model of self-control, McGee is as susceptible to temptation as the next man, and although he ordinarily resists most such enticements of the flesh, he is human enough to have on more than one occasion succumbed to his baser urges. (In one brief period in *Turquoise*, for example, he goes through in rapid succession "two tourist ladies, the new hostess at the Beef'n It, one stewardess, one schoolteacher, and, God save us and help us, one Avon lady.") But McGee is fundamentally monogamous in that he remains faithful to the one woman with whom he is currently involved. MacDonald is not interested in trumpeting McGee's priapic prowess at the expense of his morality; he wants a virile hero, one attracted to and attracted by women, but he doesn't want a *Playboy*-inspired stud who considers women to be little more than gifts from a beneficent God for his exclusive pleasure. McGee's relationships with women, and his constant assessment of their authenticity, comprise a key feature in the novels for they represent a significant measure of his ethical stance.

Early in the series McGee expounds the basic tenet of his sexual philosophy: "Bed is the simplest thing two people can do. If it goes with a lot of other things, it can be important, and if it goes with nothing else, it isn't worth the time it takes." In other words, physical compatibility or mere "interludes of frictive pleasure" aren't enough; he insists on emotional involvement of some sort (and, with increasing frequency in the later novels, on love). Women to McGee are not "pneumatic, hydraulic, terrace toys" designed for his pleasure; a self-described "incurable romantic who thinks the man-woman thing shouldn't be a contest on the rabbit level," he subscribes to the old-fashioned notion that "grabbing something because it looks great is kind of irresponsible. Life is not a candy store."

The other facet which contributes so much to the in-depth portrayal of McGee is that he is more than a simple narrative voice, he is a complete personality with a variety of voices, subject to diverse moods, capable of experiencing the full spectrum of emotions. In addition, thanks to his wide-ranging interests, which encompass far more than a simple fascination with the opposite sex, he is a veritable encyclopedia of almost professional-level knowledge about an impressive array of subjects: animal behavior (including the habits of sharks, Antarctic penguins, bald eagles, Tibetan geese); knife throwing; stamp collecting; photography; hot-air ballooning; treasure hunting; sailing; physiology; art; and a score of other subjects. Such information is not only interesting in its own right, it also serves to depict McGee as a bright and knowledgeable man whose active intelligence is as important as his fists, and as much responsible for his successes as are his more physical attributes.

Unlike Raymond Chandler and Ross Macdonald, who employed their protagonists as devices for handling emotionally charged and deeply personal issues, MacDonald uses McGee as a spokesman for his views and opinions on more public issues. MacDonald had used his fictional protagonists as vehicles for his own views before, but McGee offered him a unique opportunity to employ an effective spokesman in an ongoing forum. According to MacDonald, McGee "whips my dead horses," although he is quick to add that he is not therefore to be identified with his hero in every respect. For one thing, he confesses that he sees the world in shades of gray whereas McGee is able to "see things in black and white and make pronouncements that, heavens, I would never dare say." Moreover, while acknowledging that to give McGee an important opinion with which he did not agree would be "grotesque," that doesn't mean he hasn't allowed his hero a certain amount of individuality, some quirks and habits not his own. "He may like a certain kind of shirt or jacket—that doesn't mean that I like it. He may like a mode of travel that I don't particularly care for. I wouldn't drive that damn car of his around the block."

McGee is fundamentally a maverick, an outsider, a rebel against creeping conformity and standardization and his narratives are spiced with his pungent criticisms of the overwhelming evidence of what he calls our "toboggan ride into total, perfectly adjusted mediocrity." It is in his nature to avoid credit cards, refuse to join organizations, drive a one-of-a-kind car, and even spurn organized religion (which he likens to "being marched in formation to look at a sunset"). McGee was a confirmed individual long before "doing your own thing" became a watchword in the late 1960s. From his nonconformist perspective, he casts an observant—and often jaundiced—eye on his society, voicing frank and iconoclastic opinions on such controversial matters as America's racial crisis, the severity of its drug laws, the declining quality of its educational system, the pervasive danger of handguns, etc. Furthermore, he expresses his anger whenever he encounters examples of blatant debasement of America's culture. His stinging comments on mass media, local television newscasts, contemporary architecture, *Playboy* magazine, rock music, the convenience of modern restrooms, and the like reveal his conviction that the price of progress is all too often an inevitable and deplorable decline in quality. Nothing symbolizes his disillusionment better than the sad fate of his beloved Plymouth gin, formerly bottled in England, but now bottled in the United States as a result of its growing popularity. As he opens his final bottle of the original gin, he bemoans its fate:

> There is something self-destructive about Western technology and distribution. Whenever any consumer object is so excellent that it attracts a devoted following, some of the slide rule and computer types come in on their twinkle toes and take over the store, and in a trice they figure out just how far they can cut quality and still increase the market penetration. Their reasoning is that it is idiotic to make and sell a hundred thousand units of something and make a profit of thirty cents a unit when you can increase the advertising, sell five million units, and make a nickel profit a unit. Thus the very good things of the world go down the drain, from honest turkey to honest eggs to honest tomatoes. And gin.

But McGee's strongest feelings and harshest words are reserved for the subject his creator cares most deeply about; namely, the dangers to our threatened planet. Throughout his entire writing career, beginning with some of his early science-fiction stories and suspense novels (*A Flash of Green* was one of the earliest American novels to tackle the theme of our threatened environment openly) and including several nonfiction essays in publications like *Life, Holiday,* and *The Conservationist,* MacDonald has been outspoken on the subject of ecology. In an afterword to a recent collection of his science-fiction tales, *Other Times, Other Worlds,* he states in no uncertain terms his opinion about the urgency of the problem:

> We should think of ourselves as a virulent infection eroding this green planet even while we use it to sustain our teeming life form. When at last it dies—when at last we kill this planet—we die with it. We do not escape the consequences of our own barbarous acts by sailing off into the future. What we do here, we must live with. We must control our numbers and guard our environment or we shall all die, sooner than we might care to guess.

This is essentially the same dire warning that McGee sounds time and again in his narratives.

In MacDonald's view the dangers to our planet are manifold, although each can be traced to what he calls in *A Flash of Green* "the plague of man": overpopulation (according to Meyer's dire observation in *The Green Ripper*, "Of all the people who have ever been alive on Earth, more than half are living right now. We are gnawing the planet bare, and technology can't keep pace with need"); heedless consumption of raw materials; the destruction of natural beauty in the name of progress; the widening gap between the rich and poor nations of the world; unchecked materialism; the poisoning of the very air we breathe. Thanks to the "perpetual farting of the great god Progress," McGee finds that no matter where he travels the air is filled with "smodge, fugg, and schlutch." In *Turquoise* he becomes so outraged at the sight of chemical poisons being belched into the air by a Borden phosphate plant in Bradenton that he climbs atop his soapbox and attempts to enlist the reader directly in his cause: "Anybody can walk into any brokerage house," he advises, "and be told where to look to find a complete list of the names of the directors and where they live. Drop the fellows a line, huh?"

MacDonald is particularly vexed by what he sees happening to Florida. In their shortsighted quest for the tourist dollar, Florida merchants and vendors have all but destroyed those very qualities that attracted newcomers to the state in the first place, in the process turning the state into an ugly network of asphalt, highrises, fast-food restaurants, and littered beaches. It has become so bad in some coastal areas that, according to McGee, "Had I not seen a boat for sale every few hundred yards, I would never have known I was within five hundred miles of salt water." MacDonald's forecast for the future of his adopted state is bleak: "I could not in all conscience paint anything except a most gloomy picture of the future of Florida as a place to live," he recently wrote. "Our growth will stop when Florida, at last, becomes as desirable a place to live as Wheeling, WV, or Scranton, PA, or Jersey City." McGee's unhappiness at presiding over the sad and sorry decline of Florida is as deeply felt and as passionately expressed as the similar lamentations of Philip Marlowe and Lew Archer over the same fate that befell Southern California a generation earlier.

MacDonald has acknowledged that McGee's sermonizing does not appeal equally to all of his readers:

I get as many letters from people saying "Get off your damn soapbox
and get on with the story," as I get letters from people who say,
"Gee, I love all those asides. I don't like the plots and I don't like
all that violence. I just read the books because I like what you say
about things."

But he has no intention of ceasing to use McGee as a mouthpiece for
his views. Indeed, McGee's colorful opinions have become as integral
a part of the fabric of the series as the beautiful women, the seaside
setting, or the pervasive presence of money. Besides, MacDonald is
not about to abandon his conviction that the writer has a certain
responsibility as a citizen to do what he can in his writing to better
society. One of his admitted aims as a writer is to reach those of his
readers who do not read *Audubon, Conservation Digest,* or other such
publications and inform them about such things as the dangers to our
environment. "I know that I'm involved in entertainment," MacDonald
acknowledges, but if the entertainment is built upon "some solid
foundations of awareness of the world," then, he believes, the work
will achieve a resonance that can "alter the internal climate and the
outward perceptions of the reader."

Despite his profound believability, McGee is, like most fictional
heroes, a fantasy figure. His carefree life-style excites our envy, his
amorous adventures with beautiful women fuel our erotic fantasies,
his courage and bravery in action earn our admiration. However,
ethical in behavior, sensitive in personal relationships, and responsible
in social attitudes, McGee is far more complex than a simple two-
dimensional superhero. In his capacity for indignation, his anger at
injustice, his ravings about mediocrity, and his apprehensions about
the future of society, he expresses our hurts, experiences our sadness,
articulates our concern more effectively than we can. It is this, coupled
with his honorable struggle to be a good and decent man, that
convinces us that heroism comprises more than simple courage and
physical strength. Exemplifying as he does the possibilities for morally
sensitive behavior and socially responsible attitudes, he raises our
hopes for ourselves by reminding us of the best that is in us.

8

MacDonald's Artistry

In an introduction to *Night Shift*, a collection of stories by Stephen King, MacDonald advised budding authors to read everything they could get their hands on but cautioned them to reserve contempt for those writers who "conceal ineptitude with long words, Germanic sentence structure, obtrusive symbols, and no sense of story, pace, or character." Contained in his advice is a listing of the very ingredients that make MacDonald's own prose so effective: concrete diction; clear and direct sentences; an avoidance of obtrusive rhetorical devices; brilliantly believable characters; and mastery of story and pace.

To begin with, MacDonald is a gifted storyteller, a talent he learned early in his career as a young writer trying to break into the pulp market, which placed a premium on fast-paced, action-filled narratives. Neither as byzantine as Ross Macdonald's nor as loose and desultory as Raymond Chandler's, MacDonald's plots are well-woven, artfully constructed arrangements of action sequences. They are neither needlessly complex nor do they exist simply to obscure the identity of the villain until the final chapter. A master at creating and sustaining mystery, suspense, tension, and drama, MacDonald understands all the tricks of readability; turning the pages in one of his novels is always a pleasure, never a duty. And although each of the McGee books adheres to the general outlines of a simple recurring pattern— McGee is roused from *The Busted Flush* to retrieve or restore some valuable item for a person in distress, usually a woman, and then retires to his boat again at the completion of his mission—MacDonald is skillful enough to avoid duplicating situations. Finally, his plots generate enough narrative energy to keep the reader moving at a brisk pace throughout the books, yet are flexible enough to allow for the inclusion of quiet, gentle scenes, as well as the many mini-sermons that have become such a characteristic feature of the McGee books. MacDonald is especially careful with his digressions, usually waiting, he confesses, "until I hit a point where you have to know what's going to happen next—then I can back off and propagandize you, knowing that you'll stay there," and thus insuring that the narrative momentum is not interrupted too seriously.

As important as story is, however, it isn't everything to MacDonald; his novels always feature believable characters about whom, thanks to his skill in making them real as well as interesting, the reader comes to care deeply. His success in achieving such credibility in his characterizations can be traced to the same feature that makes his prose so effective—concretization of detail. Normally he introduces a character by focusing on a single vivid detail in order to give that figure a substantial presence on the page. "If a vague gray truck hits a vague gray man, his blood on gray pavement will be without color or meaning," MacDonald once observed. To avoid such haziness, he relies on specific details to give clear outlines to his characters, thereby securing a more deeply felt response in the reader, for, according to MacDonald, "when a real yellow truck hits Melvin, man or rooster, we feel that mortal thud deep in some visceral place where dwells our knowledge of our own oncoming death."

According to one accounting, there are over 130 female characters alone who have speaking or functional roles in the McGee series— which gives some idea of the challenge facing MacDonald of individualizing his characters, especially the female ones. As quickly as possible, he gives each a physical description providing specifics as to size, heft, skin texture, hair color, manner of laughing, sound of voice, and the like. It is such concrete details as skin "the color of weak butterscotch," eyes that are "crystal mint, that clear perfect green of childhood Christmas, the green you see after the first few licks have melted the sugar frost," hair that is "red-blond-gold-russet," a body aroma tinged with "a slight coppery odor of perspiration," eyelashes "like little curved and clipped bits of enameled black wire," or chests that are "styled for abundant lactation" and blouses that are not, that remain in the mind. Once a visual picture is established, MacDonald can then turn to the more subtle elements that differentiate the female characters not by their endowments but by their individual hopes, dreams, fears, beliefs, values, experiences, etc., all the things that make them separate, unique, and interesting individuals and which allow us to respond to them on an emotional level.

Blessed with a finely tuned ear for the sound of authentic speech, MacDonald can also define and differentiate characters by such things as dialect (Boo Waxwell in *Orange*, for example, speaks in a backwoods dialect unlike any other character in MacDonald's works: "You gone go hot up some food for ol Boo. He's gone loose these boys for a time, and you play any games, he goes eenymeenyminey, and whichever one it comes out, ol Boo blows his kneebones to pebbles") or verbal eccentricity (Mansfield Hall in *Turquoise* punctuates all his statements with loud "haws"). Sometimes he uses a single memorable physical feature (Al Stanger in *Gray* has breath that smells "like a cannibal bat") or a striking image to render a character on a single stroke. For example, McGee's description of Arthur Wilkinson's new bride's smile as being as brilliant "as a brand-new vermin trap ordered from Herter's catalogue" succinctly captures her soon-to-be-revealed duplicity. Sometimes a character is capsulized in terms that elevate him to the level of an archetype, as in this brief description of a typically handsome but incompetent local television newscaster: "A youth with many tricks with the eyebrows barked world affairs at us. He's the one that pronounces it Veet Nee-yam."

MacDonald is much too interested in his characters, however, to stop at the physical details that distinguish one from another. Once he succeeds in creating a strong initial impression of a character's appearance, he moves on to capture, in his words, "the glories and the stinks, the shame and the pride, the doubts and the angers, the deceits and the pity" of humankind. As a creator of character, he displays an anthropologist's curiosity about man and the various structures of his communities, a psychologist's fascination with the myriad complexities of personality and motivation, a poet's sensitivity to the needs and desires of the human heart, and a philosopher's ultimate concern with the meaning of it all. Although one encounters the full spectrum of humanity in his novels, it is possible to divide his characters into two main groups: manipulators, usually men, who are driven by the need to accumulate, compound, launder, or extort money; and victims, usually women, who are conned, abused, and mistreated by them. By concentrating on these two types, MacDonald is able to examine in novel after novel two of his primary interests: the focus on victimized women allows him to display the wondrous variety of the female species while exploring the ecstasies of male-female relationships; the focus on the manipulators allows him to depict in gloomy detail the moral grubbiness of everyone from unsavory con men and common swindlers to respectable real estate agents and fast-buck merchants who are out to cheat the unwary, defraud the unsuspecting, exploit the consumer, ravage the land, and debase the quality of modern life.

But whether they be heroes or villains, saints or sinners, featured performers or background figures, MacDonald's characters are invariably believable and interesting. Thanks to his instinctive choice of the right gesture, mannerism, speech pattern, quirk, and tic, even the most insignificant character is allowed his brief and shining moment in the limelight before being retired to the obscurity of the background once more. In the richness of his characterizations and the perceptive delineation of their innermost selves, MacDonald creates a world of recognizable beings who are driven by the same emotions—fear, love, hate, greed, loneliness, compassion—that compel us all. More than any other feature, it is MacDonald's skill in creating credible and convincing characters that gives his work the look and feel of solid reality.

An emphasis on the concrete and specific also distinguishes his prose style. His descriptions, for example, illustrate the effectiveness of the carefully chosen word and the telling detail. Although some of his best descriptions are pithy, as in this striking picture of people walking along a wintry Chicago street—"All the trees looked dead, and all the people looked like mourners"—or in this brief portrait of a small Adirondack mountain town—"It was the sort of town that you do not particularly want to live in, but wish you had come from"—his impressionistic talents are best displayed in his more extended descriptions, which crackle and gleam with sensuous detail. In the first of these, from *The Beach Girls* (1959), MacDonald is simply describing the intense heat of a summer day:

The breeze died. The high white sun leaned its tropic weight on the gaudy vacation strip of Florida's East Coast, so that it lay sunstruck, lazy and humid and garish, like a long brown sweaty woman stretched out in sequins and costume jewelry. The sun baked the sand too hot for tourist feet. Slow swells clumped onto the listless Atlantic beach. The sun turned road tar to goo, overheated the filtered water in the big swimming pools of the rich and the algaed pools of the do-it-yourself clan, blazed on white roofs, strained air conditioners, turned parked cars into tin ovens, and blistered the unwary. A million empty roadside beer cans twinkled in the bright glare. The burning heat dropped a predictable number of people onto stone sidewalks, of which a predictable number died, drove the unstable further into the jungly wastes of their madness, exposed the pink tongues of all the dogs in the area, redoubled the insect songs in every vacant lot, set the weather-bureau boys to checking the statistics of past performance, and sent a billion billion salty trickles to flowing on sin-darkened skins.

Here, McGee is describing his impressions of another Florida scene:

We went out and explored the city in the fading light of evening, drifting the gray Dodge back and forth through the social and commercial strata, snuffling the flavors of change, the plastic aromas of the new Florida superimposed on the Spanish moss, the rain-sounds of the night peepers in the marsh, the sea smell of low tides, creak of bamboo in light winds, fright cry of the cruising night birds, tiny sirens of the mosquitoes, faraway flicker of lightning silhouetting the circus parade of thunderheads on the Gulf horizon—superimposed on all these old enduring things, known when only Caloosas made their shell mounds and slipped through the sawgrass in their dugouts. Here now was the faint petro-chemical stinkings, a perpetual farting of the great god Progress. And a *wang-dang* thudding of bubblegum rock from the speakers on the poles in the shopping-plaza parking lot. And screech-wheeling vans painted with western desert sunsets. And the lighted banks and the savings-and-loan buildings, looking like Bauhaus wedding cakes.

In passages like these, which are typical examples of his rich evocative prose, the sights, sounds, and smells of the scene all but leap off the page at the reader. In his writing, MacDonald pays close and careful attention to the kind of sensory details that evoke the palpable reality of a scene. Thus his prose resonates with the ever-present sounds of chain saws in the distant woods, bodies smacking into backyard swimming pools, the faint rumble of high-altitude jets, or the barely heard melodies of meadowlarks, sounds that convince us on an instinctive level of the reality of McGee's world.

MacDonald is equally effective in describing scenes of a less tangible nature, such as the intense emotional and physical sensations of a man and woman engaged in lovemaking:

> For a little time she was a separate thing, an object for his hands, something he could be aware of as separate as she flexed and jerked and panted under his touch, as he peeled the gunmetal fabric back from the moonlight white bursting of flesh. And then soon he lost his own identity as never before. They became one creature, wise and knowing in its own sweet uses of itself, catching its breath in the slow hesitant ecstasy of union, then tipping and tilting into itself with a long deep sweet pulse of purpose, blended and knowing and growing. A thin voice called him, in a rising joy and plaintive impatience, and he lifted to it and roared his response and went tumbling after, to die very savagely and then very gently, and then with no movement at all in the deep clench of moonlight, adrift in a silence of bug-whine and toad-sound and distant farm dog, their hearts sobering, a deep breath catching from time to time, and the little symbolic offerings of kisses for the cooling flesh, caresses like the last echoes of a great sound that had filled the world.

Or the distorted perceptions of a mind that has been altered by a dose of an hallucinogenic drug, as McGee's is in *Pink*:

> I was woven into delicious clouds, high and ecstatic on softened hilltops, taking the slow, sweet, aching suffusions of the warm slow drift of great masses of pure color, which moved across me and through me and changed in almost imperceptible ways. I was one, united to pure sensation, everything about me becoming a part of me, a fabulous unity, so that I knew at last the ultimate fact of all existence, knew it and knew that there were no words with which it could be expressed because it was beyond words. I rolled over and stretched my arms into a strange grass, more like hair than grass, metallic blue-green in color, springing out of the soft white earth-flesh; hair-grass thick as pencils, half as tall as a man, making a strange electric tingling wherever it touched my flesh. I rolled and saw leaning to me a golden reaching softness of limbs and

ancient Martian trees—reaching, grasping gently, curling, caressing, taking me up and through brightness and then into a dusky feathery hollow between enormous breasts, into a stroking and fitting and long long gentle never-ending orgasm. . . .

Although one can find numerous examples of colorful similes in MacDonald's writing (for example, shoes that are described as being "worn to a condition as flexible and pliable as an Eskimo wife"), they are not as characteristic of his prose as they are of Chandler's or Macdonald's. Because a striking simile often stands out so vividly on the page that it draws all the attention to itself, MacDonald rejects such rhetorical devices as being overly intrusive: "The flamboyant overblown simile or analogy is like tapping the reader on the shoulder and saying, 'Look how beautiful I'm writing, fella!'" He favors the kind of extended analogy in which the emphasis is not so much on the shock of the image as on the appropriateness of the comparison. In his hands, such comparisons are made less for rhetorical effect than as a way of expressing ideas in imaginatively new terms. Whether he is describing the city of San Francisco as a woman of fading beauty:

> She was like a wild classy kook of a gal, one of those rain-walkers, laughing gray eyes, tousle of dark hair—sea misty, a lithe and lively lady, who could laugh at you or with you, and at herself when needs be. A sayer of strange and lovely things. A girl to be in love with, with love like a heady magic.
> But she had lost it, boy. She used to give it away, and now she sells it to the tourists. She imitates herself. Her figure has thickened. The things she says now are mechanical and memorized. She overcharges for cynical services.

Or how the mind solves a nagging puzzle:

> There is a hairy chimp caged in the back of the mind. The bananas hang out of reach. If you can make him stop leaping and chittering and clacking his angry teeth, make him settle down and look around the cage, usually he can find some boxes which he can pile on top of each other, and some sticks, and some string to tie the sticks together. Then he can climb onto the top box and knock down some bananas.

Or how McGee's head feels when someone gives him a good crack:

I stood up and somebody hit my head on a line drive to third, where it was fielded on one hop and hurled across to force the base runner at second, but he came in spikes high to break up the double play, and the second baseman threw my head over the first baseman and smack into the wall in front of the box seats along the first base line. My head rolled dead, eyes turned completely around so that they looked back into the blackness of my brain where fireworks were on display.

Or simply describing the distinctions of our currency:

A one-dollar bill has a humble and homely look. A five-dollar bill has a few meek pretensions. A ten is vigorous and forthright and honest, like a scout leader. A twenty, held to the ear like a seashell, emits the far-off sound of nightclub music. A fifty wears the faint sneer of race track. It has a portly look, needs a shave, wears a yellow diamond on the little finger. And a hundred is very haughty indeed.

MacDonald achieves striking effects by concretizing and personifying abstract entities.

He also uses his picture-painting facility with words to throw fresh light on complicated and often shopworn subjects, as in this parable in *A Flash of Green* in which he explains how the fast-buck operators have transformed parts of Florida from patches of paradise into scrap heaps:

Once upon a time there was a mountain peak with a wonderful view, so that people came from all over to stand on top of the mountain and look out. The village at the foot of the mountain charged a dollar a head to all tourists. But so few of them could stand on top of the mountain at the same time, they leveled the top of the mountain to provide more room and increase the take. This seemed to work, so they kept enlarging the area on top of the mountain. Finally they had a place up there that would accommodate ten thousand people, but by then the mountain was only forty feet high, and suddenly everybody stopped coming to see the view. This convinced them people were tired of views, so in the name of Progress and a Tourist Economy, they turned the flattened mountain into a carnival area, and every night you could see the lights and hear the music for miles around. They still attracted customers, but it was the kind of people who like carnivals instead of the kind of people who like beauty.

In this manner MacDonald is able to express a complex problem in a clear and effective manner without either patronizing his reader or oversimplifying the issue.

MacDonald once admitted that as a reader what he looked for in the prose of other writers was "a bit of magic . . . a bit of unobtrusive poetry . . . words and phrases [that] really sing." At its frequent best, his own prose possesses this same kind of verbal magic that causes it to sing on the page. The following passage from *Brown*, where McGee is describing the exuberant lovemaking efforts of Helena Pearson, is instructive here, not so much because it illustrates MacDonald's prose at its best but because it evokes an attitude that closely parallels his whole approach to writing:

> There was no cloying kittenishness about her, as that was a style that would not have suited her—or me. She was proud of herself and as bold, jaunty, direct, and demanding as a bawdy young boy, chuckling her pleasures, full of a sweet wildness in the afternoon bunk with the heavy rain roaring on the decks over us, so totally unselfconscious about trying this and that and the other, first this way and that way and the other way, so frankly and uncomplicatedly greedy for joy that in arrangements that could easily have made another woman look vulgarly grotesque she never lost her flavor of grace and elegance.

MacDonald addresses the act of writing with the same boldness, confidence, and unbridled joy that characterizes Helena's lovemaking and yet, like her, he never loses that "flavor of grace and elegance" even when describing the seamier side of life. His aim is economy, his effects achieved by "the careful and selective simplicities"—the result of language that is concrete, vivid, and simple: "The more simple, the more elegant and effective. The more complex and intricate, the more self-conscious and ineffective." Like Hemingway, MacDonald chooses the concrete over the abstract; relying on language that is simple, distinct, and vivid, he constructs passages of simple grace and clarity whose fluidity is perfectly suited to the telling of his fast-paced tales and whose versatility is revealed in prose that can be as gentle as an ocean breeze or as forceful as a fierce hurricane.

Neither as characteristically lean as Hammett's prose nor as extravagantly colorful as Chandler's nor as elegantly poetic as Ross Macdonald's, MacDonald's prose is an effective blend of elements of all three styles. By combining concrete details, unpretentious diction, colorful images, and rhythmically balanced sentences, MacDonald produces a zesty and energetic prose that is enlivened by one of the most authentic and distinctive voices in the genre. As imposing as the figure of McGee is, as exciting as his adventures are, and as socially relevant as his commentaries are, it is MacDonald's crisp, clean prose that gives the books their distinctive flavor. The sheer quantity of his fictional output is evidence that MacDonald is a hardworking writer; the exceptional quality of his vigorous and energetic prose (whose appearance of effortlessness should not lull us into taking it for granted) is evidence that he is a superior craftsman. Only a writer in love with words and enamored of the particular beauties of the language could have produced the richly textured, supple prose that is one of the special pleasures of each MacDonald novel.

In the final analysis, however, MacDonald is no mere storyteller, psychologist, social critic, philosopher, or poet; he is a *novelist*, who combines all these separate interests and talents into works of art that capture and evoke the spirit of his age as effectively as those of any other contemporary writer. Anthony Boucher once observed that "Good detective stories are, as I have often quoted Hamlet's phrase about the players, 'the abstracts and brief chronicles of the time,' ever valuable in retrospect as indirect but vivid pictures of the society from which they spring." For the past three decades, in dozens of novels, MacDonald has been an acute chronicler of the American Dream as it has moved south and taken up residence in the Sun Belt. If his works can be said to have a central theme, it is money: there is perhaps no writer who knows better than he how money works and how it weaves its magic spell over people. His concern is not with the very rich or the very poor but with that segment of the populace driven by avarice to accumulate, often by shady means, all it can. It is such con men, swindlers, and hustlers who provide him with his plots, serve as his villains, and produce the victims for his keenly observed chronicles which, thanks to his concentration on the human factors of each situation, achieve a powerfully compelling emotional resonance.

Like many of his mystery-writing colleagues, MacDonald is

ultimately interested in something more than mere escapist entertainment. Flatly rejecting Jacques Barzun's notion that "anyone who attempts to improve on the mystery genre and make it a real novel suffers from bad judgment," MacDonald asserts with confidence and ample good reason that "No one can tell me that it is not within my authority to try to move my suspense novels as close as I can get to the 'legitimate' novels of manners and morals, despair and failure, love and joy." Whether for the sake of convenience one categorizes his works as mysteries, adventures, or thrillers, it is clear that such labels are inadequate in conveying the full extent of his accomplishment. By creating a substantial body of thoughtful and provocative entertainment for an enormously diverse and widespread audience, MacDonald has justly earned for himself the right to be considered a serious American novelist worthy of the highest distinction.

Notes

References are identified by the page number and the last three words of each quotation. Notes to MacDonald's works are included only where the reference cannot be readily determined from the text. Unless otherwise noted, all references to MacDonald's novels are to the Fawcett editions.

Chapter 1

PAGE	QUOTE	SOURCE
1	and still do	"Master of Suspense," *MD Medical News-magazine*, November 1978, p. 117.
2	with several employers	"John D. MacDonald," *World Authors*, edited by John Wakeman (New York: H. W. Wilson Co., 1975), p. 904.
2	Grande (Big Mouth)	MacDonald, "An Author with a Fan Club," in *Maybe You Should Write a Book*, edited by Ralph Daigh (Englewood Cliffs, N.J.: Prentice-Hall, 1977), p. 136.
2	me. Not ever.	Ibid.
3	before retiring them	MacDonald, *The House Guests* (Garden City, N.Y.: Doubleday, 1965), p. 24.
3	and *do it*	Joseph Haas, "Maestro of the Mystery," *Panorama–Chicago Daily News*, September 6–7, 1969, p. 4.
3	letters of rejection	MacDonald, *The House Guests*, p. 25.
5	improved were sold	MacDonald, "Introduction and Comment," *Clues* 1 (Spring 1980), p. 65.
5	practice this way	*JDM Bibliophile* 23 (January 1979), p. 18.

PAGE	QUOTE	SOURCE
7	Great American storyteller	Quoted on cover of *The Scarlet Ruse* (Greenwich, Conn.: Fawcett Gold Medal, 1973).
7	novelist in America	Quoted on cover of *The Empty Copper Sea* (New York: Fawcett Gold Medal, 1978).
7	tomb of Tutankhamen	Kurt Vonnegut, Jr., "He Comes to Us One by One and Asks What the Rules Are," *Chicago Tribune Book World*, July 15, 1973, Section 7, p. 3.
7	than Saul Bellow	Quoted by Clarence Petersen in "A MacDonald Festival: Happy Number Sixty-three, John D.!," *Chicago Tribune Book World*, July 15, 1973, Section 7, p. 1.
8	is greatly reduced	*JDM Bibliophile* 11 (August 1969), p. 14.
8	the words appear	MacDonald, interview with Robert Cromie, 1969.
8	in every way	Ed Hirshberg, " 'Sherlock Holmes Was a Smart-Ass' and Other Diverse Opinions," *1979 Writer's Yearbook* (Cincinnati: Writer's Digest Publications, 1979), p. 38.
9	of each day	Daigh, *Maybe You Should Write a Book*, p. 139.
9	to feel wrong	Ibid.
9	out of writing	Petersen, "A MacDonald Festival," p. 5.
10	my machine going	Daigh, *Maybe You Should Write a Book*, p. 141.

Chapter 2

12	get the profits	Petersen, "A MacDonald Festival," p. 2.
12	craftsmen of crime	Anthony Boucher, *New York Times Book Review*, November 3, 1957, p. 57.
12	instead of telling	MacDonald, "The Institute," *New York Times Book Review*, August 22, 1976, p. 18.
13	are too glib	Wakeman, *World Authors*, p. 904.
13	calls "terminal reassurance"	Thomas Doulis, "John D. MacDonald: The Liabilities of Professionalism," *Journal of Popular Culture* 10 (Summer 1976), pp. 38–53.

PAGE	QUOTE	SOURCE
15	crime-suspense field	Anthony Boucher, *New York Times Book Review*, February 12, 1956, p. 28.
21	sex and violence	Jacques Barzun and Wendell Hertig Taylor, *A Catalogue of Crime* (New York: Harper and Row, 1971), p. 292.
26	and safety engineers	Vonnegut, "He Comes to Us," p. 3.
38	of the 1960's.	Anthony Boucher, *New York Times Book Review*, December 3, 1967, p. 12.
41	and lonely heart	*JDM Bibliophile* 17 (July 1972), p. 9.

Chapter 3

44	to moody violence	MacDonald, "How to Live with a Hero," *The Writer*, September 1964, p. 14.
44	Travis, in California	Michael J. Tolley, "Color Him Quixote: MacDonald's Strategy in the Early McGee Novels," *The Armchair Detective*, January 1977, p. 13.
44	very angry reader	Letter to author, September 17, 1980.
44	trite through repetition	MacDonald, "How to Live with a Hero," p. 16.
47	all rational analyses	MacDonald, "Introduction and Comment," p. 69.

Chapter 4

83	right words together	MacDonald, "Introduction and Comment," p. 67.

Chapter 5

106	But what isn't?	Quoted in Petersen, "A MacDonald Festival," p. 1.
107	about the book	*JDM Bibliophile* 14 (August 1970), p. 27.

Chapter 6

148	international political realities	MacDonald, "John D. and the Critics," *JDM Bibliophile* 24 (July 1979), p. 11.

PAGE	QUOTE	SOURCE
		Chapter 7
157	corrode the magic	MacDonald, "Introduction and Comment," p. 68.
158	saint, or psychopath	MacDonald, "How a Character Becomes Believable," in *The Mystery Writer's Handbook*, revised edition (Cincinnati: Writer's Digest Publications, 1976), p. 117.
159	a structured society	*Nightmare in Pink*, p. 21.
159	to his name	*The Quick Red Fox*, p. 41.
159	unregimented, unprogrammed, unimpressed	*A Purple Place for Dying*, p. 27.
159	grey-eyed iconoclastic hustler	*A Deadly Shade of Gold*, p. 25.
159	Yogi Bear hat	*Nightmare in Pink*, p. 133.
160	the hifi installation	*A Tan and Sandy Silence*, p. 151.
161	your own lawn	*Bright Orange for the Shroud*, p. 28.
161	a meaningless house	Raymond Chandler, *Playback* (New York: Ballantine, 1977), p. 166.
161	flagship of life	*The Deep Blue Good-By*, p. 92.
161	of the fire	*The Scarlet Ruse*, p. 264.
162	the money is	*Nightmare in Pink*, p. 8.
162	the original sin	Ibid., p. 35.
162	couple of minutes	*Pale Gray for Guilt*, p. 157.
163	HATE ALL HATE	*A Tan and Sandy Silence*, p. 83.
163	enjoy anything else	Dashiell Hammet, *The Big Knockover* (New York: Vintage, 1972), p. 34.
164	it at all	*A Tan and Sandy Silence*, p. 249.
164	of total risk	*The Empty Copper Sea*, p. 236.
164	over my shoulder	*The Green Ripper* (New York: Lippincott, 1979), p. 192.
164	he almost disappears	Ross Macdonald, "Writing *The Galton Case*," in *On Crime Writing* (Santa Barbara: Capra Press, 1973), p. 41.
165	time it takes	*The Quick Red Fox*, p. 32.
165	the rabbit level	*The Deep Blue Good-By*, p. 155.
165	a candy store	*One Fearful Yellow Eye*, p. 148.
166	never dare say	Haas, "Maestro of the Mystery," p. 5.

PAGE	QUOTE	SOURCE
166	around the block	Hirshberg, " 'Sherlock Holmes Was a Smart-Ass,' " p. 35.
166	perfectly adjusted mediocrity	*A Deadly Shade of Gold*, p. 41.
166	at a sunset	Ibid., p. 96.
167	tomatoes. And gin	*The Dreadful Lemon Sky*, p. 32.
167	care to guess	MacDonald, "Afterword," to *Other Times, Other Worlds*, edited by Martin Greenberg (New York: Fawcett Gold Medal, 1978), p. 281.
168	great god Progress	*The Empty Copper Sea*, p. 32.
168	smodge, fugg, and schlutch	*The Dreadful Lemon Sky*, p. 27.
168	of salt water	*The Turquoise Lament*, p. 167.
168	or Jersey City	*JDM Bibliophile* 26 (July 1980), p. 48.
169	say about things	"Master of Suspense," p. 120.
169	of the reader	Daigh, *Maybe You Should Write a Book*, p. 140.

Chapter 8

171	pace, or character	MacDonald, "Introduction" to *Night Shift*, by Stephen King (Garden City, N.Y.: Doubleday, 1978), p. viii.
172	you'll stay there	MacDonald, interview with Robert Cromie, 1969.
172	color or meaning	MacDonald, "Creative Trust," *The Writer*, January 1974, p. 44.
172	of weak butterscotch	*The Scarlet Ruse*, p. 59.
172	the sugar frost	*Bright Orange for the Shroud*, p. 158.
172	blond-gold-russet	*Dress Her in Indigo*, p. 54.
172	odor of perspiration	*The Green Ripper*, p. 143.
172	enameled black wire	*The Long Lavender Look*, p. 202.
173	for abundant lactation	*The Deep Blue Good-By*, p. 115.
173	from Herter's catalogue	*Bright Orange for the Shroud*, p. 16.
173	it Veet Nee-yam	*Darker Than Amber*, p. 68.
173	and the pity	MacDonald, "How a Character Becomes Believable," p. 118.
174	looked like mourners	*One Fearful Yellow Eye*, p. 125.
174	had come from	*The Quick Red Fox*, p. 66.
175	Bauhaus wedding cakes	*The Empty Copper Sea*, p. 32.

PAGE	QUOTE	SOURCE
176	filled the world	MacDonald, *On the Run* (Greenwich, Conn.: Fawcett Gold Medal, 1963), p. 77.
177	an Eskimo wife	*Pale Gray for Guilt*, p. 186.
177	"I'm writing, fella"	Daigh, *Maybe You Should Write a Book*, p. 140.
177	for cynical services	*The Quick Red Fox*, p. 83.
177	down some bananas	*One Fearful Yellow Eye*, p. 107.
178	were on display	Ibid., p. 115.
178	very haughty indeed	MacDonald, *Soft Touch* (New York: Dell, 1958), p. 48.
179	who like beauty	MacDonald, *A Flash of Green* (New York: Simon & Schuster, 1962), p. 189.
179	[that] really sing	Hirshberg, " 'Sherlock Holmes Was a Smart-Ass,' " p. 35.
179	self-conscious and ineffective	Daigh, *Maybe You Should Write a Book*, p. 141.
180	which they spring	Quoted by Allen J. Hubin in "Introduction" to *Boucher's Choicest*, selected by Jeanne F. Bernkopf (New York; E. P. Dutton, 1969), p. 10.
181	from bad judgment	Jacques Barzun, quoted in MacDonald, "Introduction and Comment," p. 73.
181	failure, love and joy	MacDonald, "Introduction and Comment," p. 73.

Bibliography

I. Works by MacDonald

A. NOVELS (WITH FIRST AMERICAN PUBLICATION INDICATED)

The Brass Cupcake. Greenwich, Conn.: Fawcett Gold Medal, 1950.
Murder for the Bride. Greenwich, Conn.: Fawcett Gold Medal, 1951.
Judge Me Not. Greenwich, Conn.: Fawcett Gold Medal, 1951.
Weep for Me. Greenwich, Conn.: Fawcett Gold Medal, 1951.
Wine of the Dreamers. New York: Greenberg Publishing Co., 1951.
The Damned. Greenwich, Conn.: Fawcett Gold Medal, 1952.
Ballroom of the Skies. New York: Greenberg Publishing Co., 1952.
The Neon Jungle. Greenwich, Conn.: Fawcett Gold Medal, 1953.
Dead Low Tide. Greenwich, Conn.: Fawcett Gold Medal, 1953.
Cancel All Our Vows. New York: Appleton-Century-Crofts, 1953.
All These Condemned. Greenwich, Conn.: Fawcett Gold Medal, 1954.
Area of Suspicion. New York: Dell, 1954.
Contrary Pleasure. New York: Appleton-Century-Crofts, 1954.
A Bullet for Cinderella. New York: Dell, 1955.
Cry Hard, Cry Fast. New York: Popular Library, 1955.
You Live Once. New York: Popular Library, 1956.
April Evil. New York: Dell, 1956.
Border Town Girl. New York: Popular Library, 1956.
Murder in the Wind. New York: Dell, 1956.
Death Trap. New York: Dell, 1957.
The Price of Murder. New York: Dell, 1957.
The Empty Trap. New York: Popular Library, 1957.

A Man of Affairs. New York: Dell, 1957.
The Deceivers. New York: Dell, 1958.
Soft Touch. New York: Dell, 1958.
The Executioners. New York: Simon & Schuster, 1958.
Clemmie. Greenwich, Conn.: Fawcett Gold Medal, 1958.
Deadly Welcome. New York: Dell, 1959.
Please Write for Details. New York: Simon & Schuster, 1959.
The Crossroads. New York: Simon & Schuster, 1959.
The Beach Girls. Greenwich, Conn.: Fawcett Gold Medal, 1959.
Slam the Big Door. Greenwich, Conn.: Fawcett Gold Medal, 1960.
The End of the Night. New York: Simon & Schuster, 1960.
The Only Girl in the Game. Greenwich, Conn.: Fawcett Gold Medal, 1960.
Where Is Janice Gantry? Greenwich, Conn.: Fawcett Gold Medal, 1961.
One Monday We Killed Them All. Greenwich, Conn.: Fawcett Gold Medal, 1961.
A Key to the Suite. Greenwich, Conn.: Fawcett Gold Medal, 1962.
A Flash of Green. New York: Simon & Schuster, 1962.
The Girl, the Gold Watch, and Everything. Greenwich, Conn.: Fawcett Gold Medal, 1962.
On the Run. Greenwich, Conn.: Fawcett Gold Medal, 1963.
I Could Go On Singing. Greenwich, Conn.: Fawcett Gold Medal, 1963.
The Drowner. Greenwich, Conn.: Fawcett Gold Medal, 1963.
The Deep Blue Good-By. Greenwich, Conn.: Fawcett Gold Medal, 1964.
Nightmare in Pink. Greenwich, Conn.: Fawcett Gold Medal, 1964.
A Purple Place for Dying. Greenwich, Conn.: Fawcett Gold Medal, 1964.
The Quick Red Fox. Greenwich, Conn.: Fawcett Gold Medal, 1964.
A Deadly Shade of Gold. Greenwich, Conn.: Fawcett Gold Medal, 1964.
Bright Orange for the Shroud. Greenwich, Conn.: Fawcett Gold Medal, 1965.
Darker Than Amber. Greenwich, Conn.: Fawcett Gold Medal, 1966.
One Fearful Yellow Eye. Greenwich, Conn.: Fawcett Gold Medal, 1966.
The Last One Left. Garden City, N.Y.: Doubleday, 1966.
Pale Gray for Guilt. Greenwich, Conn.: Fawcett Gold Medal, 1968.
The Girl in the Plain Brown Wrapper. Greenwich, Conn.: Fawcett Gold Medal, 1968.
Dress Her in Indigo. Greenwich, Conn.: Fawcett Gold Medal, 1969.
The Long Lavender Look. Greenwich, Conn.: Fawcett Gold Medal, 1970.
A Tan and Sandy Silence. Greenwich, Conn.: Fawcett Gold Medal, 1972.
The Scarlet Ruse. Greenwich, Conn.: Fawcett Gold Medal, 1973.
The Turquoise Lament. New York: Lippincott, 1973.
The Dreadful Lemon Sky. New York: Lippincott, 1975.
Condominium. New York: Lippincott, 1977.

The Empty Copper Sea. New York: Lippincott, 1978.
The Green Ripper. New York: Lippincott, 1979.
Free Fall in Crimson. New York: Harper and Row, 1981.

B. SHORT-STORY COLLECTIONS

End of the Tiger and Other Stories. Greenwich, Conn.: Fawcett Gold Medal, 1966.
S*E*V*E*N. Greenwich, Conn.: Fawcett Gold Medal, 1971.
Other Times, Other Worlds, edited by Martin Greenberg. New York: Fawcett Gold Medal, 1978.
(For a complete listing of MacDonald's stories and their publishing history, see *A Bibliography of the Published Works of John D. MacDonald,* edited by Walter and Jean Shine [Gainesville, Fla.: University of Florida, 1980].)

C. NONFICTION

The House Guests. Garden City, N.Y.: Doubleday, 1965. Amusing autobiographical account of life with MacDonald's two cats.
No Deadly Drug. Garden City, N.Y.: Doubleday, 1968. On murder trial of Dr. Carl Coppolino.

D. ESSAYS, ARTICLES, AND OTHER PUBLICATIONS

"Afterword" to *Other Times, Other Worlds,* edited by Martin Greenberg. New York: Fawcett, 1978, pp. 279–82.
"The Aging of Travis McGee." *JDM Bibliophile* 20 (March 1975), pp. 3–4.
"An Author with a Fan Club." In *Maybe You Should Write a Book,* edited by Ralph Daigh. Englewood Cliffs, N.J.: Prentice-Hall, 1977, pp. 135–41.
"Compulsion and Butterflies." *The CEA Critic,* December 1967, pp. 6–7.
"Coppolino Revisited." In *I, Witness,* edited by Brian Garfield. New York: Time Books, 1978, pp. 294–300.
"The Creative Person and Some Dangerous Streets." *Writer's Digest,* June 1969, pp. 58–61.
"Creative Trust." *The Writer,* January 1974, pp. 13–15.
"The Florida Keys in Hurricane Alley." *Holiday,* December 1968, pp. 76–79.
"He's Not Talking to Me." *Writer's Digest,* July 1953, pp. 12–15.
"How a Character Becomes Believable." In *The Mystery Writer's Handbook,* revised edition. Cincinnati: Writer's Digest Publications, 1976, pp. 113–22.
"How to Live with a Hero." *The Writer,* September 1964, pp. 14–16.
"The Institute." Review of *The Institute,* by James M. Cain, *New York Times Book Review,* August 22, 1976, p. 18.

"Introduction" to *Night Shift*, by Stephen King. Garden City, N.Y.: Doubleday, 1978, pp. vii–x.
"Introduction and Comment." *Clues* 1 (Spring 1980), pp. 63–74.
"John D. and the Critics." *JDM Bibliophile* 24 (July 1979), pp. 4–12. Responses to the papers read at the John D. MacDonald Conference on Mystery and Detective Fiction, University of South Florida, November 18, 1978.
"Last Chance to Save the Everglades." *Life*, September 5, 1969, pp. 58–61.
The Lethal Sex. New York: Dell, 1959. Anthology of mystery stories by women writers, edited and with an introduction by MacDonald.
"Quiet Times." *The Conservationist*, April–May 1974, pp. 18–19.
"Reflections on China." *JDM Bibliophile 24 (July 1979)*, pp. 13–21.
"*The Successful Writer*." The Center for Cassette Studies. Tape of 1969 interview with Robert Cromie.

II. Selected Works About MacDonald

Abrahams, Etta. "Cops and Detectives." *Clues* 1 (Spring 1980), pp. 96–98.
———. "Visions and Values in the Action Detective Novel: A Study of the Works of Raymond Chandler, Kenneth Millar, and John D. MacDonald." Unpublished doctoral dissertation, Michigan State University, 1973.
Benjamin, David A. "John D. MacDonald and the Life and Death of the Mythic Hero." Unpublished doctoral dissertation, Harvard University, 1977.
———. "Key Witness." *The New Republic*, July 26, 1975, pp. 29–31.
Campbell, Frank D., Jr. *John D. MacDonald and the Colorful World of Travis McGee*. San Bernardino: Borgo Press, 1977.
Cook, Wister. "John D. MacDonald: A Little Ecology Goes a Long Way." *Clues* 1 (Spring 1980), pp. 57–61.
Doulis, Thomas. "John D. MacDonald: The Liabilities of Professionalism." *Journal of Popular Culture* 10 (Summer 1976), pp. 38–53.
Gindin, James. "John D. MacDonald." In *Twentieth-Century Crime and Mystery Writers*, edited by John M. Reilly. New York: St. Martin's, 1980, pp. 979–83.
Green, Martin. "Our Detective Heroes." *Transatlantic Patterns: Cultural Comparisons of England with America*. New York: Basic Books, 1977, pp. 101–30. Comparison between Travis McGee and Lord Peter Wimsey.
Grimes, Larry E. "The Reluctant Hero: Reflections on Vocation and Heroism in the Travis McGee Novels of John D. MacDonald." *Clues* 1 (Spring 1980), pp. 103–8.
Haas, Joseph. "Maestro of the Mystery." *Panorama–Chicago Daily News*, September 6–7, 1969, pp. 4–5.
Hills, Rust. "The Awesome Beige Typewriter." *Esquire*, August 1975, p. 68.

Hirshberg, Ed. " 'Sherlock Holmes Was a Smart-Ass' and Other Diverse Opinions." *1979 Writer's Yearbook*. Cincinnati: Writer's Digest Publications, 1979, pp. 32–38.

Holtsmark, Erling B. "Travis McGee as Traditional Hero." *Clues* 1 (Spring 1980), pp. 99–102.

Hoyt, Charles Alva. *"The Damned:* Good Intentions: The Tough Guy as Hero and Villain." In *Tough Guy Writers of the Thirties,* edited by David Madden. Carbondale: Southern Illinois University Press, 1968, pp. 224–30.

JDM Bibliophile. A journal devoted to MacDonald's works. Between 1965 and 1978 the journal was edited and published in California by Len and June Moffatt. Beginning with issue No. 23 (January 1979) it has been edited by Ed Hirshberg and published by the University of South Florida.

"John D. MacDonald." *World Authors*, edited by John Wakeman. New York: H. W. Wilson Co., 1975, pp. 904–5.

Kelley, R. Gordon. "The Precarious World of John D. MacDonald." In *Dimensions of Detective Fiction*, edited by Larry N. Landrum, Pat Browne, and Ray B. Browne. Bowling Green: Popular Press, 1976, pp. 149–61.

Mallory, Margaret I. "The Heroes of John D. MacDonald's Novels of Violence." Unpublished master's thesis, Southwest Texas State University, 1976.

———. "John D. MacDonald's Criminal Heroes." *Popular Culture Scholar* 1 (1976), pp. 57–74.

"Master of Suspense." *MD Medical Newsmagazine*, November 1978, pp. 117–22. Reprinted in Shine, Walter and Jean, *A Bibliography of the Published Works of John D. MacDonald*, pp. 145–150.

Moffatt, Leonard J. and June M. *The JDM Master Checklist*. Downey, Calif., 1969. Includes brief biography.

Moran, Peggy. "McGee's Girls." *Clues* 1 (Spring 1980), pp. 82–88.

Nelson, John Wiley. "Travis McGee, Tarnished Knight in Modern Armor." *Your God Is Alive and Well and Appearing in Popular Culture*. Philadelphia: Westminster Press, 1976, pp. 170–92.

Nevins, Francis M., Jr. "The Making of a Tale-Spinner: John D. MacDonald's Early Pulp Mystery Stories." *Clues* 1 (Spring 1980), pp. 89–95.

Nolan, William F. "John D. MacDonald." *The Human Equation*. Los Angeles: Sherbourne Press, 1971, pp. 141–45.

Peek, George S. "Conquering the Stereotypes: On Reading the Novels of John D. MacDonald." *The Armchair Detective*, Spring 1980, pp. 90–93.

Petersen, Clarence. "A MacDonald Festival: Happy Number Sixty-Three, John D.!" *Chicago Tribune Book World*, July 15, 1973, Section 7, pp. 1–2.

Pratt, Allan D. "The Chronology of the Travis McGee Novels." *The Armchair Detective*, Spring 1980, pp. 83–89.

Sanders, Joe. "Science Fiction and Detective Fiction: The Case of John D. MacDonald." *Science-Fiction Studies*, July 1980, pp. 157–65.

Shine, Walter and Jean. *A Bibliography of the Published Works of John D. MacDonald, With Selected Biographical Materials and Critical Essays.* Gainesville: University of Florida, 1980.

————. "The Special Confidential Report." A thirty-four-page supplement issued in conjunction with issue No. 25 of *JDM Bibliophile*.

Tolley, Michael J. "Color Him Quixote: MacDonald's Strategy in the Early McGee Novels." *The Armchair Detective*, January 1977, pp. 6–13.

Vonnegut, Kurt, Jr. "He Comes to Us One by One and Asks What the Rules Are." *Chicago Tribune Book World*, July 15, 1973, Section 7, p. 3.

Wall, Donald C. "Ecology and the Detective Novel: The Contribution of John D. MacDonald." *JDM Bibliophile* 21 (February 1976), pp. 3–10.

INDEX